CHILD ABUSE AND PROTECTION

C000233496

Literature in the child abuse and child protection arena has tended to adopt either a practice or legal perspective. Drawing on their expertise as researchers and leaders in their field, Julia Davidson and Antonia Bifulco offer a comprehensive and cohesive book on child abuse and child protection, drawing on both criminological and psychological perspectives on all forms of child maltreatment and child protection practice together with impacts on the victims.

This book considers a range of areas, from definitions of child abuse and discussions of its prevalence, to an examination of the experiences of children in care, to international perspectives on children within the criminal justice system, to the emergence of online child abuse and the increasing awareness of historical abuse. Each chapter draws together key elements in the field, including prevalence and definition, different disciplinary approaches; different practice challenges; international impacts; and technological issues. Brief case studies throughout the book reflect the voice or experience of the child, ensuring that the focus remains on the child at the centre of the abuse.

Balancing coverage of theory and research and considering implications for practice and policy, this book will appeal to a range of disciplines, including criminology, psychology, psychiatry, social work and law.

Julia Davidson is Professor of Criminology at the University of East London and Honorary Professor at the Centre for Abuse and Trauma Studies, Middlesex University, UK.

Antonia Bifulco is Professor of Lifespan Psychology and Head of the Department of Psychology at Middlesex University, UK. She is Director for the Centre for Abuse and Trauma Studies at Middlesex University.

CHILD ABUSE AND PROTECTION

Contemporary Issues in Research, Policy and Practice

Julia Davidson and Antonia Bifulco

Routledge
Taylor & Francis Group

LONDON AND NEW YORK

First published 2019
by Routledge
2 Park Square, Milton Park, Abingdon, Oxon OX14 4RN

and by Routledge
711 Third Avenue, New York, NY 10017

Routledge is an imprint of the Taylor & Francis Group, an informa business

British Library Cataloguing-in-Publication Data
A catalogue record for this book is available from the British Library

Library of Congress Cataloging-in-Publication Data
Names: Davidson, Julia C., author. | Bifulco, Antonia, 1955- author.
Title: Child abuse and protection : contemporary issues in
    research, policy and practice / Julia Davidson and Antonia Bifulco.
Description: 1 Edition. | New York : Routledge, 2018. | Includes bibliographical
    references and index.
Identifiers: LCCN 2018019013 | ISBN 9781138209985 (hardback) |
    ISBN 9781138209992 (pbk.) | ISBN 9781315456256 (ebook)
Subjects: LCSH: Child abuse. | Child abuse—Prevention.
Classification: LCC HV6626.5 .D38 2018 | DDC 362.76—dc23
LC record available at https://lccn.loc.gov/2018019013

ISBN: 978-1-138-20998-5 (hbk)
ISBN: 978-1-138-20999-2 (pbk)
ISBN: 978-1-315-45625-6 (ebk)

Typeset in Interstate
by Apex CoVantage, LLC
Printed and bound by CPI Group (UK) Ltd, Croydon, CR0 4YY

For

Glenn and Rhys Davidson

Lucia Bifulco and in memory of Vincent Bifulco.

CONTENTS

PREFACE

Much is known about child abuse and its long-term impacts, and the wide-scale damage it causes to individuals, families and society. But each era faces different challenges in understanding and communicating key facts about this complex phenomenon, and effectively preventing or intervening to reduce harm. From the current perspective (2017-18) awareness about and arguably the reach of child abuse particularly via the Internet has grown in ways previously not envisaged: to the *past* in relation to historical abuse and that occurring in institutional, establishment and celebrity settings, and to the *future* in relation to technological change and online grooming and entrapment of children for abuse. Understanding of abuse impact has also widened: damage to the child is now known to include hampered development of the neurological, hormonal and brain-systems with the possibility of epigenetic change to the genetic inheritance across generations. This is in addition to the well-documented social adversity and psychological and mental health damage entailed. All these have implications for childhood, adolescent and later life development which can extend to childbirth/parenthood, menopause, ageing experience and early mortality. It is shown to relate to illness such as diabetes and cardiovascular disease, as well as emotional and behavioural disorders. This places child abuse as a central public health concern given its still high prevalence and its impact on the population's mental and physical health. The concerns are international, with a European focus on harmonising policy and legislation on child protection, but with acknowledged major gaps in the wider international field in measuring, recognising and intervening in child abuse. With high population mobility, and easy online contact across national borders, the scope of abuse links both international and local concerns.

Knowledge of child abuse has grown exponentially. This places a large burden on professionals: not only the social workers, police, psychologists and paediatricians directly involved, but also on teachers, youth and playgroup workers and any who have formal contact with children who need to be aware of safe-guarding issues. It takes a toll individually on practitioners required to face the reality and emotional burden of witnessing child abuse or its impacts daily. This can lead to serious shortages of professionals robust enough to agree to work in child protection services and to high staff turnover of staff engaged in work in this demanding area. This dips after serious case reviews when blame for child deaths is directed at professionals by the media. There are serious respon-sibilities involved. Social workers, police and judges need to determine beyond reasonable doubt that abuse may have occurred. This can lead to the child being taken away from the family with parents or carers potentially being pros-ecuted. This is hurtful to the child as well as to the wider family. Alternatively, actions may be taken to add support to the family to enable better parenting and family functioning to ameliorate the effects. For this, social work teams need to decide on the probability of evidence whether a child is in danger or not. For this, they need accurate collection of information and a precise knowl-edge of abuse thresholds to judge likelihood of future harm.

Yet there are many varieties of abuse to understand. These can be related to each other and usually in complex combinations. Some are known to be hard to assess, such as emotional abuse. Many abuses occur in the context of family conflict and domestic violence, fuelled by poverty, immigration, drug and alcohol misuse, parental stress, or in non-traditional families where there maybe isolation (e.g. single parents) or schisms (reconstituted families). Oth-ers come with diverse cultural practice (such as female genital mutilation) or through migration (child trafficking). The assessment brief becomes increas-ingly demanding, covering a range of specialisms, and requires the assistance of multi-disciplinary teams with broad expertise and knowledge. This require-ment brings its own challenges in terms of professional working practice and communication and record keeping. It can also at times lead to delays and the danger of families and children falling between the 'cracks' where services are not joined-up.

There is a wide research, policy and practice literature to cover, much 'grey' literature – reports commissioned by services or agencies and policy doc-uments. In addition, there are government enquiries usually based around serious case review when child deaths occur in the face of agency shortcom-ings. More recently this concerns police investigations when abuse reaches a national scale or involves institutional failure to recognise and respond to child abuse. The amount of detail involved in covering all such information is in danger of losing sight of the child at the centre of the abuse. In this book we strive to encompass the breadth of implications of child abuse and protection, in order to derive key messages about contemporary issues, in a form which is readily digestible by practitioners and researchers alike. In this way we feel the book will have best impact and be an aid to teaching and training in this area. In an ever-shifting professional context, our aim is to develop key themes which are relatively enduring, and which can help or hinder intervention with, or prevention of abuse. Therefore, the chapters all indicate key elements in the field (prevalence and definition, different disciplinary approaches; different practice challenges; international impacts; technological issues). In key places we have included brief case studies to reflect the voice or experience of the child. This keeps the child at the centre of the focus.

We draw on our two careers spent researching child abuse over three to four decades with our various psychological (AB) and criminological (JD) expertise. We have drawn on our own research in this area which we know in depth, and at times our own case examples. This is in addition to a scoping of other key sources of published information. We do not consider this a systematic review – rather we have selected our themes in terms of those most pertinent, comprehensive and enduring, and covered the key findings which have influenced the field, and those cases which have changed policy and practice. It is possible in this we will miss some important aspects and publications. But our aim is less for complete coverage but rather to provide a focused and digestible account which can help with thinking about abuse issues in both a critical and knowledgeable way, to aid with looking to the future state of the field and society in general.

Antonia Bifulco & Julia Davidson

March 2018

ACKNOWLEDGEMENTS

With thanks to our research team at CATs and to our colleagues who have helped us investigate child abuse over the decades. Also thanks are due to the various funders, and partner organisations which have been an integral part of our research and knowledge exchange work. We also greatly appreciate the helpful editorial input by Professor Jenny Pearce.

FOREWORD

This excellent and important book gives us a unique overview of child abuse and protection. It brings different academic disciplines together to give a comprehensive study of child abuse research, policy and practice in both the UK and in relevant international contexts. Importantly, it maintains a consistent reminder that children's rights to safety and well-being must be at the core of our thinking about child abuse and protection.

For too long child abuse and protection has been seen as the sole property of child protection agencies, rather than an issue that everyone has a responsibility to identify and prevent. Similarly, it has been seen as a problem for adults to solve on behalf of children, rather than 'with' children as active agents of social change. There is increasing recognition of models of working with children to understand the range and nature of abuse and the impact that it has on them, their friends, families and communities. Similarly, and importantly, it is through engagement with children that we learn of better ways to identify and address the range of forms of child abuse, be it abuse and neglect within the family or care home, peer on peer abuse, on and off line abuse, abuse within the school or community; or be it institutional abuse against children at local, national or international levels. This engagement with children reinforces the fact that prevention and response is everyone's business: that individuals, families, communities and businesses in the private as well as the public sectors have a part to play. Also, that all aspects of local, national and international governance play a role putting steps in place to prevent perpetration in the first place, and to identify and support those impacted.

The book helpfully outlines research that shows that while there are specific vulnerabilities to becoming a victim, perpetrator or both of child abuse, this must not overshadow awareness that child abuse can impact on boys as well as girls and can be perpetrated by children, and by women as well as men. It can occur in all communities irrespective of social class or ethnicity, economic resources or geographical location, and can take a variety of forms through different on and off line methods. The thorough and detailed information in this book picks up these themes, giving an overview of what we know, what we still need to know and do about child abuse and protection, and how it is best addressed through multi-disciplinary, multi-agency collaboration at local, national and international levels.

This is timely as the recent work of international initiatives such as End Violence Against Children (www.end-violence.org) and Know Violence In Childhood (www.knowviolenceinchildhood.org) repeatedly stress the negative impact of the range of different forms of abuse of children. Kumar and Stern, the co-chairs of the End violence campaign 2017 report noted that

> *at least three out of every four of the world's children – 1.7 billion – had experienced some form of inter-personal violence, cruelty or abuse in their daily lives in a previous year, regardless of whether they lived in rich countries or poor, in the global North or the global South.*
> (Know Violence in Childhood. 2017. Ending Violence in Childhood. Global Report 2017. Know Violence in Childhood. New Delhi, India.ii)

This increasingly important relationship between international and national initiatives is needed to address the forced movement of children and their exploitation by international, national and local criminal networks. As the book explores, our understanding of what is happening in the UK is dependent upon our awareness of the context of global change. Through this understanding we prevent the development of isolated responses to complex questions.

The book is also timely because, at a national level the UK government has, since 2015, identified child sexual abuse, which includes child sexual exploitation, as one of the top three national threats. This responded to the public outrage of revelations of the sexual exploitation of children in specific local authorities and of the extent of harm caused by some celebrities, particularly Jimmy Saville. Subsequent revelations about the sexual and emotional abuse of football players by their coaches, and of the extent of abuse perpetrated by people holding positions of trust in religious and community institutions created a recognition of hitherto hidden child abuse taking place outside of the family home, often under the noses of those deemed to be protecting children and working in their best interest. The creation of the UK Independent Inquiry into Child Sexual Abuse (IICSA) and the Child Sexual Abuse Centre of expertise (CSA Centre) is helping to build evidence and raise awareness of the forms and nature of sexual abuse and related violence against children, raising public awareness of the extent of, and damage caused by, child abuse. Recognising the need for national policy to reflect the changes in forms and nature of child abuse and protection, the 'Working Together to Safeguard Children' is now revised and updated, with changes for local regional safeguarding arrangements being made as a result of the Children and Social Work Act 2017.

These international, national and local initiatives can only be effective if implemented by trained and supported staff and if accompanied by a larger, public recognition of the important role that we all play in consulting and engaging with children in child protection matters. While child protection services and agencies do need support to identify, engage and work with the impact of abuse, this book helpfully highlights that these concerns impact on us all. It is an essential read for all interested in child abuse and protection; for those who are studying the topic; actively working with cases of child abuse; developing policy and practice in the field; or assessing the role they can play as an individual citizen. This refreshing and stimulating text is unusual as it brings different academic disciplines together to cover the range of issues involved. Through informed work as outlined within this book, joint work between all concerned can help prevent child abuse and better protect children.

Jenny Pearce,
Professor of Young People and Public Policy

1 Introduction to child abuse

Introduction

Most adults in the UK are now aware of the dangers of child abuse, whether as parents, professionals or those concerned for the health and well-being of members of our own society. Risks are openly discussed, people working with children are all required to complete criminal checks and to have a working knowledge of safeguarding and its procedures, whether in education, health, criminal justice, youth work or many other settings. Yet, despite this, recent years have highlighted a range of high profile cases, both current and historical, which give the impression that all the preventative actions have had negligible effect. This is unlikely to be the case, since registers of new cases of child protection show rates of child abuse are declining in most (but not all) categories yearly in the UK; however the accuracy of reporting rates is questionable and those registered do not reflect actual levels of abuse. But given a high number of historical abuses have come to light, together with convictions in relation to abuse in institutions, it seems that child abuse cases are increasingly a media topic.

The aim of this book is to examine contemporary issues in child abuse involving its scope and range; its definition; the role of varied services involved; challenges for research and practice; and current policies nationally and internationally aimed to prevent and combat maltreatment. Certain aspects are new to our era, for example the prevalence of online abuse and exploitation with increased social media, or due to increased internationalism aspects such as child trafficking or harmful cultural practices such as female genital mutilation. The role of the media can also be significant in terms of stirring public emotions; attributing blame and causing instances of 'moral panic' so recent cases become important, but the media can also play a helpful role in raising awareness about key issues, for example the MeToo Campaign[1] which has raised awareness about sexual harassment and violence. The area of child abuse has grown, in terms of time (ongoing and historical abuse rates), its acknowledged international setting, new types of abuse and *modus operandi* (e.g. psychological abuse or online exploitation) and increased understanding of lifelong and complex health, psychological and social impacts on the child. These have all served to make the area more complex, more difficult to combat but also of the highest importance in understanding and trying to improve our society.

This chapter seeks to therefore introduce the topic of child maltreatment/abuse by first examining the twin themes guiding policy responses to child maltreatment in terms of human rights and damage to a child's health and development. It will then examine the modern scope of abuse and the current public attention through some recent high-profile cases. It will then provide summary definitions of abuse used in the UK and the recorded prevalence rates. This will then be broadened internationally and to those less well documented. All issues will then be described in greater detail throughout the book. However, the aim is to signal the contemporary issues emerging right from the fore. This will then link to the themes arising to those developed throughout the book.

Ethics and the rights of the child

One of the main reasons for combatting child abuse is on ethical grounds since it contravenes a child's rights and is a cruel and unwarranted aspect in a civilised society. A basic underpinning of our notion of child protection and safeguarding children is based in the United Nations Convention on the Rights of the Child (UNCRC, 1989).[2] This comprises 54 articles that cover all aspects of a child's life and set out the civil, political, economic, social and cultural rights to which all children everywhere are entitled. It also sets out the need for adults and governments working together to ensure these are followed. It states that every child has rights, whatever their ethnicity, gender, religion, language, abilities or any other status. The rights listed are linked and no right is more important than another. The right to relax and play (Article 31) and the right to freedom of expression (Article 13) have equal importance as the right to be safe from violence (Article 19) and the right to education (Article 28). All UN member states except for the United States have ratified the Convention which came into force in 1992 (the implications of the UNCRC is discussed in detail in Chapter 2).

The identification of child rights was originally influenced by the work of Dr Janusz Korczak, a paediatrician who instigated novel methods of education in Poland early in the twentieth century. He ran a Jewish orphanage in Warsaw along experimental lines involving social pedagogy. This included identifying rights of the child: the right to die, the right to live for today and the right to be oneself. Whilst written before the invasion of Poland in World War II, these were prescient of later events, with Korczak forced by the Nazis into the Warsaw Ghetto with the children he had taught. He refused earlier opportunities to escape, remained with the children and finally accompanied them with his co-worker Stefa Wilczynska, to Treblinka concentration camp (Eichsteller, 2009). His work, initiated in Poland, led to the UN 1989 Convention.

Connected to these rights is the concept of the child having a 'voice', i.e. that children should be able to tell others if abused both to get help, but also ultimately to make sense of their experience and work through it therapeutically. One aid to this was Childline,[3] a confidential and free telephone line started in 1986 by Esther Rantzen. Starting as a charity, three years later it became international[4] and then was partnered by the National Society for Prevention of Cruelty to Children (NSPCC) in 2006. Its aim was to offer free counselling and a confidential way for children to disclose abuse. It now has a million calls a year dealt with by volunteer counsellors.

There are a number of barriers to children disclosing abuse. Apart from the conflict of loyalties where a parent is involved, there is also fear of threatened harm and reprisals. In addition, they are often schooled in the secrecy of the abuse and its normalisation, and the ensuing mistrust of adults can hamper seeking help elsewhere. For young children there is often no adequate frame of reference for describing the nature of the abuse. Whilst there are sometimes claimed to be language difficulties due to age or culture, it is much more likely the silence is down to fear of further harm. For this reason, teachers, social workers and others are trained to look for signs of possible abuse in changed behaviour, symptoms and evidence of poor care. However, these signs can sometimes be wrongly attributed. There are well-known cases where child illness/accident were not the result of parental behaviour. It is considered critical to listen to the child and to develop a trusting relationship with the child to learn of their experience. But it is also necessary to have good investigative skills and tools for identifying where abuse has occurred and at what level of severity and frequency to take necessary action.

However, it should be noted the UN convention has no 'teeth' in terms of its legal standing. Each country must determine and implement its policies on child protection and safeguarding and to determine what happens to children and families where abuse is deemed to have taken place.

Victim focus and terminology

In this book the term 'victim' refers to the child or adolescent who is the *target* of neglect or abuse. In other words, the child is the victim of that abuse, not a victim in a more general sense, for example by their behaviour or other characteristics. The term 'victim' is not intended to carry with it an idea of passivity or submissive behaviour or lowered status. Many support agencies prefer the term 'survivor' to imply resilience. However, this is avoided because while it is clear the child is an innocent victim, the extent of psychological survival varies from one person to another. In fact, most victims of neglect or abuse are also survivors in terms of becoming resilient to the negative impacts over a lifetime and amenable to social and psychological interventions. But many suffer dire consequences, even mortal ones (either death at the hands of the abuser or self-inflicted).

Victims can also be perpetrators. This particularly relates to sexual abuse (although it can also relate to physical aggression to peers and younger children). The triggers for this behaviour are varied but this can occur when a child has been sexually abused most usually by family members and/or friends and has come to see that behaviour as 'normal', perpetrating similar offences most frequently against siblings. Such cases are complex and difficult for CJS or social care services to unravel and provide appropriate support. They also result in distinct ethical conflicts.

In outlining abuse and its impacts, it will be necessary to also describe resilience and the fact that many, if not most of those who experience abuse in childhood, survive with relatively good functioning and do not pass risk onto their own children. It is important to realise that children and young people often do take 'agency' in managing the after effects of their maltreatment and can take positive cues from the rest of their social environment – find love and support – and work through the emotions associated with their trauma. Some do this psychological work many years later, finding the help and conditions to overcome any damage done. It is important not to stigmatise those who have experienced childhood abuse, the shame often experienced is that transmitted from the perpetrator and mistakenly by other society members. There should be no shame, culpability or stigma attached to those too young and immature to understand the nature of the maltreatment and to comprehend why they have been chosen for attack – particularly when it comes from those trusted close others who should be protecting them. Often those experiencing abuse will feel shame and self-blame, but this is a distortion of thinking which needs to be corrected, and it is important that the rest of society does not collude with this false view.

Researching the impact of child abuse

Research over the last 30 years into child abuse and its consequences has been very successful in being able to measure abuse and identify outcomes with some precision. Theoretical and causal models have been able to explain much of the cause and consequence in some detail. However, the area has become more complex – this is because the impacts are social, psychological and bio-logical, and these can be different at all ages. Damage goes into adult life, even older age and inter-generationally. It has immense scope. Box 1.1 summarises challenges to research in child abuse.

Box 1.1

Challenges to researching child abuse

- Ethics – investigating children and sensitive issues, difficult to perform in some subcultures and particularly with young children and in getting the voice of the children themselves;
- Research funding – this is increasingly competitive, and the scale and scope of the research internationally potentially requires substantial investment, as well as inter-disciplinary research teams to investigate all the ramifications of abuse;
- Measurement issues – abuse is difficult to research and assess given constraints on reporting both psychological and age-related. Accuracy of accounts and the problem of under-reporting are issues;
- Cultural and international dimensions – abuse is not easy to study in some developing countries where poverty makes all children's lives problematic. Cultural issues are also present in relation to some cultural forms of abuse (e.g. female genital mutilation); the developmental and ethical approach needs to overcome cultural relativism;
- Technology and Online abuse – modern abuse can happen via social media, with research and practice needing technological sophistication.

Nevertheless, there has been substantial research over decades on the issue of child abuse within different disciplines and at project and policy levels. This has consistently and unremittingly shown that the negative effects of abuse are very substantial and can last for a lifetime and be transmitted inter-generationally. The effects also hold internationally. The challenge now is to bring all that is known together to effect policy and practice worldwide.

There are various theoretical models applied to the investigation of child abuse impacts which cover social, psychological and biological domains. All are implicated with an intersection of all required for modern investigation. These are briefly outlined below to provide a background for subsequent chapters.

A socio-ecological context

Different models explaining child abuse and its impacts will be provided in later chapters (e.g. see Chapter 3). However, common to all the chapters and the range of issues involved for children, families and society is the reference to a socio-ecological model to encompass the various levels at which need exists, and which services and national policy need to penetrate. Bronfenbrenner's notion of these multiple levels, with the child at the centre and different levels of society in concentric circles, is utilised here to identify these levels in relation to the issues outlined in this book (Bronfenbrenner, 1995). Figure 1.1 provides a schematic model.

The socio-ecological model refers to both the cause of abuse, and to its later impacts. In terms of the cause of abuse, it is well documented that many types of known child abuse are more common in areas of deprivation and in disadvantaged families (Belsky, 1980, Farrington, 2006; Fergusson, Woodward, & Horwood, 2000). The actual level of association of abuse to social disadvantage varies for each type of experience; neglect and physical abuse show the highest levels (DuMont, Widom, & Czaja, 2007; Ney, Fung, & Wickett, 1993) with sexual abuse and psychological abuse less related (Finkelhor, 1984a; Moran, Bifulco, Baines, Bunn, & Stanford, 2003). This is not to say that abuse does not occur among those with affluence and power, and here it might escape detection. The drivers of deprivation and stress are key to many types of abuse, but it is also known that abuses are associated with each other. For example, where neglect is present then other abuses are likely to follow; this has implications for abuse rates, adversity and neighbourhood characteristics, for example where conflict and violence are common (Ney, Fung, & Wickett, 1994). Whilst online abuse is separate from such physical context, there is also some emergent research to suggest that those children who are the most vulnerable to online abuse are most likely to have experienced it offline (Livingstone, Davidson, & Bryce, 2017; Webster, Davidson, & Bifulco, 2015).

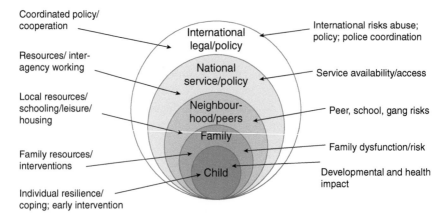

Figure 1.1 A socio-ecological approach to child abuse

An acknowledgement of the role of social deprivation in the causation of child abuse has been made by UK policies. For example, the Early Intervention initiative as embodied in Sure Start was targeted initially on deprived neighbourhoods (Anning, 2004). More recently, the 2012 the Troubled Families Programme[5] was launched to support disadvantaged families as a means of averting abuse and increasing well-being. It identified the following problems as relevant to risk for children: parents or children involved in crime or anti-social behaviour; children who are not attending school regularly; children of all ages, who need help, are identified as in need or are subject to a child protection plan; adults out of work or at risk of financial exclusion or young people at risk of worklessness; families affected by domestic violence or abuse; and parents or children with a range of physical and mental health problems.[6] The model also highlights issues of inequality in terms of impact of abuse. Those abused have reduced life chances, and recent reports on health inequalities identifies intervention in early years as a means of overcoming such inequality (Marmot, 2010). Therefore, public health issues and those concerning child maltreatment become combined in early years' intervention.

The socio-ecological model is complicated by the issue of time. As depicted, it indicates a snapshot of an individual, family or neighbourhood, with repercussions for the wider social milieu. However, it should perhaps be three dimensional, with the concentric circles indicating the various influences over time – over a year or decades or even historical periods. This would help conceptualise historical abuse and its changing ramifications for levels of impact in the present. Second, it would help for determining the journey of a child or family through their abuse investigation and service planning and cascading impacts. The model is used in this book for mapping social policy and international aspects of abuse in relation to the experience of the child, its family and neighbourhood as targets of abuse.

A subset of the social model is the feminist model. This has a focus on the gender disparity, particularly in sexual abuse, of female victims and male perpetrators (Warner, 2009). This is attributed to still existing male hegemony and patriarchal family and society structures which leaves women disadvantaged and unable to have a voice in disclosing their abuse (Angelides, 2004). This approach at times objects to the term 'victim' applied to women who have experienced abuse because it denotes weakness. The term survivor is preferred. Whilst there is a gender issue in some forms of abuse (for example female genital mutilation; child witch accusations; institutional sexual abuse), this is by no means the case across all abuse categories. Neither is it only men who perpetrate abuse. Therefore, when all abuse categories are considered, the feminist critique has somewhat limited application.

However, it is acknowledged that in societies where women are educated and have a voice, the welfare of their children is improved.[7] The wider issue of sexual harassment endemic in many cultures including our own, and silence about this, has been highlighted in the media recently given high profile cases such as Harvey Weinstein.[8] Sexual harassment is defined as:

> Unwelcome sexual advances, requests for sexual favors, and other verbal or physical conduct of a sexual nature that tends to create a hostile or offensive work environment. Sexual harassment is a form of Sex Discrimination that occurs in the workplace.[9]

The media concerns about the Weinstein case, and others like it, involve its longevity, the silence of others in the organisation who witnessed it but did not report it, the inability or constraints of women victimised to disclose, and the ripple effect when it was made public of how many other victims came forward. Whilst this is not itself child abuse, it has many features in common and indicates that inequality of the sexes may have a direct bearing on certain types of abuse, especially in societies where secrecy and barriers to disclosure is maintained.

There are of course other models of abuse in both its intergenerational transmission and impact which will be examined in Chapter 3. These encompass social, psychological and biological models.

The chapters in this book will seek to encompass the distinct levels of challenge in combatting child abuse, as well as the understanding of these distinct levels in contributing to abusive experience or identifying their impacts.

The next section deals with the definition, scope and prevalence of child abuse in the UK and associated issues. International aspects are discussed in Chapter 2.

The scope of child abuse

Defining childhood

The very first parameter of child abuse – is what constitutes the childhood period. This varies internationally. In the UK the legal definition of childhood/age of consent is 16 although the UNCRC has been ratified under which under 18s are defined as children, thus including both childhood and adolescence. Services now extend to age 20 and 25 for children in care, and impacts in 'emerging' adulthood are a source of concern (Arnett, 2007). Its earliest point can apply *in utero* with the foetus deemed to be at risk in relation to the mother's characteristics (for example her young age, or her substance abuse). This means that newborn babies can be taken away from their mothers if deemed to be at high enough risk. There are various definitions of childhood in sociological approaches. This includes structural approaches with childhood a permanent feature of society, social constructionism which highlights historical and cultural perspectives to a more changing definition and interactionist sociology which looks at children as agents in the social world, but also as a minority group (James & Prout, 2015). A major focus here is on psychological approaches, whereby childhood is defined in terms of a period of child and adolescent development, such development dictating later adult functioning. However, even here the year attributed to the end of childhood is somewhat arbitrary, linked traditionally to first point at school-leaving, but with slightly older ages also utilised as denoting the transition to adulthood: for example voting starting at 18 as the age of majority and as mentioned earlier, with developmental psychologists now examining the age group 18-25 as denoting an 'emerging adulthood', a period which still involves biological and social development. In terms of childhood and social roles, teenage is still for many a time of dependence on family and full-time education, so there are now many similarities in role and lifestyle between 15 and 19 years of age. Leaving the parental home is usually taken to denote a step towards adult autonomy, but in areas where the cost of housing is very high and in short supply, many young people remain in the family home until far into their 20s. Another aspect in the definition of childhood concerns the age of consent for sexual activity (this issue is discussed fully in Chapter 2). This is a legal definition, and in the UK is age 16, now applying equally for heterosexual and homosexual sexual activity since 1999. However, this age of consent varies across Europe (usually between age 14 and 18). For example, Portugal has 14 as the age of consent with Malta 18 years of age. Spain has just raised the age of consent from 13 to 16, with Belgium seeking to *reverse* theirs from 16 to 13 due to concerns about consensual peer sexual activity in adolescence. In the US the age of consent varies between 16 and 18 depending on State. The lowest age of consent is age 12 in Nigeria and the Philippines, and 13 in Japan (although here local statutes usually invoke age 16). The Middle Eastern countries have no age of consent, although they ban sexual relations outside of marriage but allow marriage from age 9 or 10. Conversely the highest age of consent for sexual intercourse is Bahrain at age 21, with South Korea at age 20. So, definitions of the age at which childhood ends vary, but the period from being a foetus, birth to the end of the 16th year (the legal age of consent) is used in this book, with the term 'childhood abuse' also including adolescent experience. It is recognised that children's services work with children and young people up to 18 years and in some arenas (such as care leavers) this is extended to 25.

Defining child abuse

Child abuse involves actions of maltreatment which injure the child in a variety of ways and violates their human rights. The NSPCC gives the following definition on their website:

Child abuse is any action by another person – adult or child – that causes significant harm to a child. It can be physical, sexual or emotional, but can just as often be about a lack of love, care and attention. We know that neglect, whatever form it takes, can be just as damaging to a child as physical abuse. An abused child will often experience more than one type of abuse, as well as other difficulties in their lives. It often happens over a period of time rather than being a one-off event. And it can increasingly happen online. We estimate that over half a million children are abused in the UK each year.[10]

The term child abuse usually conjures up either physical abuse where the child is the victim of violence, or sexual abuse where the child is the victim of imposed sexual activity. As such these are 'events' which occur on certain dates and times, most often with a particular frequency. Thus, evidence of their occurrence would include reports of perpetrator behaviour (verbal and physical) either by victims or witnesses. Both types of abusive action carry stigma for the victim and associated shame, which can preclude disclosure, and often occur in private or secret settings where there are no witnesses. The child will find it difficult to report on these experiences, may fear reprisal, and may not even be aware the actions constitute abuse. However, there are other formal categories of child maltreatment, mainly in the family sphere, such as neglect or emotional abuse which can be harder to pin down, either because of more diffuse activity, harder to date and to determine frequency (e.g. neglect) or because the definitions and indicators are vague (e.g. emotional abuse). Neglect, which has very serious impacts, is a different type of maltreatment, involving the lack of necessary care actions (omission) rather than presence of abusive acts (commission) and yet still requires evidence for its severity and chronicity.

There are other familial experiences sometimes included in abuse experience, to do with the child's witnessing of parental conflict or parental mental health problems. This would constitute trauma, which now includes witnessing of life-threatening incidents (AmericanPsychiaricAssociation, 2013). Whilst child abuse is a form of trauma, not all traumas constitute child abuse – for example, fires or car accidents which constitute trauma experience but not abuse. Child abuse is always interpersonal. However, some research and services include witnessing trauma events within the range of significant harm to children. This broad range of experiences – often termed Adverse Childhood Experiences or ACE – include domestic violence, parental substance abuse and parental psychological disorder and are now researched in terms of later life impact (Larkin, Felitti, & Anda, 2014). These factors can also be seen in terms of the socio-ecological model as the family context for abuse, induced in part by the strain and deprivation experienced by families. For the purposes of this book, abuse experiences will include maltreatment directed towards the children. The more common ones in the UK are Sexual Abuse, Physical Abuse, Psychological/Emotional abuse as well as problems in care around Neglect. These are all directed to the target child in question throughout childhood up until the end of the 16th year. Taking a wider international and cultural view, other experiences such as female genital mutilation, child trafficking, child labour and forced begging will also be included. The term 'abuse' will be used to cover any of these experiences unless otherwise specified. Aspects of parent/carer context such as domestic violence, discord, parental substance misuse or other psychological disorder and social deprivation/poverty will be termed 'familial or neighbourhood context' and considered risks for abuse. Similarly, verbal or physical attacks from peers will be included under 'bullying', another contextual risk with negative impacts but not termed child abuse per se. These will be examined separately from the targeted abuse labelled.

Perpetrators of child abuse can be known to the child or can be strangers. It depends to some extent on the type of abuse. Usually perpetrators are adults with caregiving roles for the child or are known to the child (Gekoski, Davidson, & Horvath, 2016), typically birth parents but also substitute parents (e.g. stepparents or other kin) or foster or adoptive parents. This can also include carers in residential care in 'loco parentis'. But perpetrators can also include those younger, including siblings in the household and other friends, and strangers who are peers under 18 years of age[11] (Allnock & Miller, 2013). Both males and females are implicated in perpetrating abuse but contribute to different victimisation risk. For example, child neglect is often focused on mother's (female carer's) behaviour, because of their traditional caregiving role, whilst physical abuse often shows fathers being responsible for more severe and aggressive attacks, although mothers are also implicated (Bifulco & Moran, 1998).

However sexual abuse (and child sexual exploitation) is wider in terms of the range of perpetrators involved. This is because it is not only linked to distortions in parenting and care (incest or familial sexual abuse), but also to exploitative sexual attention which can come from a range of individuals singly or in concert, either related or unrelated to the child/adolescent and sometimes with relatively little age difference. 'Stranger' sexual abuse is common, and whilst this is usually through face to face contact, increasingly it also encompasses contact made online. Perpetrator profiles are different for sexual abuse – this has its own diagnostic criteria in terms of paedophilic or paraphilic behaviour and is most often (although not exclusively) by males. Research in this area not only looks at relationship to perpetrator (including people in authority such as teachers or priests) but also gender and whether the abuse is conducted by a group of perpetrators and whether exploitative networks are involved. It also looks at the period of seduction or grooming which can precede the abuse. This serves to make the child compliant, to normalise sexual behaviour between the child and adult and to coerce the child. The grooming process itself could be termed emotional/psychological abuse.

Measuring child abuse

Accurate research findings require good measurement of the experiences being investigated. For studies of child abuse, this often occurs in adolescence or later since there are a number of both measurement and ethical issues about assessing children.

There are a number of standardised research assessments of childhood neglect and abuse applied retrospectively – most are brief and self-report a few intensive interviews. The more intensive ones capture higher rates of abuse, its chronicity and multiplicity more effectively (Bifulco, Brown, & Harris, 1994; Fink, Bernstein, Handelsman, Foote, & Lovejoy, 1995). Interviews can elicit more information, aid with recall of abuse in their structuring of experience chronologically and collect relevant context, timing, severity and change in experience. Self-reports have less depth, but some are validated against interviews (Bifulco, Bernazzani, Moran, & Jacobs, 2005) and can effectively categorise individuals as experiencing likely abuse or not experiencing it. Issues concerning self-report measures include limited range of abuse experiences covered (many do not include emotional abuse for example); the issue of under-reporting (this more evident in self-report) and the problem of single screening questions (these have been seen as unreliable) (Widom, Czaja, Bentley, & Johnson, 2012). In children's services, standardised measures are rarely used, instead practitioners utilise definitions derived from policy documents and use practitioner-experience to determine likely severity and danger to the child (Munro, 2011). Medical practitioners look for injuries to the child that could be caused by a physical attack, or signs of failure to thrive which could be the result of neglect. Educationalists look for changed behaviour in the child, or signs of the child being uncared for (e.g. by clothing, or weight), and of course whether they show signs of injury.

But effective quantitative causal research has more technical demands for measurement. This is to allow specificity, to differentiate the types of experience, their severity, the relationship to perpetrator, the timing and so on. These aspects are needed to correctly identify the presence of abuse at severe levels and to determine characteristics that may increase risks for negative health outcomes. There are various standardised self-report measures of care which determine care and control in childhood (e.g. Parental Bonding Instrument) (Parker, 1990). There are others which determine specific abusive experiences (e.g. Conflict Tactics Scale CTS for physical abuse [Straus, 1979]) and others broader such as Childhood Trauma Questionnaire (CTQ) (Bernstein et al., 1994). American studies utilise the Adverse Childhood Experiences (ACE) question-naire which covers a broad range of adverse childhood experience, not only abuse (Felitti, 2002). The UK Childhood Experience of Care and Abuse Ques-tionnaire (CECA.Q) is one of the few validated against an intensive interview to cover neglect and physical, sexual and emotional abuse (Bifulco et al., 2005).

There is a potential problem with measuring abuse long after it has hap-pened, in order to investigate its long-term impacts. There may be a number of reasons why memory of the experience is difficult to access by the individ-ual involved, or why there is biased reporting due to conflicting loyalties or from low mood at point of measurement. However, childhood abuse measures have proved unexpectedly robust when tested. This is particularly for the more intensive interview measures such as the CECA. In a study to investigate retro-spective reporting, a sample of 100 pairs of sisters interviewed independently was used to examine the similarity of their accounts. Each spoke of their own experience and then they were asked to describe their sister's experience and both given scorings on different abuse types, to reflect severity (Bifulco, Brown, Lillie, & Jarvis, 1997). When sisters were asked to corroborate one another's accounts, the experiences were well corroborated – particularly for neglect (.70 correlation) but also for physical abuse (.57) and sexual abuse (.52). Other shared experiences (e.g. partner violence, discord, housing and financial dif-ficulties) also had high agreement (ibid.). In an earlier project looking at loss of mother, finding death certificates allowed for corroboration of age at loss, cause of death and family location using the same interview approach (Bifulco, Harris, & Brown, 1992).

Therefore, when investigating childhood abuse and its longer-term impacts, there are a range of research measures that can be used. Most are not how-ever used in services, in part because they are not adapted for children. At the time of the Assessment Framework (DCSF, 2007a) being introduced for chil-dren's services, there was an aim of standardising assessment of child abuse and related aspects in a complex developmental model (Bentovim, Cox, Bingley Miller, & Pizzey, 2009). This led to the development of a range of tools which could be used. However, with much of the assessment ultimately computerised, this was later seen as an over-reliance on technology with too little interaction with the children and their families. Munro called for greater development of practitioner judgement (Munro, 2010) and more flexible use of assessment tools which put the child at the centre. So currently practitioners have choices about assessment, but with no single approach used. Current developments include a project to install the CECA as a scoring system to aid with rating severity of neglect and emotional abuse in Isle of Man children's services. This follows a successful pilot project in a London authority (Bifulco & Jacobs, 2012).

The next section will look at policy definitions of child abuse to establish what experiences count.

Defining child significant harm

The Children Act 1989 set out the legislative framework for the welfare and protection of children for England and Wales. This requires the judgement of a threshold of abuse or neglect, which for familial abuse would justify intervention in family life. It would justify court intervention and for the state to undertake actions to protect the child to meet their human rights and the requirements for normal healthy development. Thus, the court must decide on the basis of child protection social worker evidence, whether there has been 'significant' harm to the child as a result of parental/carer actions. The term 'harm' refers to ill treatment directly related to the impairment of normal, age appropriate health or development (Bentovim et al., 2009). Development is taken to mean physical, intellectual, emotional, social or behavioural functioning of the child, and is required to be at the normal or average level for the age group. Health includes both physical and mental health where it is damaged by maltreatment. Maltreatment refers to neglect, physical, sexual or emotional abuse and the form(s) of maltreatment need to be identified in the social worker reports, court judgements and for child protection procedures. For family court cases this includes an assessment of the extent to which the child's needs have been failed, the incapacity of parents or carers to meet those needs and the negative impact of family or social context on the child.

However, the Adoption and Children Act 2002 updated the definition of harm to include impairment suffered from witnessing the maltreatment of another such as through domestic violence between parents or the physical abuse of a sibling. This is often placed under the category of 'emotional abuse'. This does extend the social work remit to examine family context in broader detail but could be argued to over-broaden the definition of emotional abuse, which also has distinct characteristics targeted directly on the child.

There are dangers in defining abuse in terms of the *observed* harm to the child. There have been several disputed child abuse cases where children show physical effects considered to be harm from abuse, but where the causes have been mistaken. Investigations in the US review some of the rare diseases that had led to child abuse misdiagnoses relating to blood disorders that can lead to bleeding and/or bruising (Kirschner & Stein, 1985). Mistaken child abuse allegations based on poor medical diagnosing of physical disorder were investigated and shown to be interpreted as harm. Angelo Giardino,[12] documenting such cases in the US, states:

In all injuries, the major differential diagnosis is between accidental and inflicted injury. Determination of accident versus abuse is best accomplished by pairing thoughtful, thorough medical evaluation with information gathered through a multidisciplinary investigation, often involving child protective services (CPS) and law enforcement agencies.

James Garbarino, in defining child abuse, also argued as early as 1991 that not all bad developmental outcomes are the result of child abuse (Garbarino, 1991). Whilst his focus is on psychological/emotional abuse (the terms used in the United States and UK respectively) his points are relevant to defining abuse in general. He particularly differentiates the 'standards of conduct' approach to the 'probability of consequences' approach. For example, he argues sexual abuse is mainly attributed to the first criteria. Thus, sexual contact with a child is sexual abuse regardless of intent or outcome.

> The child is 'off limits' sexually to adults – regardless of any individual child's understanding, complicity or vulnerability or the adults' intentions.
>
> (Garbarino, 1991, p. 46)

However physical abuse is often judged in terms of the 'probability of consequences'. Given the prevalence (and legality in the UK) of some degree of physical chastisement, the minimal standard of conduct is blurred. It is the extent or severity of the physical assault that identifies it as inappropriate with consequences in terms of immediate physical damage to the child and a violation of rights. These thresholds have changed over time and culture. Garbarino (1991) gives the example of changes in minimal standards around neglect for children as car passengers, which have changed radically from the 1950s with the requirement of seat belts and child car seats for the very young, and now in the UK a ban on smoking in the car with a child. These are now taken to transgress minimum standards of care, but in past decades would not have.

If only the consequences of parent behaviour are utilised, this can lead to false diagnoses of child abuse. Problem behaviour in the child, physical signs of bruising or other injuries, can be due at times to other causes. It is therefore necessary to differentiate *perpetrator behaviour* from signs or symptoms in the child. Alleged behaviour of the perpetrator needs to be determined to see if physical attacks occurred and if these constitute physical abuse. Often child protection services start with signs and symptoms in the child and may have poorer evidence of parent or perpetrator behaviour. In order for the evidence to be accurately determined, careful definitions are therefore required which document parent/perpetrator actions towards the child.

Sexual abuse is often differentiated from other abuses, because it can have a wider range of perpetrators and can be part of organised criminal behaviour and therefore is usually investigated by police. Sexual abuse therefore, has greater legal and CJS ramifications in criminal courts than family courts. However, it should be noted that it can be accompanied by emotional abuse (for example through grooming, or threats to child or its family) and does occur more commonly with children who have been neglected and is often related to physical violence (Buist & Janson, 2001; DiLillo, Tremblay, & Peterson, 2000; Lightfoot & Evans, 2000). Therefore, it can be closely associated with other forms of abuse.

Assessment of children and families is critical to accurate decision making in terms of child protection from what are currently Local Child Safeguarding Boards (LCSBs). Definitions are central, but so are standardised tools and assessments, and operational definitions of indicators that can help practitioners identify abuse and judge its severity (Bentovim et al., 2009). Some are more nebulous, for example emotional abuse (Moran et al., 2003) and even in some cases neglect. Child and Family Training have produced materials on Neglect[13] with the Graded Care Profile for neglect also becoming popular.[14] Child sexual exploitation is another category considered difficult to assess. Here the Child Sexual Abuse Centre of Expertise has just published a report on tools for identification and assessment in CSE.[15] To ensure an effective new partnership working for children's services, health and the police, reliable assessments available for practice are critical, with a shared language, definition and severity grading between services needed. In particular these are needed in differentiating children experiencing significant harm, and those who are children in need.

Child in need

There are two relevant categories in investigating child abuse in social services: significant harm usually leading to the child being removed from the family for safety; and 'child in need' (CiN) where family support is deemed appropriate for keeping the child with the family but improving the level of care.

CiN is defined under the Children Act 1989 (revised 1993)

A child who is unlikely to achieve or maintain a reasonable level of health or development, or whose health and development is likely to be significantly or further impaired, without the provision of services; or a child who is disabled.... Where an assessment takes place, it will be carried out by a social worker... When assessing children in need and providing services, specialist assessments may be required and, where possible, should be coordinated so that the child and family experience a coherent process and a single plan of action.

(Department of Health, 1993, p.18)

The purpose of practitioner assessment is first to gather important information about a child and family; second to analyse their needs and/or the nature and level of any risk and harm being suffered by the child; third to decide whether the child is a child in need (section 17) and/or is suffering, or likely to suffer, significant harm (section 47); and to provide support to address those needs to improve the child's outcomes to make them safe. The predominant guidance in the UK has been through the Common Assessment Framework (2007).This identifies three dimensions relevant to assessing children: parenting capacity, family context and child impacts (DCSF, 2007a). This involves an inter-agency approach, effected currently through LSCB's in current arrangements and soon to be through a three-way partnership between children's services, health and police under the Children and Social Work Act 2017 (DfE, 2017b).

However, as well as determining significant harm, the professionals involved in child abuse cases also need to be able to assess 'standards of care' (Garbarino, 1996). The fact that not all harm that occurs to children comes through abuse, and the fact that not all children may equally show the effects of significant harm in the short term, means that perpetrator actions need to be established in identifying whether abuse has taken place. It is also necessary to document this to know the severity of the abuse. Therefore, documentation of what are expected standards of care provided to children is also important to establish. In previous policy, this led to identifying the needs of all children in Every Child Matters (Department of Education, 2003), which also formed the basis of early intervention actions focused on early years of development. However, it should be noted that this Department has now closed, and the ECM agenda has been abandoned, with parts of its legacy around well-being evident in the recent Social Work and Children Act (DfE, 2017b).

The next section will examine the national rates of child abuse in the UK to determine prevalence and change over time.

Prevalence of abuse in the UK

The question of how commonly child neglect and abuse occurs in the UK, and how rates change over time, is complex. This is because not all abuse is reported to children's services, but much remains hidden. Also, to determine change over time, the definition of child neglect/abuse needs to be consistent. Finally, abusive experiences are highly associated, so the experience identified to children's safeguarding services may in fact not be the most extreme one and may mask other severe experiences, for example of emotional abuse.

There are two sources of national figures. First is the national registration of child protection cases reported. The second comprises research estimates using representative surveys. The likely prevalence of childhood neglect and abuse will be discussed and how this has changed over time. This is impacted by changes in social policy definitions and procedures and increased public awareness, but also by new modes of abuse emerging, such as that online and through social media. This chapter will draw mostly upon the latest UK research in this area including the recent panel report on prevalence produced by the NSPCC (Radford et al., 2011). But reference will also be made to successive US child victimisation surveys (Finkelhor & Kendall-Tackett, 1997; Finkelhor, Ormrod, Turner, & Hamby, 2005). Of course, estimates of abuse depend on the definitions and thresholds for inclusion used, so there can be wide variation. Those reported here are those in the UK, the ones most similar in severity thresholds, and those most recent.

The most recent population research findings are from the NSPCC comprising a national survey using telephone interviews which used established abuse definitions and severity ratings, giving rates for 'serious' maltreatment by age and gender up to the age of 25. The questions on neglect were drawn from various measures including the shortened PARQ and the earlier NSPCC maltreatment survey but are also consistent with CECA thresholds. The figures are shown in Table1.1 for three different age groups, the latter (18-24) being outside the range of registered child abuse.

It can be seen that any maltreatment/abuse affects 9 per cent under age 11 and 22 per cent aged 11-16 - an overall rate of 16 per cent. However, neglect was substantially more common, particularly in those under age 11 (50 per cent) with an overall rate of 32 per cent; this was identified as the most common form of maltreatment. The category of mixed abuse had an overall rate up to 17 of 14 per cent. The NSPCC were able to compare rates with those investigated ten

Table 1.1 Lifetime rates of maltreatment[16] by parent or guardian in the community, NSPCC study

Maltreatment type	% Total under age 11	% Total age 11-17	% Total age 18-24
Emotional Abuse	4% (74)	7% (116)	7% (131)
Neglect	50% (130)	13% (229)	16% (303)
Physical violence	1% (34)	7% (119)	8% (159)
Maltreatment - mixed	7% (188)	21% (358)	23% (436)
Sexual abuse	1% (2)	1% (2)	1% (2)
All maltreatment	9% (229)	22% (379)	25% (465)

(Radford et al., 2011, p. 40).

Table 1.2 England[17] 2011–15 numbers on Child Protection Registers and category of abuse registered in the UK

Category of abuse	2011	2012	2013	2014	2015
Neglect	18,600	18,220	17,930	20,970	22,230
Physical abuse	4,800	4,690	4,670	4,760	4,350
Sexual abuse	2,400	2,220	2,030	2,210	2,340
Emotional abuse	11,400	12,330	13,640	15,860	16,660
Multiple	5,500	5,390	4,870	4,500	4,110
Total	**42,700**	**42,850**	**43,140**	**48,300**	**49,690**

years earlier. All categories were lower in the recent survey by at least a few percentage points. The conclusion was that rates do seem to be reducing.

National statistics of children registered with Child Protection services are another way of documenting change over time. Thus, the figures in Table 1.2, for England show generally slight reductions over time, except for neglect which rises and emotional abuse which rises substantially. This is likely to be due in part to better identification of these care aspects.

The figures relate to the initial category of abuse assigned to the child protection plan rather than the most recent category of abuse. Neglect is by far the most common, followed by emotional abuse and both have risen rather than diminished over time in relation to interventions available. It can therefore be seen that child abuse has vastly increased in its scope in recent times. This is due to widening of definitions to include more types of maltreatment and exploitation, for indicators of such maltreatment to have been updated for modern expectations and exploitation and expansion of time to include historical as well as ongoing abuse, and to encompass the child's life from as early as in the womb.

In order to consider contemporary issues, and those in the mind of the public and policy makers, it is also helpful to summarise some recent high-profile cases in the UK which have influenced both public perception and policy.

Recent UK high-profile cases

Serious case reviews

There have always been deaths of children at the hands of their parents or carers, and it seems unlikely that these can be totally eradicated despite intervention. For example, in 2013 there were three high profile Serious Case Reviews of children who had died in the UK. Daniel Pelka was a 4-year-old living in Coventry who was singled out for abuse and neglect by his mother and her partner until his death from a blow to the head in March 2012. What was missed by services was chronic neglect despite the little boy's very low weight, physical and psychological abuse. It was also despite numerous police calls to the house due to domestic violence and visits to hospital Emergency Department's with Daniel's injuries. The parents were skilled at covering up the truth of their actions and the services were misled or failed to investigate sufficiently to prevent Daniel's death. The second involved Keanu Williams, an infant living in Birmingham who died with 37 separate injuries on his body, inflicted by his mother in early 2011. The last was the conviction of Amanda Hutton in Bradford Crown Court for the severe neglect and manslaughter of her 4-year-old son, Hamzah Khan. The boy's mummified remains were found in his cot in September 2011, two years after his death in the squalid flat where other children were living. Neglect was a major element of these cases even though it is more common to name this as abuse in child deaths. Another issue was the deceit by parents and the response of social workers. Nushra Mansuri, professional officer with the British Association of Social Workers, commented on the Serious Case Review (SCR) evidence:

> In all three cases, the mothers were actively deceitful, often antagonistic and convincing liars when explaining away injuries or keeping professionals away from their door. In addition, both SCRs identified that professionals had succumbed to the "rule of optimism". This highlights how effective some abusive parents can be at averting blame and the high demands on social workers to keep relevant scepticism, at the same time as wanting to help the child, and potentially the parents too. It is also important to remember that children are killed by parents and carers – yet frequently it is practitioners involved in the cases of child death that are blamed and even vilified.[18]

The National Society for Prevention of Cruelty to Children (NSPCC)[19] provides figures to show that in 2015 alone, 65 children in the UK either died from injuries or were left seriously impaired, yet many of these do not reach media attention. There is a wide age range in cases subject to case review – ranging from month-old babies, to those aged 17 who had suffered abuse over some years. The cases are from all parts of the country, reflect different care arrangements (some with their birth parents, others in foster care) and from different ethnic communities. The deaths/serious impairments are the result of neglect, physical abuse, psychological abuse or sexual abuse, usually in combination. Some cases came to light when the child concerned committed suicide. Many were in the context of deprivation – teenage mothers barely coping, parents' substance abusing, elevated levels of poverty and housing need, parents unemployed and a number who had other children removed from their care. Clearly the range of circumstances and actions in these cases is broad and complex. Some cases are highlighted by the media, and some lead to national Inquiries, but others do not have such a spotlight. Most point to some failing of services, but also to criminal actions of parents or perpetrators. But in general, the death of a child from neglect or abuse is relatively uncommon, despite abuse occurring on a day to day basis around the country in family settings. However, there are abuses, particularly involving sexual abuse and exploitation, that are not necessarily family-based and can involve large numbers of children and young people. These are often highly secret and perpetrated by groups of abusers and many only come to light after tens if not hundreds of young people have been damaged.

Institutional sexual abuse cases 2010-16

There have been several high profile sexual abuse cases in recent years, many focused on young people in residential care where services, including the police, failed to act on the victim's complaints with some in family homes. For some, race was implicated in terms of perpetrator ethnicity which for many was of Asian origin, as well as social worker inaction due to mistaken ideas about teenage autonomy and what was perceived as a 'lifestyle choice'. In most cases there were police and other children's services inaction, this in part due to perceiving these young people (mostly girls) as being unreliable witnesses with unapproved life styles, their reputations tarnished by being in residential care. Thus, the negative judgements about teenage behaviour and stigma, as well as over-sensitivity to acknowledging race aspects due to fear by practitioners of being called racist, can be seen as a factor in enabling abuse and exploitation to continue.

There were four cases of multiple sexual abuse identified in Rochdale, Oxfordshire, Derby and Rotherham between 2010 and 2016, all with characteristics in common. The case in Derby 2010 (Operation Retriever)[20] was the earliest of these abuse scandals and involved approximately 30 teenage girls who had been systematically groomed, given alcohol or drugs and forced to have sex in cars, rented houses or hotels by ten men who were mainly of Asian origin, aged between 26 and 38 in Derbyshire. The undercover investigation by Derbyshire police charged 13 men, with 11 tried for a string of charges, not all sexual, relating to the case. Of the original 13, a total of nine were convicted of offences against vulnerable girls ranging from rape to false imprisonment. They were jailed in total for up to 22 years for 70 offences. One of the girls was in a care home, another with council foster parents and many were known to social services in the city. Perpetrators deliberately targeted children who seemed vulnerable. The girls disappeared overnight or for several days and may have generated missing person's reports. This case raised concerns about the apparent prevalence of men of Asian origin victimising white girls. This was followed by another investigation in Derby in 2012 (Operation Kern) when 15 teenage girls aged around 15 were raped by eight middle-aged men (these however all acted independently and did not know each other.)[21] Some of these girls were also in care homes. The perpetrators in this incident however were all white.

Rochdale in 2012 found gang members who were mainly men of Asian origin, targeting vulnerable girls, plying them with fast food, alcohol, drugs and gifts.[22] Some of the girls were raped and physically assaulted and some were forced to have sex with several men in a day, several times a week. One 13-year-old victim became pregnant and had the unborn child aborted. All of the perpetrators acted together to sexually exploit the girls. The nine defendants were jailed for a total of 77 years and were convicted of a wide range of offences which included trafficking, sexual assault, trafficking for sexual exploitation, rape and physical violence, and the charge of sexual activity with a child.

The difficulty of reaching a clear and shared definition of CSE has been noted recently by academics writing in this area (Beckett & Pearce, 2017). However, in 2017, Child Sexual Exploitation was defined as a form of child sexual abuse by the Department for Education (2017) as follows[23]:

> Child sexual exploitation is a form of child sexual abuse. It occurs where an individual or group takes advantage of an imbalance of power to coerce, manipulate or deceive a child or young person under the age of 18 into sexual activity (a) in exchange for something the victim needs or wants, and/or (b) for the financial advantage or increased status of the perpetrator or facilitator. The victim may have been sexually exploited even if the sexual activity appears consensual. Child sexual exploitation does not always involve physical contact; it can also occur through the use of technology.
>
> (DfE, 2017a, p. 5)

The guidance goes on to state that:

> Like all forms of child sexual abuse, child sexual exploitation: Can affect any child or young person (male or female) under the age of 18 years, including 16 and 17 year olds who can legally consent to have sex; can still be abuse even if the sexual activity appears consensual; can include both contact (penetrative and non-penetrative acts) and non-contact sexual activity; can take place in person or via technology, or a combination of both; can involve force and/or enticement-based methods of compliance and may, or may not, be accompanied by violence or threats of violence; may occur without the child or young person's immediate knowledge (through others copying videos or images they have created and posting on social media, for example); can

be perpetrated by individuals or groups, males or females, and children or adults. The abuse can be a one-off occurrence or a series of incidents over time, and range from opportunistic to complex organised abuse; and is typified by some form of power imbalance in favour of those perpetrating the abuse. Whilst age may be the most obvious, this power imbalance can also be due to a range of other factors including gender, sexual identity, cognitive ability, physical strength, status and access to economic or other resources.

(DfE, 2017a, p. 5)

In Rotherham in 2016 (Operation Clover)[24] two women who were local foster carers and again members of a gang, pretended to be trustworthy and sympathetic to the vulnerable girls and they let them stay at their home while providing access to them by men who abused them. Many of the girls had unsettled home lives, had suffered previous ill treatment or abuse and some were in local authority care. All were vulnerable to predatory behaviour. Gang members were found guilty of 55 serious offences including rape, forced prostitution, indecent assault and false imprisonment, some of which have been undetected for almost 20 years. The Rotherham case highlights the collective failure of police, social services and the local council to act despite repeated complaints from the girls. In 2013, the police received 157 reports concerning child sexual exploitation in the Borough. By May 2014, the caseload of the specialist child sexual exploitation team was 51 with more CSE cases held by other children's social care teams. There were 16 looked after children who were identified by children's social care as being at serious risk of sexual exploitation or having been sexually exploited.

The numbers of victims: young people (mainly girls); perpetrators; and offences seem staggering. Yet there was a longer history to at least one of these investigations: that of Rotherham sexual exploitation. The Jay Report (2014) on abuse cases found 1400 children were sexually exploited over the full Inquiry period, from 1997 to 2013. In just over a third of cases, children affected by sexual exploitation were previously known to services because of child protection and neglect. They were raped by multiple perpetrators, trafficked to other towns and cities in the north of England, abducted, beaten and intimidated. There were examples of children who had been doused in petrol and threatened with being set alight, threatened with guns, made to witness brutally violent rapes and threatened they would be next if they told anyone. Girls as young as 11 were raped by large numbers of male perpetrators. Services – both police and social services – were blamed as lacking leadership and underplaying the importance of sexual exploitation. This indicates that the recent Rotherham case was in fact just the tail end of a much longer case of institutionalised abuse and exploitation which occurred in that area.

There were a number of characteristics common to these institutional abuse cases in England. First, the perpetrators were often (but not exclusively) men of Asian origin, who systematically groomed, sexually tortured and trafficked (mainly white) teenage girls under the age of 18. Second, the police did not believe victim's prior complaints or take any action. Third, parents or social workers did not distinguish what they considered 'typical' teenage behaviours from sign of abuses and even referred to the victim's 'life choices' in being prey to abuse. Fourth, social workers were not monitoring children's missing days from home or school carefully and were largely unaware of the extent or chronicity of the abuse. What is striking about these cases is the numbers involved, many hundreds of victims and offences, although with lower numbers of perpetrators, and the longevity of the abusive actions (up to 20 years).

Whilst the ethnicity was observed and taken to be important, and again highlighted by the media, Ray McMorrow, a health specialist at the National Working Group reported that whilst the proportions of Asians involved in the Rotherham sex abuse was higher than their proportion in the population, it would be irresponsible to dwell on ethnicity. He pointed out that other similar abuses were conducted by white men but not given the same publicity.[25]

Operation Pallial[26] in 2012 began inquiries into abuse in the care system in North Wales at the request of North Wales Chief Constable Mark Polin. The investigation has so far resulted in the conviction of eight men, including care home owner John Allen who was sentenced to life in prison in December 2014. A total of 340 people have made contact with the investigation and 84 complaints are still being actively investigated. Institutional abuse can also come under the category of historical abuse. In 2017 the Historical Institutional Abuse Inquiry Northern Ireland[27] published findings on child abuse in residential homes and institutions from 1922 to 1995.

It is clear that historical institutional abuse has been rife for many years across different sectors; the emerging findings from the Institutional Inquiry into Child Sexual Abuse (IICSA) provides evidence of this.[28] The other impetus behind IICSA was the high profile investigation of the abuse over decades by celebrities such as Jimmy Savile, another example of organisational failure to investigate complaints of abuse.

Savile and abuse by well-known figures

Another contemporary concern involves not only the knowledge that historical sexual abuse was widespread in older generations, but much was effectively hidden within the organisations where it took place. These historical abuses took place within institutions including schools, children's homes and religious institutions. They also included medical establishments, community institutions and guest houses. The abuses were also highly secret and often perpetrated by prominent people and in the context of networks. In 2015 the public was made aware of the uncovering of alleged historical sexual abuse by politicians and those in eminent social positions.[29] This involved more than 1500 suspects, many high profile. Those implicated included politicians, and prominent people from the entertainment, music or sport industry. This followed on the footsteps of the notorious Jimmy Savile case, investigated in 2013 and published in the Operation Yewtree report, two years after the perpetrator's death with first allegations taken seriously just one year after his death. The media reports stated:

> Sir Jimmy Savile OBE (1926-2011) was, in his lifetime, a high-profile radio and television presenter, media personality and major fundraiser for charity. Although there were some unsubstantiated allegations of indecent assault made against him while he was alive, in the two years since his death, Savile has come to be known as one of the UK's most prolific sex offenders, with claims of historical abuse going back 60 years, involving the BBC, a number of care homes and schools and as many as 33 NHS institutions. When the NSPCC and Metropolitan Police published their joint report in January 2013, 450 people had made complaints against Savile; since the publication of Operation Yewtree's report, 10 additional public figures have been investigated by the police and one (the broadcaster, Stuart Hall) has been given a prison sentence.[30]

'Giving Victims a Voice'[31] was published jointly by the Metropolitan Police and the NSPCC on the Operation Yewtree findings. There was no criminal investigation into Savile, since he was no longer alive at the time his abusive behaviour became known. This large investigation considered abuse allegations which were often historical ones, pertaining to many previous decades, the earliest in 1955 in Manchester. The peak of his known offending was between 1966 and 1976 when Savile was 40-50 years old. Of offences by Savile which were reported, 73 per cent were against those aged under 18 years. The victim age range of those who have come forward was between eight and 47 years old (at the time of abuse). Of those, 82 per cent were female and most were in the 13 to 16 age group.

Many issues were raised. It is now clear that Savile was 'hiding in plain sight' and using his celebrity status and fundraising activity to gain uncontrolled access to vulnerable people across six decades. For a variety of reasons, the vast majority of his victims did not feel they could speak out and it's apparent that some of the small number who did had their accounts dismissed by those in authority, including parents and carers and the police. This in turn, along with other factors, has led to the 'Independent Inquiry into Child Sexual Abuse', currently led by Professor Jay and underway since 2015.[32] Its remit is to investigate whether public bodies and other non-state institutions in England and Wales have taken seriously their responsibility to protect children from sexual abuse and make meaningful recommendations for change in the future. Its first report in December 2016[33] set out its brief and progress. It includes both criminal and research investigation, incorporating the Truth Project which listens to the voices of victims. The recommendations for change will revolve around cultural, structural, financial and professional/political domains. This will be further described in later chapters.

In 2016 the Football Association[34] began an internal review into child abuse following allegations of abuse led by Clive Sheldon QC, and the National Independent Safeguarding Board[35] for adults and children was established to strengthen and improve the work of safeguarding boards across Wales. Also, this year the BBC Trust published the report by Dame Janet Smith, DBE, of the inquiry into the BBC's culture and practices during the 1970s and 1980s (Jimmy Savile and Stuart Hall).[36] The Review was first established in October 2012 to conduct an impartial, thorough and independent review of the culture and practices of the BBC during this time. A further investigation, into the conduct of Stuart Hall, was undertaken by Dame Linda Dobbs, DBE,[37] and was published as part of the report. Dame Janet Smith's report states:

> My conclusion is that a number of BBC staff were aware of specific complaints about Savile's conduct and in two cases were aware of his sexual interest in teenage girls, some of whom might have been underage. All of these people ought to have reported their awareness to their line managers or to someone in a more senior position. None of them did so. The result is that I must conclude that there is no evidence that any senior member of staff (of Head of Department status or above) was aware of Savile's conduct. It follows that I have found no evidence that the BBC as a corporate body was aware of Savile's conduct.
>
> (2016, p. 14)[38]

This conclusion allows the BBC to avoid any blame for acts perpetrated on its premises and in the knowledge of members of staff. The fact that these members of staff did not report the allegations is beside the point; this will be small comfort for those victimised by Savile and others.

There are many implications of historical abuse on this scale. First is recompense due to victims, but also acknowledgement that provision of interventions and treatments on a large scale is required for those who may still be hampered by their early life abuse. Another is the aim to set up safeguards to ensure this is never repeated on this scale, and to have systems in place where secrecy of such abuse cannot be maintained. Other issues implicated are around inter-generational transmission of risk from abuse which may have further damaged children of these victims. The ramifications could be very great for damage to large numbers of individuals with requirement of professional and public acceptance that cultural change is needed. In response, Operation Hydrant,[39] a coordination hub, was established to deliver the national policing response, oversight and coordination of non-recent child abuse investigations concerning persons of public prominence, or in relation to those offences which took place historically within institutional settings.

Abuse in the church

Other high-profile abuse cases have come to light in recent decades including those perpetrated by those working for churches internationally. Cases of child sexual abuse by Catholic priests, nuns and members of other religious orders, together with their subsequent cover-ups, in the twentieth and twenty-first centuries have led to numerous allegations, investigations, trials and convictions (Bruni, 2002). The abuse has included both boy and girl victims, some as young as 3 years old, with the majority of victims between the ages of 11 and 14. The accusations began to first receive wide publicity in the late 1980s. Many of these involved cases in which a figure has been accused of abuse for decades; such allegations were frequently made by adults or older youths years after the abuse occurred. Cases have also been brought against members of the hierarchy in the Roman Catholic Church who were found to have covered up sex abuse allegations of priests and also been complicit in moving abusive priests to other parishes or even abroad, where abuse continued.

The extent of this is worldwide, with particular focus on Roman Catholic countries – for example, very prominent investigations in Boston in the US (2004) and more recently in Ireland (Garrett, 2013). On 31 January 2002, the *Boston Globe* published a report that sent shockwaves around the world. Their findings, based on a six-month campaign by the 'Spotlight' investigative team, showed that hundreds of children in Boston had been abused by Catholic priests, and that this horrific pattern of behaviour had been known – and ignored – by the Catholic Church. Instead of protecting the community it was meant to serve, the Church exploited its powerful influence to protect itself from scandal – and innocent children paid the price.

The cases received significant media and public attention internationally with Ireland, Canada, Australia and the US highlighted. Members of the Church's hierarchy have argued that media coverage was excessive and disproportionate, and they have also argued that such abuse also takes place in other religions and institutions. From 2001 to 2010 the central governing body of the Catholic Church considered sex abuse allegations involving about 3,000 priests dating back 50 years. Cases reflect worldwide patterns of long-term abuse as well as the church hierarchy's pattern of regularly covering up reports of alleged abuse.

Some studies claim that priests in the Catholic Church are no more likely than other men to commit abuse. In addition, the studies claim that the rate of abuse by priests had fallen sharply in the last 20 to 30 years, and that some 75 per cent of the allegations in the United States were of abuse between 1960 and 1984. However, the Australian Royal Commission into Institutional Responses to Child Sexual Abuse found that the average time it took between the sexual abuse of a victim by a Catholic priest and its disclosure, reporting or seeking redress, was 33 years. For this reason, there is insufficient data to be able to accurately ascertain current rates of child sex abuse, or to claim that abuse in the Catholic Church has fallen in recent decades. The Commission revealed 7 per cent of Australian priests between 1950-2009 were accused of abusing children, and that one Catholic order had 40.4 per cent of their non-ordained members with allegations against them in this period.

The Inquiry into Institutional Child Sexual Abuse (IICSA) is the most far-reaching independent statutory inquiry into CSA in UK history set for October 2018. The Inquiry was set up due to serious concerns that some organisations had failed, and were continuing to fail, to protect children from sexual abuse. The Inquiry has so far launched 13 investigations into a broad range of institutions identified on the basis of the Panel's criteria for selection of investigations which include the Internet, custodial institutions, local authorities, Westminster, the Anglican and Roman Catholic Churches and residential schools. The investigations will give a voice to victims and survivors of child sexual abuse, enable the Inquiry to understand how institutions have failed to protect children from sexual abuse and make practical recommendations to ensure better institutional protection for children in the future. The Inquiry's investigative work underpins the Public Hearings which will be held during the course of most, if not all, of the investigations. Each investigation will conclude with a report that will set out the Inquiry's conclusions on institutional failings and identify practical recommendations for change. These 13 investigations constitute the first phase of the Inquiry's work and further investigations will be announced as the Inquiry progresses. The Inquiry also includes an ambitious research programme that will underpin the work.[40] The publication cites reliable studies from the United States (John Jay College of Criminal Justice Study) and Australia (Royal Commission) evidencing that between 4 per cent and 7 per cent of Catholic priests have been the subject of allegations of child sexual abuse. The findings from the IICSA Rapid Evidence Assessment state that:

1   The structure of the Catholic Church and the authority vested in individual bishops is a factor which has allowed child sexual abuse to occur in some

dioceses and has meant that responses to child sexual abuse have been inconsistent;

2　Clericalism, the belief that the clergy is superior to the laity, has been identified in the literature as a factor which may enable child sexual abuse to occur and hinder an effective response;

3　Attitudes towards sexuality within the Church have also been suggested as factors explaining the incidence of child sexual abuse in the Church and the Church's response;

4　The Church's response to allegations of child sexual abuse has been characterised by a range of sources as one of secrecy which seeks to protect the Church's reputation, this has been placed above the welfare of individual children;

5　Certain alleged practices, such as the relocation of offending priests to new dioceses, have seemed to put the needs of the perpetrator first and prioritise the perpetrator over the needs of victims and survivors and safety of children;

6　The literature suggests that the response to victims by the Church has not met their needs.

Source: (IICSA, 2017, p.1)

The IICSA Inquiry is currently hearing evidence in respect of abuse perpetrated by priests in the Anglican Church; evidence has been taken from victims recounting their experience in public hearings. The Inquiry will investigate the nature and extent of, and institutional responses to, child sexual abuse within the Church of England, the Church in Wales and other Anglican churches operating in England and Wales (collectively referred to here as 'the Anglican Church'). The inquiry will incorporate case specific investigations and a review of information available from published and unpublished reports and reviews, court cases and previous investigations in relation to child sexual abuse by those associated with the Anglican Church. The Inquiry will consider the experiences of victims and survivors of child sexual abuse within the Anglican Church, and investigate the prevalence of child sexual abuse within the Anglican Church; the adequacy of the Anglican Church's policies and practices in relation to safeguarding and child protection, including considerations of governance, training, recruitment, leadership, reporting and investigation of child sexual abuse, disciplinary procedures, information sharing with outside agencies, and approach to reparations and the extent to which the culture within the Church inhibits or inhibited the proper investigation, exposure and prevention of child sexual abuse.

Recent research undertaken in late 2017 by the IICSA Research Team into abuse in the Anglican Church suggests that although there is a wide range of literature on abuse perpetrated within the church, there is little robust research regarding prevalence (IICSA, 2017).[41]

Forced child migration from the UK 1940-1970

The scandal concerning British children sent without their parents' consent to Commonwealth countries, notably Australia, in the postwar period but as recent as the 1970s, was made public and championed by Nottingham social worker Margaret Humphreys. Her experiences in 1987 during her regular family case work found that families had been forcibly separated by a government initiative to send children in care abroad in secret. Her work led to the uncovering of this forced migration, and ultimately the reuniting of many hundreds of families. The forced migration (itself psychological abuse as children were fed misinformation about parental death) led frequently to slave labour and experiences of neglect, physical and sexual abuse. Church organisations and other charities were heavily involved. Humphreys published her experience and findings in 'Empty Cradles' (Humphreys, 2011) and created huge publicity for the case. Overall very large numbers are estimated as having been involved over the decades (150,000) the youngest as young as 3 years old. Most emphasis recently has been on the 40,000 sent to Australia, the latest of the migrations. Humphreys was in time recognised for her work, and apologies from British and Australian governments were given in 2009 and 2010 to the families involved.

Recently this issue has come within the remit of the IICSA inquiry which has recommended financial compensation to victims.[42] Inquiry chairwoman Professor Alexis Jay said:

> Child migration was a deeply flawed government policy that was badly implemented by numerous organisations which sent children as young as five years old abroad. The policy was allowed to continue despite evidence over many years showing that children were suffering.
>
> (IICSA, 1st March, 2018a)

The inquiry said the government was 'primarily responsible' for the scheme managed by the Catholic Church and charities, including Barnardo's and the Fairbridge Society, which is now part of the Prince's Trust. The report also said the government failed to ensure children were protected; failed to respond to reports of abuse; was unwilling to jeopardise its relationship with the Australian government and did not want to upset Barnardo's or the Fairbridge Society. It also found:

● Many of the organisations 'enjoyed patronage from persons of influence and position';

- The avoidance of 'embarrassment and reputational risk was more important' than care of the children;
- Successive governments after 1970 failed to accept full responsibility;
- Other institutions involved in the scheme which have failed to apologise should so do so 'as soon as possible'.

It is hoped that the victims of the forced migration receive compensation. But it also needs to be acknowledged that many will need intensive psychological and related services to deal with the lifelong damage that might have been incurred. Whilst they may have received financial recompense, it is not clear whether such services will be provided on the potential scale needed. The implications of the IICSA inquiry into historical abuse have many such issues for how society aids those with the lifelong burden of abuse, in this case with government culpability.

The next aspect outlined here in terms of contemporary child abuse issues, which sets the scene for how child abuse is identified and countered, is the international context. This is outlined in more detail in Chapter 2.

Abuse internationally

The prevalence of abuse worldwide is important, but rates are not well established. Reliable statistics vary from country to country according to the policy requirements, legal definition of abuse and the accurate collation of figures. This is being more consistently and extensively applied in the EU, is rigorously applied in the US, Canada and Australia, but is variable in other parts of the world.

Understanding the international basis for childhood abuse can be important even for local understanding of abuse. For example, given high rates of immigration/emigration, practices involving abuse may move from country to country, with issues such as: the potential for sexual tourism of British people abroad to places like Thailand which can include child abuse; Internet-based abuse can originate in other countries with sites set up for example in Russia and the Far East which can affect children in the UK and worldwide. Immigration from non-European countries can involve more culturally bound forms of abuse such as Female Genital Mutilation, child trafficking or child labour.

The prevalence of neglect or abuse of children worldwide is unknown and can vary in different cultures and settings, and at different times, but is very likely to occur in all societies. One problem of identification involves the laws, cultural context and local thresholds applied. This is in addition to stigma, taboo and secrecy, with barriers to disclosing abuse endemic. In the international field, identification of abuse is often centred on child sexual exploitation and child trafficking, since this is the most likely to cross international boundaries.

A review of child sexual exploitation using data from 73 countries and five con-tinents showed definitions to be variable between high- and low-income catego-ries, the latter less inclusive, for example around child prostitution (Dubowitz, 2017). Yet most countries examined allowed for the removal of maltreated chil-dren from their homes, three-quarters required assessment of child and fam-ily need and required victims to receive services. Only about a third similarly required services for perpetrators.

Other studies have reviewed child abuse definitions cross-culturally, for example in South Africa (Piercea & Bozalekb, 2004). Here professionals were asked to rate categories of abuse for severity and showed that sexual abuse and child prostitution were ranked highest. It is worth noting that 'child pros-titution' is now a term not used in many countries, now being referred to as 'child sexual exploitation' (CSE) in the UK (DfE, 2017a). When lay persons versus professionals were compared in the South African study, the former evaluated categories as more serious. Other research investigators have focused on rou-tinely collected hospital data as a means of child maltreatment surveillance, for example in Australia (McKenzie, Scott, Waller, & Campbell, 2011).

It is only relatively recently that child sexual abuse facilitated through online contact has become well established. This has several facets - perpetrators can contact the children online, groom them and the meet (offline) for an abusive sexual encounter. It can also involve filming or photographing of abuse which is then distributed on the Internet as a form of currency amongst abuse offend-ers. Finally, there is also the simultaneous abuse and grooming of adolescents for abuse offending. Investigation of such abuse is complex and has led to the development of High Technology Crime Units (HTCU) in the police, and the investigation of online sources of paedophilic and other grooming behaviour. Technology has now become a new mode for predators to approach children, with a very wide geographic scope and at little cost or inconvenience to the perpetrator. Legislation has had to follow, with policy implications for the UK and EU, but also internationally (Webster et al., 2015).

Other forms of abuse internationally include child trafficking. This involves action to protect the movement of children, usually across international bor-ders for exploitation purposes, a UN Protocol, signed in Palermo Sicily 2000 and known as the Palermo Protocol.[43] As minors, children cannot consent, and the purpose of the trafficking is for sexual exploitation or begging or domestic servitude or organ removal, benefit fraud or child labour. It is often accompa-nied by neglect, physical, sexual or psychological abuse. Children are sworn to secrecy and find they have no way of escaping being alone in a foreign country. Whilst international in scope, such children can also be found living in the UK.

Another cultural practice considered abusive is that of Female Genital Muti-lation (FMG) common in regions of Sub-Saharan Africa and the Middle East. It involves the partial or total removal of female external genitalia for non-medical reasons (Cloward, 2016). Victims are numbered in the millions and the practice is considered acceptable in many communities worldwide. The Serious Crime Act 2015 extended the definition of child cruelty and introduced in the UK a legal duty for regulated health and social care professionals and teachers to report FGM in England and Wales. Also, the Modern Slavery Act 2015 consolidated and clarified existing legislation on trafficking for child trafficking and enforced child labour, introducing an anti-slavery Commissioner for England and Wales.

Another distinct form of abuse occurring in other cultures is the denouncing of the child as a witch. This is most common in Nigeria and can be related to homelessness and trafficking of children believed to be witches. Adversity that happens in a family or community is attributed to evil forces and spells, with children sees as controlled by evil spirits and being responsible for evil to other in the form of ill health and violence.

It can therefore be seen that culture and international forms of abuse can have a significant impact on children, with effects also experienced within the UK. Therefore, culture and internationalism are important contemporary issues in child abuse. These issues are discussed in Chapter 2.

The next section returns to the UK context, and examines policy reviews and their impact on services and professional working with children and families where there is abuse.

Policy-focused service provision

Statutory child protection services include social services and the police which are the focus in this book (see Chapters 3 and 4). However, because of the need for identifying abuse more widely, and the issue of early intervention, many other services are also involved. A key one is education. All schools are required to have a member of staff responsible for safeguarding children and all staff need to be alert to possible signs of abuse. Modern safeguarding now has an emphasis on early years education, with a view to taking preventative action for all children in improving their future opportunities and well-being. This also includes nursery provision. Health services are also involved. Perinatal services are important given high-risk parents having pregnancy with the potential for abusing the baby. Other services include GP services and Emergency Departments where injured children can be brought or paediatrician services for children with physical symptoms which may have a maltreatment source. Child and adolescent mental health services (CAMHS) can also been involved when children show signs of distress which may relate to maltreatment. Where abuse is recognised, children can also respond with various psychological disorders, and therefore require treatment for effects of abuse.

The influence of early intervention advocacy has arisen both from developmental research emphasising early years, and due to the potential lifelong cost effectiveness of early action for improved quality of life nationally. In recent times the Sure Start programme targeted families in poor areas to provide additional service to improve life chances from infancy. This developed into Children's Centres which work in collaboration with nursery provision and schools. The target was young children from disadvantaged backgrounds, with a remit of child support re health and cognitive development and education and family support through parenting and mental health provision. Follow-up evaluations have been undertaken with indications of positive outcomes. However, there is now indication with the 2017 Social Work and Children's Act (DfE, 2017b) that the early intervention agenda is beginning to wane with more focus on 'signs of safety'[44] and 'contextual safeguarding' for adolescents at risk from dangers outside their immediate family.[45] This move is perhaps to narrower concerns for child protection with targeted intervention into families in need and for those requiring more acute help. Figure 1.2 shows the service 'pyramid' which applies to both health and social services[46] organisation to indicate different levels of services. This is paralleled by the implied levels of need which may require each level of service.

- **Tier 1** – Universal services such as schools, health visiting, GP and so on.
- **Tier 2** – Targeted services for children and families beginning to experience – or at risk of – difficulties, for example school counselling, parenting programmes, support for teenage parents and so on.

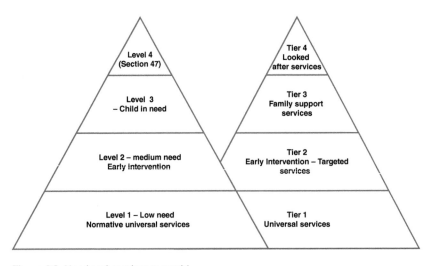

Figure 1.2 Need and services pyramid

- **Tier 3** - Specialist services for children and families with multiple needs such as intensive family support, specialist child and adolescent mental health services, and services for children with disabilities.
- **Tier 4** - Specialist services for children and families with severe and complex needs, including child protection services, inpatient child and adolescent mental health services.

At times of limited funding there is tension for children and families between these tiers who can be in competition for funds. Thus, early intervention is an important plank in improving the health and well-being of the nation starting from early years. But simultaneously the health and care needs of all other age groups need simultaneous attention either as targeted interventions or emergency/acute care or treatment. Early intervention needs a long period to establish its effectiveness, targeted interventions and emergency care have more immediate benefits. Our society aims to have both types in place, but at different times some aspects of the child welfare system is likely to be disadvantaged.

There have been many Policy reviews in recent years (see later chapters for details), many following child deaths. A number have led to analysis of service failure with recommendations for change. These raise contemporary issues around challenges in the current child protection context. These are discussed in greater detail in subsequent chapters, but some of the main features extrapolated are highlighted here.

Multi-agency working

The Laming Review, now 15 years old, has been particularly influential with its focus on how agencies work together in protecting children (Laming, 2003). The inquiry focused on the tragic death of Victoria Climbié, murdered by her aunt Marie-Therese Kouao and her then partner Carl Manning. The inquiry identified the failing of individuals, departments and services on their lack of communication and action, their 'blinding incompetence' and the complete lack of empathy and lack of focus on the vulnerable child. The report concluded that heads of local authority departments must in future be held accountable for failing to pass on or relay information about cases of abuse or mistreatment of children within their care. Many services had been involved with Victoria: the police, social services, departments of four local authorities, the National Health Service (NHS) and the NSPCC as well as local churches. All had noted the signs of abuse and on numerous occasions she could have been saved if action had been taken. In particular Harringey Council and Victoria's social worker, Lisa Arthurworrey, was singled out for blame. This was despite a range of agencies being involved in the case over time, and other professionals also being culpable.

In order to combat the causes and consequences of child abuse, it is necessary to take a multi-agency approach. This is mirrored by the inter-disciplinary approach in research investigation which serves to provide a more complete understanding of both victim and perpetrator characteristics and contexts to aid future intervention. In services, the overlap of child sexual abuse/exploitation investigation as a criminal matter can be complemented by social work investigation of maltreatment in families involving abuse, as well as educational services where signs of abuse may first be noted. Divisions between the agency processes can serve to obfuscate the factors common to both, in terms of the linked experiences, common causes and similar impacts (Munro, 2011). There are various linkages. For the child victim, sexual abuse and exploitation can be associated with parental neglect and other family abuse. The sexual offender who may be a stranger, will target neglected children and those already looked after by the state, identifying these as vulnerable and easier to victimise. Similarly, children with low self-esteem emerging from familial emotional abuse will be more prey to sexual grooming processes. Re-victimisation occurs among children made vulnerable from family maltreatment. Both neglect and CSE can be increased by neighbourhood characteristics. Equally the consequences of both types of victimisation are very serious in terms of long-term poor functioning in relationships and clinical disorder, with the combinations of abuse having even greater consequences in adult life. Therefore, despite the criminal and family court procedural divergence and the different processes and training followed by police and social workers or clinicians, a holistic picture is needed to understand the context, causes and consequences of child maltreatment.

Managing the mental health problems resulting from child abuse has proved central. The Children and Social Work Act 2017 was introduced to improve mental health provision for looked after children. This Act also requires that relationships education is to be provided to pupils of compulsory school age receiving primary education at schools in England and that relationships and sex education is to be provided (instead of sex education alone) to pupils receiving secondary education at schools in England.

The legislation stipulates that children must be informed about:

- safety in forming and maintaining relationships,
- the characteristics of healthy relationships, and
- how relationships may affect physical and mental health and well-being (Children and Social Work Act s34).

The legislation does not explicitly mention online abuse aspects, which is perhaps a missed opportunity for synthesis of policy on abuse and of providing a broader remit.

Race/ethnicity/cultural awareness

One issue raised during the Laming inquiry concerned racial aspects of the Climbié case, due to the fact that a black child was murdered by her black carers, and the social worker and police officer most closely involved in the case were black. Granham, the QC in the case, stated that race may have played a part in the case with practitioners' fears of being accused of racism leading to their inaction. In the hearings, Arthurworrey, who is African-Caribbean, also admitted that her assumptions about African-Caribbean families influenced her judgement. For example, she had assumed Climbié's timidity in the presence of Kouao and Manning stemmed not from fear, but from the African-Caribbean demonstration of respect towards one's parents.

The issue of over-caution due to presumed racial sensitivity was stated by Ratna Dutt, director of the Race Equality Unit:

> There is some evidence to suggest that one of the consequences of an exclusive focus on 'culture' in work with black children and families, is [that] it leaves black and ethnic minority children in potentially dangerous situations, because the assessment has failed to address a child's fundamental care and protection needs.
>
> (Laming, 2003, p. 345)

Ratna Dutt, later stated:

> the implicit message is that it's acceptable for ethnic minorities to receive poor services under the guise of superficial cultural sensitivity. This is absolutely shameful, as it allows people to argue that good practice is compromised by anti-racism... or a large number of black frontline staff if the finger of blame is pointed at them they don't end up in jobs in other local authorities. That's how institutional racism operates.[47]

The report also quoted Dr Nnenna Cookey, a consultant paediatrician, who said:

> I do take huge issue with the emphasis that Black families should be assessed by, or given the opportunity to have, a Black social worker. For me that detracts from the whole process. A child is a child regardless of colour. I think the social and cultural differences or backgrounds . . . of these families is crucial and should be considered as part of a general assessment. But I think if we are not careful we'll lose the whole emphasis on the child's welfare. I think if we are not very careful we will send out the very wrong message

that non-Black social workers do not have the capabilities, the standards and everything that goes with it to assess Black families. This would be a mistake.[48]

Abuse assessment and bureaucratic procedures

Whilst Laming's many recommendations were approved (see Chapter 5 for more details), there was nevertheless the death of another child, Peter Connolly (Baby P) in 2007. This child had also been involved in social services, and the death occurred in the same area of London, with Harringey Children's services. Race was not an issue in this case. Instead a subsequent review into services by Professor Eileen Munro focused on the failure of bureaucracy that had developed and burgeoned in children's services to the extent that the needs of the child were often lost. She advocated a more open and less blaming culture around safeguarding children, learning from the past and learning to manage human error systemically. She criticised the overuse of technology in assessment and completing bureaucracy which restricted time spent with children and families. She also advocated increasing professional confidence and judgement in social work. This is achieved through additional training where necessary, but also through giving the profession of social work higher status as a professional body. The Munro report 2011 focused on a systems analysis of social work with a parallel report of the child's journey through the protection system. The Munro review provided a number of recommendations. These included taking a new look at both bureaucracy and the use of technology in assessing and processing cases; the re-framing of managerialism and target setting in services; and a drive to keep experienced social workers on the frontline and make changes to the social work career to keep more working with families. She also recommended a Child Social Worker for England to advise ministers. Whilst changes were implemented, there are still issues about how practice can be most effective, and ways in which it is aided and hampered by the use of technology.

Managing error in identifying abuse

One issue concerns how to manage risk associated with child abuse, and to cope with human error and its aftermath, which can have potentially dire outcomes in terms of the life of a child. When this happens, practitioners can become hate figures in the tabloid press. Munro states (2011):

> Mistakes in assessing risk can be either of under-estimating (false negative) or over-estimating (false positive) the danger to the child. With hindsight, it

can be deemed that the child was left in an unsafe home or was removed without sufficient cause. The former kind of mistake is more easily seen so there is more pressure in general to avoid false negatives than false positives. However, there seems a predictable rhythm to society's pressure. Fluctuations in public attitudes to removing children from their birth families are linked to major media coverage of mistakes... data confirm that a shift in public attitudes influences the anxiety that child protection professionals experience when trying to avoid false negatives when dealing with a difficult case. However, people also react strongly when they see families being broken up by what they see as over-zealous professionals. Whenever it is perceived that large numbers of children are being removed from their birth parents, anxiety grows that too many families are being torn apart and professionals are getting too powerful, leading to push in the other direction.

(Munro, 2011, p.17)

Social workers are caught in the dilemma of providing care and keeping the family together when possible, to preserve autonomy and privacy in family life, but at the same time investigating harm where child removal becomes a key safety priority. The issue of how professionals manage in this difficult arena is considered a contemporary concern for further discussion.

There are some inherent contradictions in the social work role in the UK in that the parallel provision of care, alongside forensic investigation into abuse, take place side by side. Wrennall (2014) points this out:

The role of investigator and gatherer of intelligence has eclipsed the role of social worker to such a high degree that little actual social work takes place. British children and families have tended to receive police work performed by social workers rather than social work recognisable by any international standards. Britain is almost alone in adopting a model of Child Welfare in which these roles are combined. It is not the only country, but one of the few. Social workers have long been aware of the tensions and contradictions between the roles of carer and controller. The dictum, "we sometimes control because we care", quoted in the literature, was meant to resolve the contradiction. But putting words together in the same sentence is not the same as resolving the problems of irreconcilable role expectations.

(Wrennall, 2014, p.3)

Digital aspects of abuse

The Digital Economy Act 2017 was introduced to strengthen age verification measures for children online. This endows, for example, the British Board of Film Classification (BBFC) with the authority to ban adult pornography websites that do not instigate a suitably full-bodied system to verify age, by necessitating a Credit Card (CC) to be used to gain access only available to those 18+. Unfortunately, the new Act fails to deal with children who fraudulently use their parents'/older siblings' credit cards and only applies to websites. On a more positive note it will prevent children from using Virtual Private Networks (VPN's) to gain access to foreign domiciled pornography sites, beyond the reach of English law.

The Serious Crime Act 2015 extended the definition of child cruelty and made important changes to the Sexual Offences Act in respect of the online grooming of a child. Section 15 of the SOA 2003 – *'meeting a child following sexual grooming'* has done little to address the problem of online grooming as the defendant had to communicate with a child online and to meet, arrange to meet or travel to meet the child with the intention of sexually abusing the child. There would have to be evidence of sexual intent under this legislation. The offence of 'sexual communication with a child' was introduced through an amendment to the Serious Crime Act 2015; this did not actually come into force until 3 April 2017 (now s.15A of the Sexual Offences Act 2003). The new offence requires the communication to be intentionally made and either inherently sexual, objectively sexual or designed to prompt a sexual response, irrespective of whether the first communication was sexual.

Contemporary issues

This book has a focus on contemporary issues concerning child abuse. This introduction has highlighted a number of these which will be explored in following chapters. These are summarised in in Table 1.3 which also signposts the later chapters which discuss them in more detail.

It can be seen that these occur at different levels of the socio-ecological model described earlier (see Figure 1.3)

Table 1.3 Contemporary issues in child abuse identified

Issue	Brief outline	Chapter
1 **Ethics and child voice**	Force of UN rights of the child; child's voice in their care and protection.	Ch 2 Safeguarding children internationally
2 **Internationalism and culture**	International standards and abuse identification; immigration; cultural diversity and abuse	
3 **National policy response**	Accommodating a high number of policy changes to broaden the scope of abuse and extend responsibilities of practitioners. Putting policy into practice	Ch 4 Children in social care services; Ch 5 Child victims in CJS services

Issue	Brief outline	Chapter
4 **Identification and definitions of abuse**	Definitions of more common abuse types, consequences long term	Ch 3 Health and psychological consequence of abuse
5 **Impact of abuse**	Impact of abuse is now known to be more extensive – lifelong and physical and psychological disorder outcomes.	
6 **Service availability and effectiveness**	Challenges in policy and practice in social care and CJS identified in terms of multi-agency working and increased bureaucracy.	Ch 4 Children in social care services;
7 **Historical and organised abuse**	As past abuse comes to light, its investigation and recompense needed.	Ch 5 Child victims in CJS services
8 **Technology and social media**	Online harm; children's use of social media	Ch 6 Online abuse

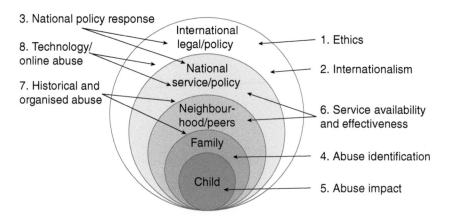

Figure 1.3 Contemporary issues in a socio-ecological model

Discussion

Every generation requires different tools to identify, understand and prevent childhood abuse. Ours has particular challenges. It also has potentially a great many resources to bear on the issue. These include greater research understanding, higher transparency of debate about, and recognition of abuse, standardised tools for assessment, cooperative professional working and an adult population largely educated in abuse and its consequences. These are necessary to reduce abuse in our society.

This chapter has shown how extensive child abuse is, both in domestic and international aspects, and the complexities of having services which can adequately act to prevent and intervene when abuse occurs. This throws up many challenges on inter-agency working, assessment and bureaucracy. It is important not to overlook the child at the centre of such action, and to attend to the child's rights and to hear their voice in describing their experience.

The following chapters will outline issues about the range of abuse (for example its internationalism and online aspects); the negative impacts of abuse on the child; and the abused child in health/social care and criminal justice services. The contemporary issues identified will run through each of these topics.

Notes

1 https://metoomvmt.org/.
2 www.unicef.org/crc/
3 https://childline.org.uk/
4 www.childhelplineinternational.org
5 http://researchbriefings.parliament.uk/ResearchBriefing/Summary/CBP-7585
6 www.gov.uk/government/news/troubled-families-programme-annual-report-published.
7 www.theguardian.com/global-development-professionals-network/2013/mar/26/empower-women-end-poverty-developing-world
8 www.bbc.co.uk/news/entertainment-arts-41594672
9 http://legal-dictionary.thefreedictionary.com/sexual+harassment
10 www.nspcc.org.uk/preventing-abuse/child-abuse-and-neglect/
11 *www.nspcc.org.uk/globalassets/documents/research-reports/no-one-noticed-no-one-heard-report.pdf*
12 Physical Child Abuse Differential diagnosis – Giardino 2015 – *http://emedicine.med scape.com/article/915664-differentialDiagnoses*
13 www.childandfamilytraining.org.uk/sites/9/pg/80/Neglect-Differing-Perceptions.pdf
14 www.partnersinsalford.org/sscb/gradedcareprofile.htm
15 www.csacentre.org.uk/research-publications/cse-risk-tools/.
16 Many use 'maltreatment' and neglect/abuse interchangeably. However it explicitly includes neglect and related problem care and is more commonly applied to abuse in the home from parents/carers.
17 Department for Education (2015) Characteristics of children in need in England, 2014-15. London: Department for Education (DfE). Table D4 www.gov.uk/government/uploads/system/uploads/attachment_data/file/469737/SFR41-2015_Text.pdf
18 www.communitycare.co.uk/blogs/childrens-services-blog/2013/10/the-lessons-to-be-learnt-from-three-recent-high-profile-child-abuse-cases/#.V-vOJMsVCpp
19 www.nspcc.org.uk/preventing-abuse/child-protection-system/case-reviews/2015/
20 www.bbc.co.uk/news/uk-11819732
21 *https://theukdatabase.com/2012/09/25/8-men-jailed-for-child-sexual-abuse-derby/*
22 *www.theguardian.com/uk/2012/may/08/rochdale-gang-guilty-exploiting-girls*
23 www.gov.uk/government/uploads/system/uploads/attachment_data/file/591903/CSE_Guidance_Core_Document_13.02.2017.pdf
24 www.theguardian.com/uk-news/2016/jun/06/rotherham-child-sexual-abuse-few-victims-identified-nca
25 *www.theguardian.com/uk-news/2014/aug/27/rotherham-child-sex-abuse-tip-iceberg*
26 www.nationalcrimeagency.gov.uk/publications/43-operation-pallial-report-eng/file
27 www.hiainquiry.org/
28 www.iicsa.org.uk
29 www.bbc.co.uk/news/uk-32812449

30 http://discoversociety.org/wp-content/uploads/2014/01/DS4_Cree.pdf

31 www.nspcc.org.uk/globalassets/documents/research-reports/yewtree-report-giv
ing-victims-voice-jimmy-savile.pdf

32 www.iicsa.org.uk/

33 www.iicsa.org.uk/key-documents/935/view/IICSA%20Review%20Report_Final_alt_
v4_ACCESS.pdf

34 www.theguardian.com/football/2016/dec/06/football-association-appoint-clive-
sheldon-qc-child-sex-abuse-review

35 *http://gov.wales/newsroom/health-and-social-services/2016/160211flynn/?lang=en*
http://gov.wales/topics/health/socialcare/safeguarding/?lang=en

36 *www.bbc.co.uk/bbctrust/dame_janet_smith*

37 www.bbc.co.uk/aboutthebbc/insidethebbc/howwework/reports/bbc_progressreport_
damejanetsmith_july2016

38 www.damejanetsmithreview.com/

39 www.npcc.police.uk/FreedomofInformation/OperationHydrant/OperationHydrant.aspx)

40 *www.iicsa.org.uk/investigations*

41 www.iicsa.org.uk/key-documents/3361/view/IICSA%20REA%20Child%20sexual%20
abuse%20in%20the%20Anglican%20and%20Catholic%20Churches%20Nov%20
2017.pdf

42 www.myonlynews.co.uk/news/iicsa-inquiry-says-uk-government-should-pay-australia-
child-migrants/

43 www.unodc.org/unodc/en/organized-crime/intro/UNTOC.html

44 www.nspcc.org.uk/services-and-resources/research-and-resources/2013/signs-of-safety-
model-england/

45 https://contextualsafeguarding.org.uk/about/what-is-contextual-safeguarding

46 www.scie.org.uk/publications/introductionto/childrenssocialcare/furtherinformation.
asp

47 www.revolvy.com/topic/Victoria%20Climbié&item_type=topic

48 www.foundationonline.org.uk/course_files/safeguarding_2016/2_safer-organisations/
2i.html

2 Safeguarding children internationally

This chapter seeks to outline issues around safeguarding internationally, considering international policy with regard to child safety as well as a wider range of abuse to children in the international context, picking up on some of the issues raised in Chapter 1. The first part of this chapter considers the range of policy and legislative measures that have been introduced at the international, EU and national UK level to respond to online and offline child sexual abuse (CSA) and child sexual exploitation (CSE). The second part of the chapter further explores the scope of child abuse and the different forms that can occur internationally and in different cultures. This includes female genital mutilation (FGM), child trafficking and sexual exploitation and enforced child begging. Other key issues such as domestic servitude and forced criminality are outlined more summarily. Finding shared international definitions of child abuse remains a challenge, given cultural perceptions and traditional practices vary greatly, making some forms of abuse both legal and acceptable in certain contexts.

International policy and legislation regarding CSA/CSE

The last three decades have seen an increasing awareness of the need to provide a global policy safety net for children; this goal has been instigated and expressed at international level by the United Nations as outlined in the introductory chapter. In 1989 the UN Commission on Human Rights appointed a Special Reporter to consider matters relating to the rights of children and consider how universal standards could be translated into action at the national level. This led to the United Nations Convention on the Rights of the Child (UNCRC) in 1990,[1] a ground-breaking international convention requiring signatories to take all appropriate measures to prevent harm to children. The UNCRC gives children a series of cultural, socio-economic and political rights, underwritten by a covenant that ensures that the child's best interest is the primary consideration for policy. All countries have now ratified the UNCRC with the exception of the US and Somalia. Since the instigation of the UNCRC, a number of international instruments have strengthened child rights further, including the ILO Convention 182 concerning the Prohibition and Immediate Action for the Elimination of the Worst Forms of Child Labour (1998),[2] the ILO Protocol to Prevent, Suppress and Punish Trafficking on Persons, especially Women and Children, supplementing the UN Convention against Transnational Organized Crime (2000),[3] the Protocol on the Sale of Children, Child Sexual exploitation and Child Pornography (2000)[4] and the protocol establishing a complaints procedure for violations of children's rights (2011).[5] The evolving capacity of children is now a significant arbiter of law and policy both nationally and internationally; however, the UK has not yet ratified the Lanzarote agreement of 2007 which seeks to criminalise sexual activity with children below the legal age of consent, regardless of the context in which such behaviour occurs. It also mandates the criminalisation of child sexual exploitation and pornography (child indecent images). The Convention sets out several measures to prevent child sexual exploitation and abuse, including the training and educating of children, monitoring of offenders and the screening and training of people who are employed or volunteer to work with children.[6]

Children's experience and expectations regarding their role in society remain dependent upon the social, cultural and political context in which they find themselves; this context lottery also unfortunately extends to the nature and adequacy of child safeguarding systems and protective legislation. It is undeniably the case that until recently, and in some cases currently, in many countries children have been and continue to be treated as second-class citizens, devoid of human rights, effectively denied a voice in matters concerning their wishes and well-being; many are still subjected to the worse forms of abuse despite moves to provide protection through the UNCRC.

The creation of an international consensus on approaches to child abuse and victimisation is an ideal embodied in the UNCRC; however, this is highly problematic given that countries have widely varying legislative structures that are underpinned by deep rooted historical, cultural and social contexts and practices. The fact that widely different interpretations of the legal age of consent to sexual relations exist across countries is indicative of the scale of the problem faced: if an agreement cannot be reached regarding the definition of '*child*', it is probably too much to hope that a consensus could be reached regarding definitions of child abuse, and should such a consensus be reached, ensuring that legislation is effectively implemented at national level is highly problematic. Some academics have argued for an internationally agreed age of consent to overcome this problem, but reaching a consensus regarding the legal age of consent remains a challenge given the obstacles discussed (Pearce, 2017).

The advent of the Internet and advancement of new technology which now penetrates even the remotest areas of the world brings with it increasing risk to children. Although, for example, Internet penetration rates remain considerably lower in Africa than rates in the Western World, a recent report in the Guardian Newspaper (2016)[7] suggests that there are approximately 38 million subscribers to cell phone technology in the African continent, where this form of technology is now more affordable and easily accessed than via desktop or laptop computers. The UNCRC was written at a time when the Internet was not so pervasive; there is an urgent need to revise the convention incorporating issues such as the right to remove online material, the right to safety and support online and the right to digital literacy.[8] There are some good international initiatives to address these issues including End Violence (UNICEF)[9] and the recently published Council of Europes recommendations on children's rights in the online environment.[10]

Childhood and consent to sexual relations

It is clear that definitions of childhood are culturally bound; however, legal definitions of childhood are intertwined with the age of sexual consent. The UN Convention on the Rights of the Child (UNRC) is clear regarding under 18 being the age of childhood, but there is geographically wide variation. Defining childhood in this way is clearly problematic as the definition is at odds with the legal definition of childhood at the national level in many countries.

As sexual activity is associated with adulthood and maturity in many societies, the age at which a person can give consent to sexual relations implies the legal end of childhood. Children and young people are seen to lack the capacity or 'competence' (Children Act, 1989,[11] 2004[12]) to make a sound judgement about sexual relations, as Finkelhor states:

> Children are deemed to lack the capacity to consent to such relationships. However, at some point in adolescence children acquire the ability to consent.
> (Finkelhor, 1984, p.26)

In many industrialised countries the age of consent has steadily increased over time, reflecting both the manner in which perceptions of childhood have changed and the extension of the state of childhood. But there remains wide disparity in the age of consent even across the EU in different jurisdictions. In Scotland, England and Wales the age of consent to heterosexual sexual relations was 10 in 1285, becoming 13 in 1875 and was set at 16 in 1885 in the Criminal Law Amendment Act (for heterosexual relations). In Canada the age of consent was 14 until as recently as 2008 when it was raised to 16 in the Tackling Violent Crime Act, for the first time since 1892.[13] This is comparable to some other countries, such as: Switzerland, New Zealand and the United States. The age of consent is as low as 14 in some countries including: Albania, Bulgaria and Germany. In many European countries the age of consent is 15: Denmark, France, Greece, Monaco, Sweden, Iceland, Romania etc., whilst in some it is set at 18: Malta, Turkey and the Vatican City.

In South Africa the age of consent for boys was set at 19, in an attempt to curb the increasing HIV problem amongst young people, high teenage pregnancy rates and the high rate of adolescent rape:

> Childhood in South Africa is seriously compromised by the HIV/AIDS pandemic and we also have very high levels of early teenage pregnancy. The age of first sexual experience has also dropped with a significant % of children having their first sexual experience between the age of 10 and 13 years. South Africa also has the dubious reputation of having the highest incidence of rape per 100 000 of the population, with 50% of all victims being children. Politicians who were motivating for the age of 18 years believed that this would protect our youth from early pregnancies and HIV/AIDS infection. Submissions to the Parliamentary Portfolio Committee on Justice and Constitutional Development strongly supported the age of consent to sexual relationships remaining at 16 for both genders.
>
> (Joan Van Niekerk, National Co-Ordinator, Childline South Africa, 2007.
> Personal communication)

Differences in the age of consent to sexual relations reflect social, cultural, political and religious differences in views about the nature and start of childhood. In some countries such as India where traditionally children have married at what would be considered a young age in Western countries, the debate regarding child abuse and the age of consent is recent and developing and in other countries, such as South Africa, the setting of the age of consent has been driven by moves to curb disease, pregnancy and sexual violence amongst young people. In some parts of Africa and the Middle East, the age of consent is not a recognised concept as such and sexual relations are illegal outside of marriage (Bahrain, Dubai, Saudi Arabia and the Sudan for example); in many countries homosexual relations are illegal (Afghanistan and the Sudan for example).

It is clear that perceptions of childhood have changed substantially over time; the definition of childhood now extends into early adulthood in some cases. This is supported by research on development ongoing up to age 25 in the period known as 'emerging adulthood' (Arnett, 2014) (see Chapter 3). Legislation does not occur in a vacuum but rather reflects the social and cultural context in which it develops; many societies have become more child centred and it is no longer acceptable to abuse and exploit children, physically, sexually or economically. Therefore, a contemporary issue around abuse, in times of globalisation, is that of a consistent age of consent so that disparities are not exploited by those in other jurisdictions, and that children from all cultures have equal access to health and well-being consistent with human rights charters.

Child abuse policy: the right to legal protection internationally

Under the UN Convention on the Rights of the Child (UNCRC) children have a right to protection from all forms of violence, which is now taken to include online violence. Article 34 of the UNCRC commits states to protect the child from all forms of sexual exploitation and sexual abuse and to take all appropriate national, bilateral and multilateral measures to that end. Article 19 seeks to protect children from all forms of abuse:

> States Parties shall take all appropriate legislative, administrative, social and educational measures to protect the child from all forms of physical or mental violence, injury or abuse, neglect or negligent treatment, maltreatment or exploitation, including sexual abuse, while in the care of parent(s), legal guardian(s) or any other person who has the care of the child.[14]

The UNCRC also contains important general principles which should be considered throughout all relevant legislation and measures, including the principle that the child's best interests should be considered in actions which affect them. There is also an Optional Protocol to the CRC on the Sale of Children, Child Sexual exploitation and Child Pornography (Lanzarote Treaty, ratified by the UK Government in 2018). It is the only universal treaty specifically addressing this topic. The Committee on the Rights of the Child has been set up to monitor the implementation of the convention by states, but it is unfortunate that the convention has no real legal teeth and cannot force states to follow its recommendations. Clearly the right to legal protection of children worldwide is a contemporary issue and a worthy aim to follow the UNCRC.

Political initiatives at European Union (EU) level

There has in recent years been a concerted attempt to enhance the protection of children through political initiatives in Europe. In 2003 the EU adopted a Council Framework Decision 'on combating the sexual exploitation of children and child pornography' committing EU member states to bringing their national laws in line with the standards it contains, including criminalising child pornography and other child sexual exploitation offences. The EU's Safer Internet Programme has also made a significant contribution including through funding the network of Hotlines, and the next generation of the Programme (2009–13) will prioritise child protection. In addition, there has recently been a European Commission proposal[15] for a revised EU Framework Decision 'on combating the sexual abuse, sexual exploitation of children and child pornography' which provides a renewed opportunity to focus the debate on sexual exploitation, improve, share and update our understandings of sexual abuse, and strive for a more consistent implementation process.

The EU Directive 2011/93/EU on combating sexual abuse and sexual exploitation of children, and child pornography has replaced the Council Framework-Decision 2004/68/JHA. This Directive sought to force member states to introduce legislation at the national level in respect of criminal offences relating to sexual abuse committed against children, the sexual exploitation of children and child pornography; the directive also includes online sexual solicitation or grooming. The directive also aims to prevent convicted child sex offenders from undertaking professional activities involving regular contact with children. Twenty offences are included in the directive divided into four categories including:

- sexual abuse;
- sexual exploitation;
- child pornography;
- the solicitation of children online for sexual purposes (online grooming).

Minimum and maximum terms of imprisonment ranging from 1 to 10 years are set out dependent upon the severity of the offence and mitigating and aggravating offence circumstances. Incitement to commit an offence is also punishable. Aggravating circumstances include for example, offences committed against vulnerable children, intra-familial abuse and where the perpetrator is in a position of trust. An offender convicted of any of the offences listed in the directive must be prevented from undertaking work involving contact with children, and this information must also be shared with other member states. The Directive provides that Member States can prosecute their citizens for CSA offences committed in other countries. The Directive requires Member States to ensure that sites which host indecent child images within their territory are promptly removed and must strive to remove those hosted abroad. It is not clear however where the UK will stand in terms of such EU initiatives post BREXIT.

Although strides have been made with the attempt to standardise practice and intervention/prevention, challenges still exist. Carr undertook a study on behalf of the EC in 2014 exploring the extent to which member States have implemented the Directive (Carr, 2014). Forty-six EU countries were approached, with a 63 per cent response rate; of those countries indicating that there was protocol in dealing with these issues, 28 per cent noted that they did not meet the terms of Article 23 – these included Belgium, Romania, Portugal and Lithuania.

Furthermore, Article 23 Treaty of Lanzarote (CETS No. 201) states:

> parties shall take the necessary legislative means to criminalise and prevent the intentional proposal through ICTs of adults to meet children.

The above can become problematic when local law and jurisdictional issues become entangled in an ongoing investigation. Age of consent laws differ from country to country as discussed. This disparity in legislative frameworks at a national level has proven to be a barrier to prosecution and conviction in CSA cases, particularly in the online sphere.

Different forms of child abuse: an international perspective

In 2010 UNICEF estimated that at least 77 countries condoned the use of corporal and violent child punishment, which is viewed as an acceptable form of punishment and remains legal in penal and other institutions. UNICEF now estimates that at least three million children aged 2-4 experience violent punishment on the part of their caregivers on a regular basis (UNICEF, 2018a).[16] Research exploring attitudes towards the physical punishment of children has been undertaken by UNICEF (2010). The UNICEF Multiple Indicator Cluster Survey (MICS) Child Discipline Items and Related Analyses project aims to describe child punishment attitudes and techniques in households in 35 middle-to-low-income countries. Findings from the analyses indicate that violent physical and psychological discipline focused on children 2 to 14 was quite common across all the countries included in the MICS country-level samples. While overall rates of violent discipline are high (39 to 95 per cent of children 2 to 14), they do not appear to be unusual compared to those found using similar methods in high-income countries. Research conducted in China and Korea in the late 1990s (Kim et al., 2000) surveyed children aged 8-12 in Shanghai (238) and Yanji (245) in China and Seoul (248) and Kimpo (241) in Korea about their experience of family violence. A substantial proportion (70.6 per cent) had experienced some form of family violence during the last year and just over half (51.3 per cent) had experienced corporal punishment at school. It was evident that Korean children experienced more severe forms of punishment in the home.

A study exploring children's experience of violence in the family has been conducted in Tanzania (United Nations Children's Fund 2011 in collaboration with

UNICEF).[17] A large, representative sample of 3,739 young people aged 13-24, equal genders, participated in the research. Geographically the respondents were in equal numbers from Tanzania and Zanzibar (UNCF_UNICEF, 2011). The vast majority of the respondents from Zanzibar identified themselves as Muslim, whilst the respondents from Tanzania were split almost equally between three religious groups (Muslim, Catholic and Protestant). The findings present a concerning picture of children subjected to sexual and more frequently physical abuse often within their own families and communities without recourse to help.

The findings indicate that approximately 30 per cent of females and 20 per cent of males have experienced sexual violence before the age of 18. Approximately 70 per cent of the sample had experienced physical violence by an adult by the age of 18, this experienced equally by boys and girls. The violence usually included being punched, whipped or kicked, with 51 per cent of respondents having experienced physical violence by a family member or a teacher prior to the age of 18. Most females reporting physical violence had been abused by their mother or father, with mothers more likely to punish female children and fathers being more likely to punish male children. There was a reluctance to report sexual abuse to parents, family, friends or authorities, with 49 per cent of females and 68 per cent of males not reporting incidents. The majority of those who did report incidents of sexual abuse after it occurred, told their parents or their friends; males were more likely to confide in friends. Many children did not report abuse due to the fear of family embarrassment/stigma or of not being believed. A small proportion of females did not tell their families for fear of being beaten. Only 22 per cent of females and 12 per cent of males sought help from services for sexual abuse. Only just over half (59 per cent) of those females seeking services received help. Other research has demonstrated females experiencing sexual abuse were more likely to describe their depression, anxiety, alcohol misuse and sexually transmitted disease. Reza and colleagues' study produced similar findings: of a sample of 1,244 females aged 13-24 in Swaziland, the researchers found that sexual violence was associated with reported lifetime experience of sexually transmitted diseases, pregnancy complications or miscarriages, unwanted pregnancy and self-report of feeling depressed (Reza et al., 2009).

It seems that those children experiencing abuse are more likely to experience multiple forms of abuse, with over 80 per cent of Tanzanians who reported experiencing sexual violence as a child also reporting experiencing physical violence. The proportion of females aged 13-17 experiencing sexual abuse on multiple occasions was approximately 38 per cent compared to 31 per cent of boys in the same age group. This group reported experiencing three or more incidents of sexual violence. When asked at what age they first experienced sexual violence, 19 per cent of females reported incidents aged 13 and under, whilst 40 per cent were aged 14-15 at first incident.

In terms of physical violence 78 per cent of females and 67 per cent of males aged 13-17 reported being physically abused by a relative or teacher, more than five times (the largest numerical category coded). The research explored attitudes towards violence. They found that 40 per cent of females and 50 per cent of males aged 13-24 thought that it was acceptable for a husband to beat his wife under certain circumstances, including for leaving the house without permission, neglecting the children and arguing. This is undeniably of concern. The authors claim that the preponderance of such views amongst young people illustrates the continuing secondary position of women in society. This problem remains a core issue in challenging prevailing attitudes towards the sexual and physical abuse of females. This gender inequality remains a contemporary issue worldwide.

Female genital mutilation (FMG)

FMG is a traditional practice in many regions across the world but in particular of Sub-Saharan Africa and the Middle East. It involves the partial or total removal of female external genitalia for non-medical reasons. It is estimated that approximately three million girls are at risk of FGM every year and that 14 million women have experienced FGM (Reza et al., 2009). FGM is an abhorrent practice that represents an attempt to control women's sexuality from a young age (usually the onset of puberty) through mutilation and is occurring on a very large scale worldwide. Categories of FMG can be seen in Box 2.1.

Box 2.1

Female genital mutilation classification

Type 1: Often referred to as **clitoridectomy**, this is the partial or total removal of the clitoris, and in very rare cases, only the prepuce;

Type 2: Often referred to as **excision**, this is the partial or total removal of the clitoris and the labia minora, with or without excision of the labia majora;

Type 3: Often referred to as **infibulation**, this is the narrowing of the vaginal opening through the creation of a covering seal. The seal is formed by cutting and repositioning the labia minora, or labia majora, sometimes through stitching, with or without removal of the clitoris (clitoridectomy);

Type 4: This includes all other harmful procedures to the female genitalia for non-medical purposes, e.g. pricking, piercing, incising, scraping and cauterising the genital area.

Source: *World Health Organisation 2017*[18]

UNICEF (2018b) describes FGM as a practice to control or reduce female sexuality and as an initiation for girls into womanhood.[19] The practice has deep cultural and historical roots in some societies where FGM is a social convention, with the social pressure to conform a strong motivation to perpetuate the practice; it is often considered a necessary part of preparation for adulthood and marriage. FGM is often motivated by beliefs about what is considered proper sexual behaviour, linking procedures to premarital virginity and marital fidelity. In many communities FGM is believed to reduce a woman's libido, and thereby is further believed to help her resist 'illicit' sexual acts. FGM is associated with cultural ideals of femininity and modesty, which include the notion that girls are 'clean' and 'beautiful' after removal of body parts that are considered 'male' or 'unclean'.

The practice is performed mainly on children between four and 14 years of age. In some countries such as Ethiopia, however, more than half of FGM is performed on infants under one year old. FGM does irreparable harm; it can result in death through severe bleeding leading to hemorrhagic shock, neurogenic shock as a result of pain and trauma, and severe, overwhelming infection and septicaemia. It is no doubt a traumatic experience. In the UNICEF study, 5 per cent of children aged 13-17 and 10 per cent of women aged 18-24 reported having experienced FGM. It is however encouraging that young people in the study were overwhelmingly against the practice with 84 per cent of females and 79 per cent of males saying it should be stopped (UNICEF, 2017).[20]

International moves to abolish FGM have included a collaborative effort on the part of the World Health Organization (WHO) which issued a joint statement with the United Nations Children's Fund (UNICEF) and the United Nations Population Fund (UNFPA) against the practice of FGM in 1997. A new statement was issued in February 2008 to support increased advocacy for the abandonment of FGM. The statement presents new evidence about the negative impact of FGM on women and the human rights/legal aspect of the practice. In 2008, the World Health Assembly passed a resolution (WHA61.16) on the elimination of FGM, emphasising the need for concerted action in all sectors – health, education, finance, justice and women's affairs. The WHO in 2017 states that when practising communities decide to abandon FGM, the practice can be eliminated very rapidly; work with communities has focused on advocacy, research and the informed development of health programmes (Cloward, 2016).[21] Other international initiatives prioritising FGM include the UNICEF End Violence programme.[22]

Recent international efforts have been made to counteract FGM through research, work within communities and changes in public policy. Progress at international, national and sub-national levels includes: wider international involvement to stop FGM; international monitoring bodies and resolutions that condemn the practice; and revised legal frameworks and growing political support to end FGM. This latter includes a law against FGM in 26 countries in Africa and the Middle East, as well as in 33 other countries with migrant populations from FGM practising countries. In 2003 the FGM Act was introduced to English law, covering the following offences: female genital mutilation; assisting a girl to mutilate her own genitalia; assisting a non-UK person to mutilate overseas a girl's genitalia; and failing to protect a girl from risk of genital mutilation.[23]

The London Safeguarding Children Board (LCSB) confers with UK guidance that defines FGM as a form of child sexual abuse, and the LCSB has produced some detailed guidance (2016) about the safeguarding responsibilities of local authorities.[24] Although there have been very few convictions under the new UK legislation (Female Genital Mutilation Act 2003 updated 2018),[25] data from the Health and Social Care Information Centre which collates data from health care providers in England provides an overview of reported cases. The Enhanced Dataset is an Information Standard (SCCI2026) that was published with data collection commencing on 1 April 2015.[26] This requires all clinicians across all NHS healthcare settings to record in the clinical notes when a patient with FGM is identified, together with what FGM Type it is. The data suggests that from January to March 2016, 1,242 new cases of FGM were recorded; 88 per cent of women and girls with a known country of birth were born in an Eastern, Northern or Western African country. Where the FGM Type was known, Types 1 and 2 had the highest incidence (38 per cent and 30 per cent respectively).

It is clear that awareness raising work with young people and community groups in the UK is needed to open a dialogue about FGM and to make sure that children are aware of their rights under the new legislation; the Government has produced a resource pack for schools and local authorities.[27]

Child trafficking and sexual exploitation

In the context of international aspects of child abuse and exploitation, this section explores the trafficking of children. This is the movement of children, usually across international borders, for the purpose of movement and exploitation. Children as minors do not have the capacity to consent to transportation and are often carried under force, coercion or deception. Article 34 of the Convention on the Rights of the Child[28] requires the State to protect children from sexual exploitation and Article 35 requires:

> States Parties shall take all appropriate national, bilateral and multilateral measures to prevent the abduction of, the sale of or traffic in children for any purpose or in any form.[29] [30]

The Convention is supplemented by two optional protocols, one addressing child pornography, child sexual exploitation and the sale of the children and the other addressing the involvement of children in armed conflict.

The Optional Protocol on the Sale of Children, Child Sexual exploitation and Child Pornography (OPSC) supplements the Convention on the Rights of the Child and is the first of two optional protocols to enter into force. The OPSC was adopted in May 2000 and entered into force in January 2002.[31] It is the first instrument defining and expressly prohibiting the sale of children, child sexual exploitation and child pornography. Accordingly, the OPSC requires these offences to be treated as criminal acts. It also requires the States Parties to: establish grounds for criminalising these prohibited acts; ensure jurisdiction over the offences; provide for the extradition of offenders; encourage international cooperation between States to pursue offenders; and provide support to child survivors of commercial sexual exploitation (the UK has signed but not ratified this).

Within two years of the entry into force of the OPSC, States parties are required to submit initial, comprehensive reports to the Committee on the Rights of the Child on its implementation.

Box 2.2

Key treaties on child labour and exploitation

- ILO Worst Forms of Child Labour Convention (No 182), which includes the trafficking, sale and sexual exploitation of children aged under 18. States parties to convention No 182 have an obligation to develop programmes to eliminate the actions covered;
- The Palermo Protocol[32] in 2000, which also covers the trafficking of children under 18. The protocol importantly provides that the consent of persons under 18 is considered irrelevant as they are

> deemed to lack the legal capacity to consent in matters concerning child pornography and prostitution;
> - The Council of Europe convention on the Protection of Children against Sexual Exploitation and Sexual Abuse (CEC, 2012).[33] The convention contains obligations to criminalise conduct that is not specifically covered by the OPSC, on using the services of a child prostitute for example.
>
> In England and Wales child trafficking is addressed through the following legislation:
>
> - the Immigration Act 1971 (the facilitation of illegal immigration);
> - the Asylum and Immigration (Treatment of Claimants) Act 2004 (which introduced a new criminal offence of trafficking people into, within or out of the UK for the purposes of exploitation);
> - the Children Act 1989; the Children Act 2004 (child protection and care)
> - the Sexual Offences Act 2003.

The Sexual Offences Act 2003 is currently the substantive piece of legislation regarding sexual offences and introduced the offence of trafficking individuals into, within, or out of, England and Wales for the purposes of sexual exploitation (the serious crime act is also of relevance as it includes organised and serious crime [Part 3] and child sexual exploitation [Part 5]).[34]

As a contemporary social problem, child trafficking is a growth area with between 500,000 and 700,000 children being sold across national borders annually. Children are now viewed by organised criminals, particularly gangs operating in the former Soviet Union and Eastern Europe, as the most profitable illegal commodity after drugs and armaments. Human trafficking is a serious, international, organised crime. The Human Trafficking Foundation estimates that $32 billion per annum[35] is generated per year from the trafficking of human beings.[36] Conditions for transported children are often appalling, with many living beyond the law without basic medical care and bereft of human rights. Children sold into the sex industry are frequently exposed to systematic sexual abuse and sexually transmitted diseases including HIV and AIDS.

The global trafficking of children is aided by the development of new technologies, and the global nature of Internet communication has facilitated the sale of children, child labour, child pornography and child prostitution. Trafficking can also be linked to domestic servitude, child soldiering and illegal adoption. INTERPOL indicates there is also an increasing trade in trafficking for the use of human organs (particularly kidneys); this is since in many countries waiting lists for human organs are very long.[37] Increasingly organised gangs are using this opportunity to exploit vulnerable people and operate illegal donor networks. Donors are often deceived about the amount of money they will receive and the associated risk as operations are often carried out in poor conditions with no medical after care.

The UN identifies human trafficking as occurring in many countries, but often from less developed countries to more developed countries, where people are rendered vulnerable to trafficking by poverty, conflict or other local conditions. Most trafficking is national or regional, but there are also notable cases of long-distance trafficking. Europe is the destination for victims from the widest range of destinations, while victims from Asia are trafficked to the widest range of destinations. The Americas are prominent both as the origin and destination of victims of human trafficking. The UN defines trafficking as follows:

> The recruitment, transportation, transfer, harbouring or receipt of persons, by means of the threat or use of force or other forms of coercion, of abduction, of fraud, of deception, of the abuse of power or of a position of vulnerability or of the giving or receiving of payments or benefits to achieve the consent of a person having control over another person, for the purpose of exploitation. Exploitation shall include, at a minimum, the exploitation of the sexual exploitation of others or other forms of sexual exploitation, forced labour or services, slavery or practices similar to slavery, servitude or the removal of organs.[38]

In 2000 the adoption by the United Nations General Assembly of the *'Protocol to Prevent, Suppress and Punish Trafficking in Persons, Especially Women and Children'* marked a significant milestone in international efforts to stop the trade in people. The custodian of the Protocol is the United Nations Office on Drugs and Crime (UNODC). The UNODC addresses human trafficking issues through its Global Programme against Trafficking in Human Beings. As discussed earlier, to date, more than 110 States have signed and ratified the Protocol, but enforcing the protocol remains problematic at a national level and very few convictions have been made. The nature of trafficking is largely hidden, and it is likely that the majority of trafficked children may never come to the attention of the authorities. Data is therefore likely to be misleading. ECPAT UK suggests that the UK's national referral system should be restructured to create a separate system that focuses only on trafficked children, every local authority should have a designated lead on child trafficking, the person should have expertise in the area and that safe fostering accommodation should be provided for all trafficked children. And this should run alongside a system of guardianship so that all trafficked children have a parental figure who acts in their best interests, provides support and aids decision making (ECPAT, 2017).[39]

Many academics have written extensively on the trafficking or forced migration of children, but the absence of valid and reliable data and research about both the scale, nature of trafficking and the experience of those who are trafficked means that arguments are often based on assumption rather than evidence (O'Connell Davidson, 2005). Findings reported should therefore be treated with caution. Research conducted by Pearce and colleagues suggests that most practitioners in the UK working with trafficked children are not familiar with the signs and indicators of trafficking and therefore fail to report, resulting in an underestimate of the extent of the problem (Pearce, Hynes, & Bovarnick, 2013). Although official definitions of trafficking are clear, in reality, it is sometimes difficult to distinguish between children who are trafficked, and those who have travelled abroad and then later become subject to exploitation. These latter, who may leave home voluntarily but then become exploited, should be afforded the same protection. The difficulty is that some of these children may be subjected to exploitation, but then may keep most or all of their earnings rather than paying a trafficker. Also, much of the policy has focused upon children who are trafficked cross-border (trans-national trafficking) and many children are in fact trafficked within their own countries (internal trafficking).

An added problem is that children may be exploited and trafficked at a local level by those working for large, reputable organisations. An example was provided in a BBC Panorama documentary (24 March 2010)[40] based upon a story written by a journalist (Paul Kenyon) who posed as a cocoa buyer in West Africa (Bradburn & Kenyon, 2010). This is a region which produces much of the chocolate sold in the UK, and he claimed that children are a central part of the supply chain and are frequently trafficked and used as slave labour. This involves children as young as seven, who are used on cocoa farms where they work long hours and have no access to education. Kenyon discovered that even when chocolate is labelled 'fair trade', there is no certainty that children have not been involved in the production process. The programme highlighted the case of a child who was sold by his uncle to traffickers and forced to work as a cocoa picker. However, sometimes children had not been trafficked but were being used by their families as pickers, with those interviewed having learnt the technique from their parents and had passed it on to their children. The Fairtrade Foundation employs a rigorous certification programme and has acted to suspend growers known to be using child labour, and the large manufacturers have policies prohibiting the use of child labour. But Kenyon points out that it's difficult to evidence where child labour has been used in the growing and production process during which the bean will pass from grower, to buyer, to manufacturer and to distributer; consequently the covert practice often slips through the net. During the programme Kenyon illustrated the ease with which beans picked by children can enter the process by undertaking a deal himself.

He travelled to San Pedro, which is host to several multi-billion-pound cocoa suppliers, with cocoa beans for sale produced using child labour. Whilst he was unsuccessful in selling the beans to a *'big player'* as documents were requested, he was successful in selling to a smaller dealer from the Lebanon who was licensed and who then sold the beans to a large company supplying international chocolate producers (referred to as *'high street names'*).[41]

It would seem that the trafficking process involves a number of steps, including:

- recruitment of the child and negotiation of the fee (assuming that the child's family or carer is complicit, on some occasions vulnerable children are simply abducted);
- removal of the child – from home or from an agreed place;
- transportation of the child – this may involve a journey through several countries before the destination is reached.

However, it seems that the process of trafficking is rarely simple. There is little direct research with victims of child trafficking, but victims' testimonies from research conducted in Eastern Europe suggest that in reality they often move in and out of exploitation throughout their early lives, often escaping from one exploitative situation and being forced into another exploitative situation by adults sometimes from their own families.[42]

There has been a recent increase in the trafficking of children from Eastern Europe. A report by UNICEF (Limanowska, 2005)[43] which states that the conflict in the former Yugoslavia during late 1990 – early 2000 resulted in the displacement of many women and girls who were trafficked into the sex trade from across South East Europe. The report is based upon documentary evidence and interviews conducted with a small number of children (22 girls and 1 boy under the age of 18 interviewed) who had been trafficked (as children) in the last three years (ibid.). The respondents were from Kosovo, Moldova and Romania. Approximately half of the respondents had been trafficked within their own country and the other half had been trafficked to another country. The report claims that two age groups of children are most likely to be trafficked from Eastern Europe, pre-pubescent boys and girls considered suitable for begging and teenage girls for the sex trade, although it is noted that due to the absence of reliable official data and research on trafficking, the assertion is based upon anecdotal evidence from those experiencing trafficking (Limanowska, 2005).

The research findings suggest that the underlying causes of trafficking are often related to the individual circumstances of the children and their families. An example is provided of a girl who leaves school and cannot find employment so decides to travel abroad with the support of her family. Members of the community put her in touch with a trafficker who offers to put her in touch with an employer in another country. The trafficker negotiates a fee and the girl is trafficked. In this study six respondents from Kosovo who were trafficked internally suggested that they wished to pursue an income opportunity and that failures on the part of social services (Centres for Social Work) and the police facilitated the trafficking (Limanowska, 2005). For example, one respondent was subjected to sexual abuse by her father and was returned to him following each failed attempt to escape. Consequently, she chose to be trafficked to avoid further abuse at home.

It is important to understand the way in which young people are approached and the circumstances that lead to trafficking, if effective awareness raising prevention work is to be developed at the local and national level. The UNICEF study described above indicates that young people were often duped by traffickers who made false promises. Some of the teenagers in the research reported had been offered marriage by boyfriends who wanted to take them to other countries; some were made bogus job offers and were instead sexually exploited. Several of the respondents were trafficked to Russia and offered a cleaning job and were then sold into the sex trade. On many occasions the young people trusted the trafficker as they were introduced by someone they knew and trusted in their own community. Two respondents were trafficked following an invitation by their female cousins. Traffickers often secure the compliance of children by threats and deceit. UNICEF currently estimates that approximately 5.5 million children have been trafficked across the world.[44]

Evidence is also available from a large UK charity whose work focuses upon the safeguarding of trafficked children in the UK, Every Child Protected Against Trafficking (ECPAT). This is a charity with 70 offices worldwide which aims to undertake an:

> on-going programme of research, training and advocacy (which) informs our campaigning efforts. ECPAT UK has been instrumental in raising awareness in government of the plight of children trafficked into the UK for both sexual exploitation and for exploitative labour.[45]

ECPAT regularly seeks the views of trafficked children in developing policy and practice, and drawing upon the experience of the children, claims that in some countries children and vulnerable adults are blamed for misfortune by communities and by their families. The misfortune might include poverty and ill health. The organisation states that some trafficked children are branded 'child witches' and threatened with ritual practices and oaths (ECPAT, 2014). These are often female, and the children are believed to be 'evil' or 'possessed' by an evil spirit (ibid., 2009, p. 1). The accusation may come from family members, members of the community or priests. The consequences for the child can be very serious as families often reject them, forcing the child to live on the streets, where they then become an easy target for traffickers.

One young person commenting in the ECPAT[46]paper described how she came to believe that she was a witch:

Case example of 'child witch'

'they told me I was evil and made bad things happen. I believed and that was my punishment and what my life would be' another child commented who had been trafficked described what happened before she was handed over to the trafficker: 'The lady came and they were talking. My grandmother suddenly said 'abomination' I was sent out and the next day I went with the lady'.

(Young People ECPAT Youth Group, 2009, p.2)[47]

The charity, Stepping Stones Nigeria,[48] states that the problem is particularly acute in the Niger Delta where large numbers of children are being made homeless and trafficked due to deeply held cultural beliefs in local communities about witchcraft. This traditional belief centres around the view that all adversity is due to evil forces and that an evil spell can be given to someone through food and drink, the soul of the person will then leave the body to be initiated into witchcraft, returning to cause destruction, ill health and violence. Children are seen to be more easily controlled by witches and more likely to harbour an evil spirit.[49] The work of the Stepping Stones charity in Africa was covered in a Channel 4 Dispatches programme in 2008 (Saving Africa's Witch Children) (Gavan & van der Valk, 2008).[50] The programme describes the way in which local priests in Akwa Ibom State in Nigeria offer 'deliverance' services for children costing an average of £170 per child. If the parents are unable to pay, the priest holds the child captive until they can. A makeshift home and school has been set up by the charity for homeless children, which estimates that 5-6 local children are accused of witchcraft every day. Children have often suffered horrendous abuse and torture, perpetrated by their families in an attempt to exorcise the evil spirit. Abuse includes the use of acid, setting the child on fire and machete wounds. One child arrived at the centre with a three-inch nail in her head. The centre aims to care for and educate the children and ultimately to educate their parents and reconcile the family; this is however difficult as children identified as witches are isolated and ostracised by the community. In 2003 the Nigerian Government passed the Child's Rights Act which makes such abuse illegal, but the difficulty is in enforcing an act that runs counter to deeply held cultural and religious belief and not every state had enacted it when the programme was made (Gavan & van der Valk, 2008).

Traffickers also resort to the use of religious and traditional practices to secure children's silent compliance; the child victims refer to these practices as 'voodoo' or 'juju' but the description varies according to the country of origin. The traffickers cast spells on the child who believes that they or their families will be harmed if they are not compliant. Herbs and potions may be used to convince the child:

> They made me drink this tea and it made me feel dizzy, that is how they got inside my head.
>
> (ECPAT, 2009b, p.1).

Ritual oaths are used with some children in the same way that debt bonds are used with others. The child places a great deal of importance on the oath made with the trafficker and feels indebted; the child may fear the consequences of attempting to escape or of telling anyone about their plight (ECPAT, 2009a). The UK Child Exploitation and Online Protection Centre (CEOP, 2010)[51] argues that although the Government has introduced recent policies to protect trafficked children and to deter trafficking,[52] children are still trafficked to the UK from many countries. CEOP produced a threat assessment in 2010 which suggested that a total of 287 children from 47 countries had been identified as potential victims of trafficking in the UK during 2009; most of the children were from Vietnam (n = 58) and Nigeria (n = 40), while some of the children were also from China and some were Roma children. The purpose of the trafficking varied enormously as follows: 35 per cent of the children had been trafficked for the purposes of sexual abuse, 18 per cent were exploited for cannabis cultivation, 11 per cent were exploited for enforced domestic labour, 11 per cent for benefit fraud, 4 per cent for enforced marriage and the remaining children were trafficked for street crime and illegal adoption. In the absence of reliable data this may not provide an accurate picture of the true breakdown of the country of origin of trafficked children in the UK, but it is however clear that the growth of cannabis farms and the use of child labour has become a key problem in the UK (ACPO, 2010). The report states that the trafficking of children from Nigeria continues to be problematic, with children being transported for the purpose of sexual abuse, benefit fraud and forced domestic labour. Most of the children were trafficked to central London and the majority were aged 14–17 years.

Child trafficking and organised crime

Children are also trafficked for a range of criminal activities including street crime such as ATM theft, pick-pocketing and forced labour and begging. In these circumstances children are the victims of crime and are usually perpe-trating the acts on behalf of an adult gang. These children do not come to the attention of the authorities until they are apprehended by the police[53][54] (CEOP, 2010; ECPAT, 2010). There is some anecdotal evidence to suggest that teenag-ers aged 16–17 (predominantly male) are increasingly being used by criminal gangs in Eastern Europe to perpetrate cybercrime in the UK, and although it is clear that these young people have been manipulated by adults and are vic-tims, they have committed offences and are receiving custodial sentences. The Internet is undoubtedly already playing a significant role in the organisation and planning of child trafficking and will continue to serve to facilitate such offences. The Internet is used to control victims, make financial transactions and for networking amongst international groups of traffickers.

Vietnamese child cannabis gardeners in the UK

The New Statesman was one of the first publications to discuss the growth of cannabis farms in the UK using children from Vietnam and China to cultivate the plants (Shackle, 2008).[55] The article suggested that with increased demand for cannabis this would become a significant problem in future. The article cited an awareness campaign launched by DrugScope highlighting the plight of the chil-dren[56][57][58] A study by the Association of Chief Police officers, now the National Police Chiefs Council, indicates that there are a large number of cannabis farms in the UK; it is estimated that the police discover an average of 500 per month as demand far outweighs domestic supply (ACPO, 2010). Farms are usually set up in private homes but are increasingly found in disused nightclubs and ware-houses as the scale of the production increases; the organisation of the business is considered to be highly professional and run by criminal gangs predominantly from the UK and Asia. During 2009 and 2010 almost 1.3 million plants had been seized with a street value of £150 million (ACPO, 2010).[59]The ACPO report also points to increased rivalry and incidents of violence as gangs compete in the market. The trend in trafficking of children for these purposes is therefore very likely to increase. The children undertake a number of tasks, including the diver-sion of electricity, plant care and breaking and entering into the factories of rival gangs. The report describes a criminal network in which small, local teams with specialist knowledge run the day-to-day operations controlled by higher level criminal networks which presumably facilitate the trafficking of children. The report also suggests that the criminal networks behind the production of canna-bis in the UK are involved with the production of other illegal drugs of all classes, counterfeit currency, illegal DVDs, dangerous dogs and stun guns (p.13) (ACPO, 2010). A later study found however that the UK pattern in the domestic cultiva-tion of cannabis is moving away from the large scale commercial cultivation, at times coordinated by South East Asian organised crime groups, to increased cul-tivation within residential premises by British citizens (p.1) (Kirby & Peal, 2015).

There is little research describing the experience of the Vietnamese children and the way in which networks operate, an exception being CEOP who has conducted a study (CEOP, 2010). The majority of children in the study were boys aged 13–17 who had been trafficked from Vietnam to work in cannabis factories in the UK (although the report suggests that the production of cannabis is dominated by white British criminals) as gardeners, where their work involves the cultivation and care of the plants. The data indicates that only Vietnamese traffickers were transporting nationals for work in their own factories. CEOP rightly points out that it is of great concern that the Vietnamese children are treated as offenders rather than victims. Many of them have been charged for the production and supply of cannabis, and it is clear that their labour is enforced (CEOP, 2010). It is also of concern that the traffickers continue to evade detection and there have been no convictions in the UK of Vietnamese traffickers to date (CEOP, 2010). The CEOP study shows how Vietnamese traffickers work with other international trafficking networks to transport the children to their final destination. Multiple routes through Europe are available with children reporting that they were often transported via lorry, swapping lorries during the journey several times: for example, one child was passed through 17 different agents in one journey. This implies a sophisticated level of international cooperation amongst criminal networks that is probably facilitated via the Internet. Lorry drivers were sometimes very much involved in the process and met covertly with agents and children in quiet locations. Traffickers would usually remove the child's illegal documentation once in the UK. A recent article in the Japanese Times states that over 150 Vietnamese children have disappeared from foster and care homes since 2016, many of whom are believed to have been trafficked for labour in cannabis farms.[60]

It is clear that trafficked children are viewed as a valuable commodity by traffickers as considerable time and funding has been expended in the selection and transportation of the children; it is therefore no surprise that many children taken into care by local authorities in the UK go missing shortly afterwards as they are reclaimed by the trafficker and forced back into labour. Of the recovered Vietnamese children in the CEOP study, 48 per cent have since gone missing (CEOP, 2010). It seems that there is simply no escape for some trafficked children particularly where there is an outstanding debt. The children were held captive in cramped living conditions; some remained in the residence for the entirety of their stay and were often subjected to neglect, emotional and physical abuse. However on a more positive note a study evaluating Barnados intervention with trafficked children showed benefits (Shuker, 2014). The Barnados Safe Accommodation Project had three core aims: to improve frontline practice through intervention with children at high risk; to build capacity/expertise within the sector and to safeguard children from harm. The evidence from the evaluation suggests that, between the outcomes achieved by the training and the specialist placement strands of the project, all three aims were achieved. The findings suggest that where placements are offered in accordance with a recommended model, sexually exploited and/or trafficked young people can be effectively protected (ibid.).

Enforced child begging

Child begging is now seen as a form of forced labour or slavery which involves psychological and/or physical coercion; all children who are forced to beg are subjected to forced labour which is prohibited under the International Labour Convention (ILO, 29). Data from the United States suggests that children are routinely trafficked into forced begging in Asia, Europe, Africa and Latin America (US Department of State, 2008). Child begging is a difficult area to research as victims are often invisible and controlling gangs operate covertly under the criminal justice radar. Some research has however been conducted by Anti-Slavery International (Delap, 2009),[61] which sheds light on the plight of child beggars in Albania, Greece, Senegal and India. The research suggests that children can be forced to beg by parents and by criminal gangs. Children are frequently beaten if they do not comply, and these children usually live apart from their families in poor conditions. Poverty is seen to be an underlying cause of much forced child begging. The begging often includes trafficking or movement of the child either across border or internally within their own country. The research is one of few studies in this area which includes direct reference to the views of trafficked children which were sought during interviews in each of the countries.

The research included in-depth interviews with a total of 381 children and over 100 parents: 162 children, 72 parents (who had supplied their children for begging) and 28 professionals working in the trafficking area in four cities in Albania and Greece: 113 children in 13 locations in Delhi; and 106 children and 76 parents in Senegal. Combined qualitative methods were used including observation of children begging, rapid interviews on the street (lasting approximately 15 minutes), in-depth interviews with children and their parents, focus groups and key informant interviews (Delap, 2009).

The research identified three different types of forced begging: children trafficked into begging by informal networks and criminal gangs, referred to as *'begging mafias'* (Delap, 2009, p. 6); forced begging linked to drug addiction, this proved to be the most common form of forced begging in Albania and Delhi; and children sent to live in Koranic boarding schools forced to beg by their teachers. The research paints a disturbing picture of parents who are often working with traffickers, or who are at least complicit in the removal and enforced slavery of their children for profit.

Some evidence of trafficking by criminal gangs was found in this research, as one child was trafficked from Albania to Greece and was forced to beg every day from early in the morning until late at night. He was part of a group of nine children who were kept in a basement by the gang. The children were beaten, whipped and kicked if they returned with insufficient money at the end of each day. An account provided by another respondent illustrates the way in which children are often sold to several people and sometimes by their own parents. Another respondent was only 4 or 5 years old when he was trafficked from Albania to Greece; he was forced into a car, but the traffickers were arrested by the police and could not prove he was their child. He was returned to his mother in Albania who then sold him to another trafficker who took him to Athens. The trafficker told the child that he owed him money and forced him to beg to repay the debt. The child escaped and was taken in by a woman with eight children; he returned to the street to beg in order to pay for his keep and was forced to sleep outside by the woman's husband; aged 21 he commented:

I lost myself as a child, I will not sell myself to anyone now.

(Delap, 2009, p.7)

As this case study illustrates, it appears that the trafficking of children and their enforced begging by third parties and enforced begging on the part of parents are two separate issues, but the reality is that the two are linked. Evidence from this research suggests that on many occasions parents have been forced to cooperate with traffickers, sometimes securing a fee for their child or negotiating a share of the profits.

Delap claims that this provides evidence that parents are increasingly forcing their children to beg, thus gaining a more substantial share of the profits and on some occasions taking on the role of the criminal gang; there is however limited evidence to support this claim. It is noted that no reference to this was found in the literature review, but this is not surprising given that researchers have not been able to interview trafficked children and their families in the past due to access issues. The idea that families are directly involved in the sale of children to third parties and criminal gangs is a contentious one. The findings from this research are confirmed by other earlier research conducted by Surtees for the International Organization for Migration (IOM) (Surtees, 2005)[62] which suggested that children are trafficked from Bulgaria usually for the purpose of enforced begging (although sometimes for sexual exploitation), all of the children were Roma and were begging before being trafficked. The recruitment process involved a kind of 'bonded labour' (Surtees, 2005, p.6) where children were sold by their parents to traffickers for a fixed sum, and it was uncommon for siblings from the same family to be trafficked to different parts of the world.

One child trafficked to Austria had siblings trafficked to beg in Vienna. Most of the Bulgarian children were recruited by a male and a female who were family members. The authors note that most of the unaccompanied children who were begging had notarised letters from their parents on their person indicating parental knowledge of their plight; it must be acknowledged however that families may well be manipulated by traffickers in this context. The Bulgarian children were trafficked to Belgium, Austria, Germany and Italy. Many were also forced into engaging in petty crime on behalf of the gangs and were often arrested by the police for stealing. Indeed some of the children were trafficked specifically to conduct petty crime.

The parents in this research who had forced their children to beg indicated that the reality is that the money earned is often seen as an essential part of the family income. In Albania the children typically spent six hours a day begging, and they would earn roughly the same as a street cleaner and most of the income would be given to the parents. Some of the children covertly retained a small amount of the income to buy treats and this was identified as giving them something to look forward to. They would have been punished had the parents discovered this covert activity. The parents claimed that poverty was the biggest factor prompting the decision to traffic a child or to force a child into begging. Some parents felt that their children would have a better life away from home:

> we send our children away to protect them from the crisis at home: It's a way to lessen our poverty.
>
> (Delap, 2009, p.14)

Another mother commented

> If they do not want to starve they have to go out begging.
>
> (Delap, 2009, p.14)

The IOM study (Surtees, 2005) indicates that some of the Bulgarian children were accompanied by their parents to another country to meet the traffickers and would therefore have entered the country of destination legally.

The research provides an interesting insight into the circumstances of the children who are forced to beg. In Senegal, Delhi and Albania children typically start to beg at age 4 or 5 and stop begging at puberty (ibid.). This is attributed to the fact that younger children are more easily controlled by adults and also to cultural issues around the shame of begging and the eligibility of girls for marriage. The research indicates that boys are more likely to be pushed into forced begging than girls and are more likely to be controlled by third parties.

None of the children were attending schools, stating that their begging work did not allow time for study. The research conducted in Delhi suggests that drug addiction is more likely to be a contributory factor in forced begging for boys than it is for girls. There is no doubt that all of the children responding experienced a gross violation of their rights, but those trafficked and begging for third parties experienced the worse abuse. Tactics involving extreme violence and coercion were employed by third parties and often parents also employed abusive tactics to control children and to punish children returning with insufficient money. In Delhi there was evidence of child drug dealers who are used to introduce other children to drugs and force them to beg through violence. Three children forced into begging by drug dealers in Delhi spent 9–12 hours per day begging to pay off drug debts and to buy more drugs to which they had become addicted. The children also reported experiencing violence on the part of other street beggars who were in competition with them in the same area.

Surtees believes that a number of contributing factors lead to enforced child begging including: family poverty; lack of access to good quality education and cultural issues (Surtees, 2005). It is suggested that in some cultures there is an acceptance of child labour and of child begging as an essential component to family survival. The majority of Albanian children in this research came from the Roma and Egyptian communities who comprise a minority of the general population (who are however amongst the poorest and most socially excluded); parents from these communities indicated that begging was a traditional form of labour passed from generation to generation. The authors state that such a cultural tradition is more likely to make children vulnerable to forced begging. Another contributory factor was identified as child abuse and neglect within the home, as several of the respondents from Delhi had fled abuse at home and had encountered drug dealers who forced them to beg.

The report concludes that government response to forced child begging should include: the protection of children via legal frameworks; effective, community-based prevention strategies and awareness raising and short term immediate help for children including access to free health care, shelter and education. It is also clear that work needs to be undertaken in communities and with parents to address cultural attitudes towards begging.

The research conducted by CEOP in the UK (CEOP, 2010) largely supports the findings from the Anti-Slavery International study (Delap, 2009) but findings are based upon stakeholders' (police officers and social workers) knowledge of cases rather than upon victims' accounts. Findings indicate that victims were living in relative poverty prior to being trafficked, and some families had been deceived by traffickers offering a better future for their child, whilst other families were complicit and had sold their children. The study identifies 'vulnerabilities' (p.17) (Delap, 2009) that were exploited by traffickers including: a sudden change in the child's personal circumstances e.g. death of a parent; parents viewing the child as a financial burden – here the trafficking was often precipitated by children being forced to work outside the home; parents or family members not wishing to support their children; and traffickers targeting poor families and offering a better life in the UK. Children trafficked from West Africa and Asia were usually provided with false travel documentation often in the name of the trafficker. Other cited research has indicated that children are usually controlled during transit via coercion and physical violence (Surtees, 2005; Anti-Slavery International, 2009).[63] The CEOP study corroborates this but adds that traffickers used a variety of other methods including: debt bondage – here traffickers hold children accountable for costs incurred in paying for their travel and accommodation, and the child is forced to work to pay off the debt to the trafficker (CEOP, 2010). Sometimes the debt can be deliberately substantial, forcing children to work indefinitely for the trafficker. On two occasions in this study Vietnamese children's debts were between £17–20,000. There were occasions when families paid the debt but usually the debt served as a means of enforcing labour and servitude. This situation is quite different to the context in which parents sell their children or receive a share of the profits from their labour, which was evident in the Anti-Slavery International study.

Trafficking of children for sexual abuse and exploitation

It is very difficult to estimate how many children are trafficked for the purposes of sexual abuse and exploitation given the hidden nature of the offence and victims' (usually forced) silence. National estimates provided by UNICEF in 2011 states that:

> between 5,000 and 7,000 Nepali girls are trafficked every year across the border to India. Most of them end up as sex workers in brothels in Bombay and New Delhi. An estimated 200,000 Nepali women, most of them girls under 18, work in Indian cities. An estimated 10,000 women and girls from neighboring countries have been lured into commercial sex establishments in Thailand. Recent Thai Government policy to eradicate child sexual exploitation means that fewer girls are being trafficked from northern Thailand and more girls and women are being brought from Myanmar, southern China, Laos and Cambodia (estimates by ECPAT [End Child Sexual exploitation in Asian Tourism]). China's Public Security Bureau reported 6,000 cases of trafficking of children in 1997, with a steady increase in girls aged 14 and 15 (Oxfam). UNICEF estimates that 1,000 to 1,500 Guatemalan babies and children a year old are trafficked for adoption by foreign couples in North

America and Europe. Girls as young as 13 (mainly from Asia and Eastern Europe) are trafficked as "mail-order brides". In most cases these girls and women are powerless and isolated and at great risk of violence'.[64] [65]

UNICEF (2013)[66] claims that approximately 5.5 million children are trafficked every year (not all for sexual exploitation); the demand for trafficked children is led not initially by the users i.e. those who pay for the sexual services of children, but by the facilitators or pimps who profit the most from the sale of the children. It is evident that a number of people in the network are often involved in the trafficking process, where roles can include that of facilitator, transporter and recipient (who may be a brothel or sweatshop owner).

A report prepared by the UNODC has explored the role of organised crime in the trafficking of human beings from West Africa to Europe (UNODC, 2011).[67] The report is based upon documentary research and 200 interviews with trafficked women and girls. The authors point to a substantial increase in the number of women and teenage girls trafficked for the purposes of sexual exploitation. It is estimated that in the region of 6,000 West African women enter Europe each year to work as sex workers. It is also estimated that approximately 10,000 Nigerian teenage girls are held captive for sexual exploitation in Libya and Morocco. These girls are frequently subjected to rape and sexual abuse and are 'bought' and 'sold' freely as commodities by traffickers. The authors suggest that female sexual exploitation is one of the few forms of illegal migration where a key role is played by organised criminal gangs. Another report published by the UNODC in 2009 suggests that the value of the West African trade in women and girls is an estimated $300,000,000 per year (UNODC, 2011).

Many of the children in the UK CEOP (CEOP, 2010) study suffered sexual and physical abuse en route to the destination country; some of the girls who were trafficked to work in brothels were sexually abused during the transportation by traffickers to break down resistance in preparation for the brothel. There is also evidence from this study of female children being trafficked from Eastern Europe to the UK. A case study is provided of a 15-year-old Romanian girl who was offered work in the UK by traffickers and on arrival was forced into prostitution. The girl was frequently moved from one location to another, was raped, beaten and threatened by the traffickers who forced her into sexual exploitation to earn her keep. The child was imprisoned and unable to escape. An anonymous phone call to the police led to the child being discovered and removed from a private brothel in Birmingham. The trafficker was convicted and received a 7-year prison sentence (p. 39) (CEOP, 2010). In the UK the National Referral Mechanism (NRM)[68] is a process that was set up by the Government to identify and support victims of trafficking; the mechanism was set up to identify victims under the Council of Europe Convention on Action against Human Trafficking in Human Beings, Treaty No.197,[69] which came into force on 1 February 2008. The National Referral Mechanism (NRM) is a framework for identifying victims of human trafficking and ensuring they receive the appropriate protection and support. The NRM is also the mechanism through which the National Crime Agency collects data about victims. At the EU level, projects have been funded to provide support for trafficked children: for example, Reinforcing Assistance to Child Trafficking Victims in Europe (ReACT) is a partnership project between ECPAT groups in the UK, France, Belgium, the Netherlands and Germany which aims to 'increase the capacity of representatives (guardians and lawyers) of child victims of trafficking to provide appropriate support and uphold the rights of trafficked children during legal proceedings in key trafficking destination countries'.[70]

Research conducted in 2002 by Hughes for the US Department of Justice (*Trafficking of children for prostitution*) states that children are trafficked to the United States for the purpose of sexual exploitation from countries such as Mexico, China, Honduras and Vietnam.[71] Hughes draws a connection between the trafficking of children and the production of indecent child images or child pornography. It is suggested that the market for indecent child images in the United States, and elsewhere, has fuelled the international trafficking of vulnerable children who are sexually abused in the production of images. Hughes points to evidence which indicates that children are often trafficked internally within countries for this purpose. A study of Aboriginal girls trafficked for the purpose of sexual exploitation in British Columbia reached similar conclusions regarding the role of the Internet (Aebi, 2001). The study indicates that children who are used for sexual exploitation are also used for pornography and points for the growing tendency to video the sexual abuse and share it on the Internet with others. For example, there appears to be a growing trend among abusers to videotape the child victim in order to upload these tapes onto the Internet to share with others. Aebi states that:

> in British Columbia children are targeted by lone individuals or by organized gangs who seek out and befriend teenage girls are 'befriended' at malls and parties or at government resources, such as group homes and detention centres, and party houses. Drugs also figure into the recruitment and coercion pattern, as do gifts. In addition, some sexually exploited girls are used to recruit others into prostitution and there is a clear relationship between running away, homelessness and vulnerability to recruitment.
>
> (Aebi, 2001, p.1)

Large numbers of children are trafficked from many countries for a variety of reasons each year. Their experiences differ but it is clear that many are often deceived, abused, isolated and indebted to traffickers. Some of the children controlled by criminal gangs are further criminalised when discovered. It is essential that these children be viewed and treated as victims rather than perpetrators. International efforts to identify and protect children are underway, but their plight remains very real and essentially hidden from view. It is unfortunate that the evidence in this area is largely anecdotal and reliant upon the accounts of professionals involved in working with victims and offenders. There is little research directly addressing the victim experience given the familiar difficulty associated with accessing trafficked victims and their families.

Discussion

This chapter has explored the policy and legislative response to child abuse at a national and international level and considered different forms of child abuse that were once geographically located, but with the movement of people across borders and with the advent of new technology, have become issues demanding an international response. The exploitation of vulnerable children and young people from poor, developing countries must increasingly become an issue of concern to the UK and other Western governments.

In the UK the last five years has seen wave after wave of child abuse revelations, often involving organisations in the active denial of abuse. The impact of this has been far-reaching with many survivors coming forward to report the abuse they have suffered, first at the hands of perpetrators and second at the hands of organisations, perhaps too concerned about their reputations to take responsibility for abuse perpetrated against children in their care. Commentators have long been concerned about secondary abuse experienced by children in the criminal justice system, but a whole new area of active organisational denial has been at play placing children at risk, denying them the opportunity to be heard and ultimately denying access to justice. The response to this has been a plethora of inquiries, policy documents changes to existing legislation and the introduction of new legislation; inquiries such as the Independent Inquiry into Institutional CSA may shed light for the first time on the scale of abuse experienced and upon the role of organisations in the concealment of child abuse.

In terms of contemporary issues deriving from international aspects of abuse, this chapter emphasises how widespread, secret, connected to organised gangs and to cultural beliefs, varieties of abuse are. This requires concerted efforts from international aid organisations in conjunction with States and legislative bodies. It widens our awareness of different contexts for abuse and exploitation. These also become local issues when children are trafficked to the UK, or when cultural groups practice FMG or accuse children of being witches. Awareness of these issues needs to be increased among the public and among professionals in order to safeguard children more generally.

Notes

1 *www.ohchr.org/EN/ProfessionalInterest/Pages/CRC.aspx*
2 *www.ilo.org/dyn/normlex/en/f?p=NORMLEXPUB:12100:0::NO::P12100_ILO_CODE:C182*
3 *www.ohchr.org/EN/ProfessionalInterest/Pages/ProtocolTraffickingInPersons.aspx*
4 *www.ohchr.org/EN/ProfessionalInterest/Pages/OPSCCRC.aspx*
5 Adopted and opened for signature, ratification and accession by General Assembly Resolution A/RES/66/138 of 19 December 2011 entered into force on 14 April 2014.
6 See the Lanzarote Convention https://www.coe.int/en/web/children/lanzarote-convention.
7 Mutiga, M., & Flood, Z. (2016, August 8). Africa calling: mobile phone revolution to transform democracies. *The Guardian*. Nairobi. www.theguardian.com/world/2016/aug/08/africa-calling-mobile-phone-broadband-revolution-transform-democracies
8 http://5rightsframework.com/
9 www.unicef.org/endviolence/
10 www.coe.int/en/web/portal/-/council-of-europe-gives-recommendations-to-member-states-on-children-s-rights-in-the-digital-environment
11 *www.legislation.gov.uk/ukpga/1989/41/contents*
12 *www.legislation.gov.uk/ukpga/2004/31/contents*
13 *http://laws-lois.justice.gc.ca/eng/AnnualStatutes/2008_6/page-1.html).*
14 *http://www2.ohchr.org/english/law/crc.htm#part1*
15 Proposal for a Council Framework Decision 'on combating the sexual abuse, sexual exploitation of children and child pornography, repealing Framework Decision 2004/68/JHA' COM(2009)135final of 25th March 2009.
16 https://data.unicef.org/topic/child-protection/violence/violent-discipline/
17 *https://reliefweb.int/report/united-republic-tanzania/violence-against-children-tanzania*
18 *www.who.int/mediacentre/factsheets/fs241/en/*
19 https://data.unicef.org/resources/no-time-to-lose-on-child-marriage-and-female-genital-mutilationcutting/
20 https://data.unicef.org/resources/no-time-to-lose-on-child-marriage-and-female-genital-mutilationcutting/
21 World Health Organization. (2017). Female genital mutilation. Retrieved October 25, 2017, from www.who.int/mediacentre/factsheets/fs241/en/
22 www.unicef.org/endviolence/
23 *www.legislation.gov.uk/ukpga/2003/31/contents*, 10/2017).
24 www.gov.uk/government/publications/female-genital-mutilation-resource-pack/female-genital-mutilation-resource-pack
25 www.legislation.gov.uk/ukpga/2003/31/contents
26 *http://digital.nhs.uk/catalogue/PUB20852 www.hscic.gov.uk/isce/publication/scci2026)*
27 *www.gov.uk/government/publications/female-genital-mutilation-resource-pack/female-genital-mutilation-resource-pack* 10/2017).
28 Compliance with the convention and optional protocols is monitored by the Committee on the Rights of the Child.
29 *www.ohchr.org/EN/ProfessionalInterest/Pages/CRC.aspx*
30 *www.ohchr.org/EN/ProfessionalInterest/Pages/CRC.aspx*
31 www.ohchr.org/EN/ProfessionalInterest/Pages/OPSCCRC.aspx
32 www.cps.gov.uk/legal-guidance/human-trafficking-smuggling-and-slavery
33 https://rm.coe.int/168046e1e1
34 www.legislation.gov.uk/ukpga/2015/9/contents/enacted
35 www.dosomething.org/us/facts/11-facts-about-human-trafficking
36 *http://humantraffickingfoundation.org/what-human-trafficking*
37 *www.interpol.int/Crime-areas/Trafficking-in-human-beings/Trafficking-in-human-beings*
38 *www.unodc.org/unodc/en/human-trafficking/what-is-human-trafficking.html 2017.*

39 www.ecpat.org.uk/Handlers/Download.ashx?IDMF=1dcfdd01-44fd-4b0f-90c3-ccbc36649a80
40 *www.bbc.co.uk/programmes/b00rqm4n*
41 See www.youtube.com/watch?v=75E54D4z3fI&feature=related for a clip from the Panorama programme. (http://news.bbc.co.uk/panorama/hi/front_page/newsid_8583000/8583499.stm)
42 www.unicef.org/protection/57929_58005.html
43 *www.osce.org/odihr/14145?download=true*
44 *www.unicefusa.org/stories/infographic-global-human-trafficking-statistics*
45 *www.ecpat.org.uk/*
46 www.ecpat.org.uk/
47 *Stolen Futures: Trafficking for Forced Child Marriage in the UK ECPAT UK, 2009*
48 www.safechildafrica.org/child-witches/
49 www.safechildafrica.org/child-witches/
50 www.youtube.com/watch?v=ooXBMU_06vg www.channel4.com/programmes/dispatches/4od#3008630
51 https://childhub.org/en/system/tdf/library/attachments/1171_Child_Trafficking_Strategic_Threat_Assessment_2010_NPM_Final_original.pdf?file=1&type=node&id=6537(CEOP, 2010b)
52 Home Office (2009) 'UK action plan on human trafficking' for example which introduced the National Referral Mechanism (NRM) a central process to aid the identification of victims of trafficking. And the 'Strategy on human trafficking' www.gov.uk/government/publications/human-trafficking-strategy.
53 *www.ceop.police.uk/Documents/ceopdocs/Child_Trafficking_Strategic_Threat_Assessment_2010_NPM_Final.pdf*
54 *www.ecpat.org.uk/sites/default/files/begging_organised_crime_briefing.pdf*
55 Shackle, S. (2008). Slavery on Britain's cannabis farms. Retrieved October 27, 2017, from www.newstatesman.com/law-and-reform/2008/11/cannabis-farms-children
56 www.drugwise.org.uk
57 www.theguardian.com/society/2017/mar/25/trafficked-enslaved-teenagers-tending-uk-cannabis-farms-vietnamese
58 www.theguardian.com/global-development/2015/may/23/vietnam-children-trafficking-nail-bar-cannabis
59 *www.acpo.police.uk/documents/crime/2010/201008CRICCC01.pdf*
60 www.japantimes.co.jp/news/2017/10/15/world/crime-legal-world/vietnamese-child-trafficking-victims-u-k-vanishing-foster-homes/#.WeYEDVu3zIU
61 www.antislavery.org/wp-content/uploads/2017/01/beggingforchange09.pdf
62 *http://publications.iom.int/system/files/pdf/second_annual_report2005.pdf*
63 *http://lastradainternational.org/lsidocs/Begging_for_Change.pdf*
64 *http://asiasociety.org/policy/social-issues/human-rights/trafficking-children-prostitution-and-unicef-response.*
65 http://asiasociety.org/trafficking-children-prostitution-and-unicef-response
66 www.unicefusa.org/stories/infographic-global-human-trafficking-statistics
67 www.unodc.org/documents/human-trafficking/Migrant-Smuggling/Report_SOM_West_Africa_EU.pdf
68 www.nationalcrimeagency.gov.uk/about-us/what-we-do/specialist-capabilities/uk-human-trafficking-centre/national-referral-mechanism
69 www.coe.int/en/web/conventions/full-list/-/conventions/treaty/197
70 *www.ecpat.org.uk/react*
71 www.uri.edu/artsci/wms/hughes/trafficking_children

3 Health and psychological consequences of abuse

Introduction

The experience of neglect and abuse in childhood has dire consequences for the longer term health of victims (Felitti, 2002). The more immediately observable consequences are psychological. For example, rates of clinical disorder in adolescence are up to five times higher amongst those who have suffered abuse (Bifulco et al., 2002; Bifulco, Schimmenti, Jacobs, Bunn, & Rusu, 2014). The effects continue into adult life – the impacts around three times higher for clinical depression and anxiety (Infurna et al., 2016). There are also similar impacts for disorders linked to crime: including conduct problems, psychopathy and interpersonal violence (Fergusson, Horwood, & Ridder, 2005). However, effects are now known to go further, with neurological and endocrinological changes and with physical illnesses such as diabetes, coronary heart disease and even dementia implicated in later life (Felitti et al., 1998). The contemporary view is that childhood abuse can cause long-term health damage, if no interventions are provided. The scale of the problem and its chronicity suggests this is a major public health issue. This is because even if perfect safeguarding policies were ever to be effected going forward, prior generations carrying the effects of untreated abuse can under certain conditions transmit risk to their offspring creating simultaneous risk across age groups and generations (Fergusson; Boden, and Horwood, 2006).

There are many mechanisms through which childhood abuse affects adverse health outcomes. These are biological, social and psychological and the resulting lifespan causal models are complex and still being developed. Thus, whilst impacts continue into adult life and middle age, child abuse is still not routinely assessed as part of diagnosis and treatment outcomes. Early causes of medical conditions can go unrecognised by GPs or medical consultants. Another issue is that reporting of childhood abuse is not simple:

historical abuse is very secret and stigmatising and undisclosed and is often perpetrated by someone known to the child, largely family, but in the instance of child sexual abuse, often by friend, neighbour or someone in authority (Horvath, Davidson, Grove-Hills, Gekoski, & Choak, 2014).[1] Some victims are themselves unaware of the extent of their own abuse. This can be through perpetrator 'normalisation' grooming, or threats around disclosure, or through psychological defences around denial or forgetting. Another obstacle to determining historical abuse concerns assessment. A detailed measure is needed which can determine the type, chronicity and severity of childhood abuse experience in order to predict or understand the impacts (Bifulco et al., 1994). Such tools are lengthy to administer, require trained data collectors and have not yet been implemented in health settings. There are also some methodological puzzles about recall and measurement - with retrospective studies of childhood abuse with adults showing strongest associations with psychological disorders, whilst prospective studies following children or young people into adult life indicate higher association with physical disorders in some studies (Reuben et al., 2016). This may be a measurement issue (prospective and retrospective approaches utilised different measures) but may also indicate differences in recall processes or in disclosure capabilities at different ages. However, neither approach disputes there are long-term ill-effects among a significant percentage of those abused. Finally, the debate needs to include issues of resilience - not all children, adolescents or adults are equally susceptible to the negative effects of abuse - some appear immediately resilient, others acquire resilience over time.

This chapter is in two parts - the first will examine models of causes and consequences of abuse; the second will discuss research into outcomes - both psychological and physical.

Models of childhood abuse and adult disorder

There are many approaches to researching and interpreting child abuse findings from a range of disciplines. These encompass social (including adversity and life events, deprivation and negative family context); psychological (highlighting attachment style, parenting, interpersonal difficulties and intergenerational transmission); affective-cognitive models (including emotional regulation, negative thinking and coping with stress) and medical/biological (e.g. through cortisol regulation or brain development). Recent understanding indicates all these are relevant, with more interactional models now popular (Cicchetti & Roisman, 2011). However, the different approaches will be examined in turn in order to scope out the different influences on child abuse and its investigation.

A social adversity model

The socio-ecological approach to the causes and consequences of abuse has already been outlined in Chapter1. This approach examines disadvantage associated both with the occurrence of abuse in childhood and with the consequences as the child grows into adulthood (Belsky, 1980). It focuses on adverse experience and of disadvantage and lost opportunity. It therefore encompasses experiences known to relate to direct abuse to the child, such as poverty, housing difficulty, parental psychological disorder and domestic violence. These are well substantiated. Abuse is known to occur more often in disadvantaged families and can be associated with stress and adversity in parents (Spence, Nunn, & Bifulco, in press). It can also lead to social disadvantage - abused children can miss out on educational and socialising opportunities which restricts their later career or partner choices. This is most extreme in those taken into care - particularly residential care. However in others the failure to increase social class, higher levels of exclusion and higher rates of life events and disadvantage associated with single parenthood, unemployment or poverty is notable (Spence et al., in press).

Therefore, within a socio-ecological model (Bronfenbrenner, 1995), childhood abuse can be seen to be an experience that limits later life chances. These in turn relate to higher likelihood of clinical disorder and this too adds to potential stigma and limited life choices. Adult trauma and adversity add to the model. Abuse is known to be open to revictimisation (Finkelhor, Ormrod, & Turner, 2007) and this extends to intergenerational transmission and increased risk of later adult partner violence (Andrews & Brewin, 1990). Studies of adult adversity show it adds to childhood maltreatment in increasing risk, with additional dose effects (Bifulco, Damiani, Jacobs, & Spence, in press) even into older age (Bifulco, Jacobs, Oskis, Cavana F., & Spence, (in press)).

However, whilst most theorists accept the influence of a socio-ecological model, this is no longer considered sufficient to explain either the occurrence of abuse (not all poor or disadvantaged parents are maltreating) or the consequences (many children are resilient, and there are different mechanisms for children succumbing to damaging consequences). Therefore, this model is built into other psychological and biological approaches to emphasise transactional models (Cicchetti & Roisman, 2011).

Psychological models

Much of the investigation of the outcomes of abuse has been undertaken by psychologists who have investigated psychological disorder as well as vulnerability factors which increase susceptibility to disorder.

Attachment models of abuse

Attachment theory, defined by John Bowlby, has been invoked to understand abuse both in its causes (through intergenerational transmission and problem parenting) and its impacts (on insecure attachment style and problem relationship formation). Bowlby viewed the bonding between mother and baby as critical to normal healthy human development (Bowlby, 1988). The focus of studies of attachment began by looking at the early relationship with mother and baby, around issues of parenting sensitivity and child response, but since then the focus has extended to the child's interpersonal behaviour with a range of close others and how this develops into adult life (Belsky, 2002). Attachment theory can be invoked to explain both causes and consequences of abuse. Disturbed attachment style in the parent can lead to hostile, over-anxious or avoidant behaviour towards the child which at the extreme involves maltreatment (Bifulco & Thomas, 2012). If the parents fail to have a 'caregiver alliance' in raising their children, their interactions with the children can be distorted and their own dysfunctional partner relationship a source of further disruption to parenting (ibid.).

But childhood maltreatment also has a direct effect on the developing child, including problem attachment development involving mistrust of others which shows in different ways. These are termed insecure or disorganised styles which can occur due to harsh or neglectful parenting and are contrasted with secure. There is a broad categorisation of four styles – secure is the functional, adaptive style; anxious is either clinging and dependent (called enmeshed) or mistrustful but anxious (fearful); avoidant is dismissive of others' help and self-reliant – this can be mistrustful with anger (angry-dismissive) or with more reserved avoidance (withdrawn) (Bifulco & Thomas, 2012). In a minority of instances disorganised attachment style is defined, variously identified as unresolved in respect to loss, or as mixed between anxious and avoidant styles, often involving both anger and fear. Most self-report studies of adults show around 64 per cent are secure, with more insecure being avoidant (25 per cent) rather than anxious (11 per cent) (Mickelson, Kessler, & Shaver, 1997). Insecure attachment styles are associated with childhood neglect or abuse in both adults and adolescents. One study shows odds ratios of around 4 from abuse to insecure styles (Bifulco & Thomas, 2012). Logistic regression suggests poor care is more an issue in anxious styles and abuse in angry dismissive. Withdrawn does not however show an association with childhood abuse (ibid.).

The attachment model is compatible with a genetic/biological model. Gene-environment interactions interpreted in terms of differential susceptibility may play a large part in the explanation of individual differences in human development (Bakermans-Kranenburg & van IJzendoorn, 2007). Reviewing studies on the behavioural and molecular genetics of attachment, evidence is found for interactions between genetic and environmental factors explaining individual differences in attachment security and disorganisation (ibid.). In particular, the DRD4 7-repeat polymorphism seems associated with an increased risk for disorganised attachment, but only when combined with environmental risk. Gene-environment (G · E) interactions may be interpreted as genetic vulnerability or differential susceptibility. There is more support for the differential susceptibility hypothesis predicting not only more negative outcomes for susceptible children in unfavourable environments, but also positive outcomes for susceptible children in favourable environments (Bakermans-Kranenburg & van IJzendoorn, 2007).

Affective-cognitive models of abuse impact

There is a body of work around 'developmental trauma' or that occurring early in life which affects aspects of emotion and cognition in a negative way as the child develops. In terms of emotion, there are issues around poor regulation of expression which can lead to angry, even violent behaviour. This can be accompanied by dissociation whereby the anger is impulsive and often outside the conscious awareness of the individual. This can then lead to anti-social behaviour, including violent behaviour. It can also lead to actions like deliberate self-harm when the individual has no release for emotions and turns the aggression on themselves. There is also a cognitive or thinking aspect, whereby the child learns mistrust, helplessness etc. which then impacts on their ability to cope with stressful events. Complex trauma (multiple and/or chronic experience) can interfere with neurobiological development and the capacity to integrate sensory, emotional and cognitive information into a cohesive whole (Van der Kolk, 2005; Van der Kolk & Fisler, 1994). Such developmental trauma sets the stage for unfocused responses to subsequent stress leading to psychological disorders, including post-traumatic stress disorder and other problems. Specifically, it leads to lack of a continuous sense of self, poorly modulated affect and impulse control including aggression against self and others and uncertainty about the reliability and predictability of others. Cumulative trauma is also encompassed through multiple incidents of abuse, which increased risk of disorder in a 'dose' effect (Bifulco et al., 2003). When such multiple threats occur it can be overwhelming and result in 'developmental trauma disorder' (Van der Kolk, 2005). This defines the worst outcome of such adversities in childhood with neurological damage resulting in modifications of the HPA axis and noradrenergic system with failure of regulation of physiological arousal and emotion exhibited by either the self or others (Shore, 2003). The child becomes entrapped in a pattern of dysfunctional responses to traumatic cues, experiencing confusion, dissociation, somatic symptoms and traumatic re-enactment, together with a persistent negative evaluation of self-attribution, characterised by self-hate and shame, and absence of trust in the protectiveness of others.

Biological models of abuse

Neglect and abuse in childhood has negative impacts on the growing child and impairs their normal development. It can occur through various means. For example, very severe neglect can lead to reduced brain and neurological development. The stress caused by abuse can, over time, lead to dysregulation of cortisol, the stress hormone. Lack of close attachment can lead to a depletion of oxytocin sometimes called the attachment hormone (Shen, 2005). All of these can increase risk of adult clinical disorder and have effects on adult risk and vulnerability.

A recent review by McCrory and colleagues summarise the current evidence on the biological impacts of childhood maltreatment (McCrory, De Brito, & Viding, 2012). First, the point is made that most clinical disorders are implicated as well as physical health and social problems in later life. Second that the neurobiological mechanisms involved remain poorly understood with a complex interaction likely between environmental experiences (such as abuse) and individual differences in risk versus protective genes, which influences the neurobiological circuitry underpinning psychological and emotional development. The review then identifies the following:

- Neuroendocrine studies indicate an association between early adversity and atypical development of the hypothalamic-pituitary-adrenal (HPA) axis stress response, which may predispose to psychiatric vulnerability in adulthood. The HPA axis represents one of the body's core stress response systems. Exposure to stress triggers release of corticotrophin-releasing hormone (CRH) and arginine vasopressin (AVP) from the paraventricular nucleus of the hypothalamus, which in turn stimulate secretion of adrenocorticotrophic hormone (ACTH) that acts on the adrenal cortex to synthesise cortisol. Feedback loops at several levels ensure that the system is returned to homeostasis since chronically elevated cortisol levels can have deleterious effects on health;
- Animal research has shown that the hippocampus plays a central role in learning and various aspects of memory and that these functions are impaired when animals are exposed to chronic stress. Studies of adults with PTSD who have histories of childhood maltreatment consistently report that these individuals have smaller hippocampal volumes. It is surprising then that structural magnetic resonance imaging (sMRI) studies of children and adolescents with abuse-related PTSD consistently fail to detect

decreased hippocampal volume. One possibility is that the impact of stress is delayed and becomes manifest only later in development;

- Brain imaging research in children and adults is providing evidence of several structural and functional brain differences associated with early adversity. Structural differences have been reported in the corpus callosum, cerebellum and prefrontal cortex. Functional differences have been reported in regions implicated in emotional and behavioural regulation, including the amygdala and anterior cingulate cortex;

- These differences at the neurobiological level may represent adaptations to early experiences of heightened stress that lead to an increased risk of psychopathology.

Interaction between social environment and the biological factors are implicated. Some may be basic due for example to poor feeding, others the effect of sustained stress on the child. But there are also potential genetic effects. There are no single genes responsible for clinical disorder, but rather a difference in the way children react to maltreatment may be due to genetic differences in their vulnerability. Such gene by environment interaction (GxE) research has demonstrated that for a range of genetic variants (known as polymorphisms) childhood abuse can increase the risk of later psychopathology for some children more than others. For example, Caspi and colleagues were the first to report on an interaction of a measured genotype (monoamine oxidase A, MAOA) and environment (abuse) for a psychiatric outcome and demonstrated that individuals who are carriers for the low-activity allele (MAOA-l) were at an increased risk for anti-social behaviour disorders following maltreatment (Caspi, 2002). Imaging genetic studies have found that the risk genotype, MAOA-l, is related to hyper-responsivity of the brain's threat detection system and reduced activation in emotion regulation circuits. This work suggests a neural mechanism by which MAOA genotype engenders vulnerability to reactive aggression following maltreatment.

Developmental neuroscience research is just one small part of a wider societal endeavour, to better understand the complex repercussions of child maltreatment, so that as clinicians working with children we become better at early intervention and prevention. There is accumulating evidence pointing to a variety of neurobiological changes associated with child abuse and early adversity. Such changes can be viewed as a cascade of damaging effects that are harmful for the child. However, if an evolutionary and developmental approach is taken, then changes can be interpreted as more or less adaptive responses to an early environment characterised by threat. For a child to respond optimally to environmental challenges, early stress-induced changes in neurobiological systems can be seen as 'programming' or calibrating those systems to match the demands of a hostile environment. However, from a clinical perspective, such adaptation may heighten vulnerability to clinical disorder, partly due to the changes in how emotional and cognitive systems affect social interaction. For example, early-established patterns of hypervigilance, which may ensure survival in an unpredictable home environment, may be problematic in other settings increasing vulnerability for emotional and social difficulties.

McCrory and colleagues conclude that effects of parenting on the child's developing brain may be substantiated in future research (McCrory, de Brito, & Viding, 2010; McCrory et al., 2012). Such efforts should focus on parenting in the normal range, experimental manipulations of parenting, differential susceptibility to parenting effects and pathway models linking parenting to brain development and, thereby, to behavioural development.

There is also research on the link between the social environment and health involving other biological processes related to ageing (Colter et al., 2014). Telomeres are an essential part of human cells that affect how our cells age. They are the caps at the end of each strand of DNA that protect our chromosomes. Without the coating, DNA strands become damaged and less effective. Telomere shortening is involved in all aspects of the ageing process on a cellular level and telomere length represents our *biological* age as opposed to our *chronological* age. Using data from a birth cohort study, Colter and colleagues examined telomere length (TL) in a study of African American boys. They found that those who grew up in highly disadvantaged environments had shorter telomeres (at age 9) than boys who grew up in highly advantaged environments. They also found that the association between the social environment and TL was moderated by genetic variation within the serotonin and dopamine pathways. Boys with the highest genetic sensitivity scores had the shortest TL when exposed to disadvantaged environments and the longest TL when exposed to advantaged environments. This helps to further document a gene–social environment interaction for TL, a biomarker of stress exposure.

All-encompassing models

The most comprehensive psychological approach to the link between child abuse and lifespan psychological disorder is that of 'developmental psychopathology' (Cicchetti & Cohen, 2006). This considers individual development throughout the lifespan, looking at factors which contribute to psychological disorder across life stages. It incorporates more specific models including those interpersonal, those organisational, those biological and aspects such as resilience (D Cicchetti, Cummings, & Greenberg, 1990). It advocates a contextualised view of child abuse, and careful assessment of individual characteristics (Toth, Cicchetti, Macfie, Maughan, & Vanmeenen, 2000) including the self (Toth, 1997).

It is of course harder to test in any individual study but proposes a sophisticated synthesis of other approaches. This is an important lead for how models are needed which speak to different aspects of development, social adversity and psychopathology.

This next part of the chapter will look at specific findings relating to child abuse outcomes, particularly those relating to adolescent and adult clinical disorder. It will also briefly examine other health outcomes, and the issue of intergenerational transmission of risk for disorder. A focus will be on London studies using the CECA interview and conducted by the author (AB).

Outcomes of childhood neglect and abuse

As discussed earlier, investigating longer term outcomes of childhood abuse requires a focus on sound measurement, and that which can encompass the complexity and dynamic nature of childhood experience viewed retrospectively. The CECA intensive interview measure will be outlined. In addition, two specific analyses of the abuse-disorder relationship will be identified. The first is the *'dose-effect'*. This states that the more abuse (the more complex, multiple and more severe) the higher the rates of disorder ensuing. The second is a *'specificity'* effect. This focuses on the *specific* outcome that might arise from particular types of abuse in terms of disorder for example, contrasting neglect with abuse, or different impact of the relationship to perpetrator, for example from mother or father figures, and in terms of different types of psychological disorder resulting. These two approaches (dose effects and specificity effects) are not incompatible, and together hold some of the answers to the relationship of abuse to disorder. Finally, the issue of resilience to abuse will be outlined.

The London studies from the Centre for Abuse and Trauma studies

The chapter will provide a particular focus on London studies by the CATS team (which the present author (AB) lead) which have used an intensive interview measure for retrospective abuse assessment (the Childhood Experience of Care and Abuse, CECA (Bifulco et al., 1994).[2] These studies have taken a lifespan perspective (Bifulco, Brown, & Harris, 1987; Bifulco et al., 2003). The CECA is an intensive measure of proven reliability and validity and often taken as a 'gold standard' with a meta-analysis indicating significant effect sizes over numerous studies internationally (Infurna et al., 2016). It is a historical or retrospective measure of the first 16 years of life, used with adolescent or adult. It is not adapted for younger children (as with most other abuse measures). It is therefore used with young people for recent abuse and with adults for longer-term abuse

The studies given main focus here include those using the CECA in interrelated London studies of families, investigating mothers as well as their male and female offspring inter-generationally. The mothers had been screened through access to GP patient lists in North London; half were representative of mainly working-class families (Bifulco et al., 2002), and the remainder for having difficulties in childhood or adult relationships (Bifulco et al., 1997; Bifulco et al., 1998). The mothers were studied for their lifetime experience of abuse, trauma and problematic relationships, as well as their attachment style and parenting. The young people studied were offspring of these women (aged 16–30, average age 20). The same measures of childhood neglect/abuse (CECA) were included. Clinical interviews were conducted with both generations – in the mothers mainly covering depression and anxiety (emotional disorder) and in the younger generation also covering conduct disorder and substance abuse (behavioural disorder) as well as deliberate self-harm. Analyses were conducted within the generations, but also across generations to examine factors in transmission of risk with the findings described as follows.

The childhood experience of care and abuse (CECA)[3]
In the introduction, the self-report measures of child abuse were outlined. There are fewer intensive interview measures; the CECA is perhaps the best established and most international in its use and will be outlined here (Bifulco et al., 1994; Gianonne et al., 2011; Infurna et al., 2016; Kaess et al., 2011). It has good inter-rater reliability (i.e. that different people using it will score the same) and has been validated by checking the reports of sisters raised together when interviewed independently (Bifulco et al., 1997). It was designed to assess an individual's childhood recollection and thus their own prior neglect or abuse before age 17. It begins by asking about parental loss, in order to determine different parent figures and households during childhood. Questions are repeated for birth parents and any household substitute parents Established techniques such as 'typical day' are utilised to ground the individual in concrete memories of events and interactions. This determines household routines, who woke the child up, cooked breakfast, got them to school, collected them from school, cooked an evening meal, played with them, and then bathed them and got them to bed This established a family context within which more focused questions are then presented.

The CECA includes a number of questions about care in childhood in terms of material care, interest in school and friends, concern about health and parental interest in child's well-being or distress. This is repeated for different household arrangements and over time to establish a dynamic scoring of peaks and troughs in childhood care. For each of these arrangements, questions are asked about care and control, with factual questions about intensity, frequency, chronicity and relationship to perpetrator. Importantly, multiples of abuse are covered. In addition to neglect and abuse directed at the child, other aspects of family context were covered, including parental violence and discord, poverty, housing difficulties and parental mental health.

Box 3.1

Summary CECA abuse definitions **(Bifulco & Moran, 1998).**

- **Antipathy** – cold or critical parenting – items include critical comments, angry hostile interaction, scapegoating, rejection. This is sometimes considered emotional abuse;
- **Neglect** – indifference to the child's physical, material and emotional needs in domains of feeding, clothing, hygiene, medical care, education, friendships and sympathetic support;
- **Physical Abuse** – attacks on the child which have the potential for harm. Severity determined by frequency, chronicity and intensity of attack;
- **Sexual abuse** – inappropriate sexual contact or solicitation by adult or older peer, either related or non-related. Severity determined by extent of sexual contact, power exerted and closeness of prior relationship;
- **Psychological abuse** – coercive control exerted through psychological or emotional means to confuse and disorientate and create submissiveness. It covers a range of techniques including dehumanisation, terrorising, emotional blackmail, deprivation of basic needs and valued objects. Severity determined by intensity, chronicity and range of strategies used.[4]

Given that emotional abuse is often considered difficult to recognise, the following example is of antipathy from mother.

Case example – emotional abuse from mother by Eloise (Bifulco & Thomas, 2012, p. 124).

'I couldn't say I felt rejected, but I always felt left out. My mother would always ridicule me, she'd use me as this battering ram. She'd use the other children to consolidate her position in the family and made very sure in her own way that I was left out. I have no memories of her ever being caring and physically affectionate or even verbally affectionate at all, very strange. Yet she was to the others. She was always changeable like that'. Eloise said she was isolated, that her mother 'ganged up' with her siblings against her and stated that her mother was doing the same with her children now in setting them against her. 'I remember many years ago there was a woman in the street where we lived, and she actually came to see my mother and told her that she ought to do more to support me and look after me and I remember my mother telling me this years later and laughing. She is very cruel. There was no support. There was nobody to come home and tell if something awful had happened to you. My aunt says my mother has no understanding at all, absolutely none.... In childhood she would ridicule me all the time. She probably didn't dislike me, and she probably loved me, and she probably still does. Because I'm very different to the others I probably was more difficult because I was a much stronger person than any of them, and I have strengths that she could probably always see but she could never compete with. I think I always did feel embarrassed about walking into a room where my mother and sisters were, so I must have had the feeling that it was odd in some way. She would threaten to send me away. My mother was always saying that my father said that I ought to go to boarding school. She always used to say that, always, always, because she said I was so difficult, awkward and unpleasant. Now that I think about it she used to say that all the time.' Her parents got on badly: 'My mother couldn't cope with my father. They had no communication at all. She isolated him and then she isolated me, but I don't know why'.

Comment

This quote refers to emotional abuse in the form of antipathy: cold, critical and rejecting parenting. This is perhaps a 'softer' version of such abuse than the sadistic coercive control indicated by psychological abuse. However, within this account there are some indicators of the latter for example the 'cruel' remarks, the threats to send to boarding school, the reference to using the child as an emotional 'battering ram'. The participant intersperses her account with evidence of her mother's behaviour but also with her own response in feeling both awkward, left out, isolated. There is some self-attribution – her mother reacting to the child being 'difficult' and different. She tries to justify her mother's behaviour 'she probably loved me' and attributes it to conflict in the marriage. She has some alliance with her father 'she isolated him and then she isolated me'. From this account it was possible to extract the factual elements of the mother's behaviour towards the child and score antipathy as marked 'severity'.

Child abuse and psychological disorder

There are a number of studies showing childhood neglect or abuse to relate to psychological disorder (Kaplan, Pelcovitz, & Labruna, 1999) in different life stages (Benjet, Borges, & Medina-Mora, 2010). Whilst initially child abuse was mostly investigated for emotional disorder (Bifulco & Moran, 1998) or for juvenile delinquency (Widom, 1989), it has since been shown to have impact on a wider range of disorders, including substance abuse and deliberate self-harm (Goldstein, Flett, Wekerle, & Wall, 2009), bipolar disorder (Agnew-Blais & Danese, 2016) and schizophrenia (H. Fisher et al., 2006). The findings using the CECA in London sample will be highlighted here. The disorders covered include emotional disorders (depression, anxiety, deliberate self-harm) and behavioural disorders (substance abuse or conduct disorder). See Box 3.2 for definitions using Diagnostic Statistical Manual (DSM) approaches(APA, 2013)

Box 3.2

Summary definitions of psychological disorder

- **Major Depression.** Affective or mood symptoms include depressed mood and feelings of worthlessness or guilt. Behavioural symptoms include social withdrawal and agitation; Cognitive symptoms, or problems in thinking include difficulty with concentration or making decisions. Finally, somatic or physical symptoms include insomnia or hypersomnia (sleeping too much);
- **Anxiety disorders** share features of excessive fear and anxiety and related behavioural disturbances. *Fear* is the emotional response to real or perceived imminent threat, whereas *anxiety* is anticipation of future threat. Fear is more often associated with surges of autonomic arousal necessary for fight or flight, thoughts of immediate danger, and escape behaviours, and anxiety more often associated with muscle tension and vigilance in preparation for future danger and cautious or avoidant behaviours. Sometimes the level of fear or anxiety is reduced by pervasive avoidance behaviours. *Panic attacks* feature prominently within the anxiety disorders as a particular type of fear response. Panic attacks are not limited to anxiety disorders but rather can be seen in other mental disorders as well. Includes Generalised Anxiety Disorder (GAD); Panic and Agoraphobia; Social Anxiety;
- **Post Traumatic Stress Disorder (PTSD).** This is explicitly defined in relation to an external trauma event. Criterion A specifies the

qualifying experience of traumatic event, four sets of symptom clusters, include – reexperiencing the event, avoidance, negative alternation in mood or cognition and increased arousal. There are also requirements around duration and impact on functioning;

- **Deliberate self-harm (NSSI); non-suicidal injury** – the intentional, direct injuring of body tissue. The most common is using a sharp object to cut one's skin, but self-harm also covers a wide range of behaviours including burning, scratching, banging or hitting body parts, interfering with wound healing, hair-pulling and the ingestion of toxic substances or objects;
- **Suicidal behaviour** – ideation towards suicidal thoughts, planning or actual attempts to end life;
- **Conduct disorder** – a prolonged pattern of anti-social behaviour such as serious violation of laws and social norms and rules in people younger than the age of 18. A repetitive and persistent pattern of behaviour in which the basic rights of others or more major age-appropriate societal norms or rules are violated, as manifested by the presence of three (or more) of the following criteria the past 12 months, with the least one criterion present in the past six months. Includes aggression to people and animals, destruction of property, deceitfulness or theft; serious violation of rules leading to significant impairment in roles, and under the age of 18 only;
- **Substance abuse/dependence** based on clusters of behaviours and physiological effects occurring within a specific time frame around the misuse of alcohol or drugs. The diagnosis of dependence always takes precedence over that of abuse and includes tolerance, withdrawal, taken in larger amounts, unsuccessful attempts to quit; large amount of time taken to get the drug, important activities reduced due to substance use; continued use despite knowledge of ill-effects. Abuse alone includes recurrent use interferes with roles, physical hazards linked to activity, legal involvement over the drug, continued use despite problems in relationships, lifestyle.[5]

The London sample – CATS study

The sample comprised an intensively studied series of 276 mother–offspring pairs in a relatively deprived inner-city London area with high rates of lone parenthood and socio-economic disadvantage. It included both representative (n = 172 pairs) and high risk (n = 104 pairs) mothers and offspring (Bifulco et al., 2002). The findings showed for 'severe' (marked or moderate levels) before age 17 in young people:

- In the representative group, rates of 16 per cent antipathy (coldness, criticism) from mother, 13 per cent antipathy father, and 7 per cent neglect,

6 per cent physical abuse mother, 9 per cent physical abuse father and 7 per cent sexual abuse. An index comprising severe neglect, or physical or sexual abuse showed 23 per cent had at least one such childhood experience;

- In the high-risk group (selected for mother's relationship problems) the rates of neglect/abuse were significantly higher in the young people. The overall index of neglect/abuse held for 39 per cent, an odds ratio of two compared to the representative group. Physical abuse from mother was three times more common (17 per cent), and from father twice as common (17 per cent). However, neglect and sexual abuse was not significantly different from the representative group (12 per cent vs 7 per cent and 6 per cent vs 7 per cent respectively);
- In the representative group of young people 8 per cent had yearly emotional disorder (major depression or anxiety) and 7 per cent had externalising disorder (conduct disorder or substance abuse). Overall 11 per cent had a clinical disorder in the year, compared with 43 per cent in offspring of vulnerable mothers (OR = 6.4, p < .001). The high-risk group had emotional disorder rates of 30 per cent and behavioural disorder rates of 21 per cent, odds ratios of 5.1 and 3.8 respectively when compared with the representative group.

Table 3.1 shows the relationship of childhood neglect/abuse to yearly clinical disorder in the total sample combined, showing the odds ratio (increased likelihood of disorder when severe abuse present vs absent).

It can be seen that all experiences related to clinical disorder and the index of neglect/abuse had an odds ratio of 5, reflecting the likelihood of disorder occurring when abuse was present. The only higher rate was for sexual abuse (7.9). Neglect was also high at odds ratio of 5.3. Other experiences were all significantly related to disorder with odds ratios of 2.5 to 3.9.

Table 3.1 Childhood experience by 12-monthly disorder in the London young adult sample

Severe CECA scale (marked or moderate)	Any disorder* Odds ratio	p <
Antipathy mother	3.2	.001
Antipathy father	2.5	.01
Physical abuse mother	3.8	.001
Physical abuse father	3.9	.0001
Neglect	5.3	.0001
Sexual abuse	7.9	.0001
Neglect, physical or sexual abuse	5.0	.001

*Depression, anxiety, conduct disorder or substance abuse (Bifulco et al., 2002).

Table 3.2 Childhood severe abuse type by perpetrator and type of adolescent disorder

CECA scale Odds ratio	Depression	Anxiety	Deliberate self-harm	Substance Abuse	Conduct disorder
Antipathy mother	1.60	3.20**	2.88**	2.27*	2.60*
Antipathy father	1.80	0.71	2.40*	4.08***	4.08***
Neglect mother	2.66**	3.22**	8.04**	2.36*	2.08
Neglect father	1.89	0.90	2.71*	2.85**	1.63
Physical abuse mother	3.01**	1.56	3.77*	2.20*	3.30**
Physical abuse father	1.61	1.81	1.24	4.69**	1.81
Sexual abuse	3.49*	2.10	2.00	15.00**	18.00***

*p < .05; **p < .01; ***p < .001 From Bifulco (2008) and Schimmenti & Bifulco (2015)

In the high-risk sample of young people, further details of disorder were recorded. Table 3.2 shows the odds ratios of the childhood experience at severe levels and different clinical disorder from age 13 to interview (Bifulco, 2008; Schimmenti & Bifulco, 2015).

It can be seen that all experiences related to at least one type of disorder, but patterning was evident. For example, whilst all the childhood experiences related to substance abuse, only three related to depression (neglect, physical abuse from mother and sexual abuse). Fewest experiences related to anxiety disorder. Problem care experiences were as prominent in relating as abuse experiences. However, the highest odds ratio was for sexual abuse in relation to substance abuse disorder (OR = 15) and conduct disorder (OR = 18).

There was further specificity in relation to parent/perpetrator, Additional analyses (see Figure 3.1) showed that and index of neglect, or antipathy or physical abuse from mother was significantly related to depression, but that from father was not; and that the same behaviour from fathers' related to substance abuse, but from mother was not (Bifulco, 2008). Therefore, some evidence of specificity of type of abuse, and from which parent were seen to relate to type of disorder.

It was clear from the interviews conducted with this sample that many of the young people had more than one type of abuse in childhood – these often from different figures and at different times. The issue of how multiple abuse effects disorder was therefore examined to check for 'dose effects'. Figure 3.2 shows in the London high risk adolescents, the presence of different disorders by the number of different types of childhood abuse experienced (0–3 neglect, physical or sexual abuse). Whilst there was evidence of dose effects for all disorders, this only held at a statistically significant level for deliberate self-harm (p < .008) and conduct disorder (p < .001) (see Figure 3.2) (Bifulco, 2008).

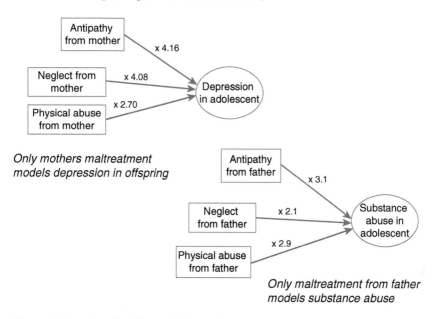

(results of logistic regression; odds-ratios shown)

Antipathy from mother — x 4.16 →

Neglect from mother — x 4.08 →

Physical abuse from mother — x 2.70 →

Depression in adolescent

Only mothers maltreatment models depression in offspring

Antipathy from father — x 3.1 →

Neglect from father — x 2.1 →

Physical abuse from father — x 2.9 →

Substance abuse in adolescent

Only maltreatment from father models substance abuse

Figure 3.1 Parent maltreating and disorder in adolescents – London study

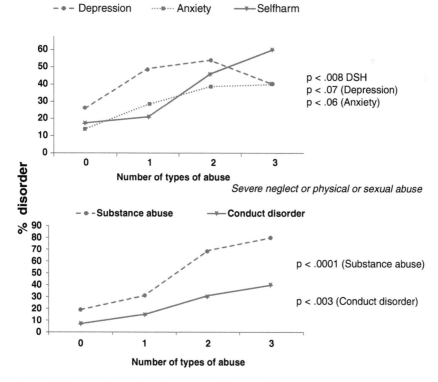

- ● - Depression   ▪▪▪▪▪ Anxiety   ─✴─ Selfharm

p < .008 DSH
p < .07 (Depression)
p < .06 (Anxiety)

Number of types of abuse

Severe neglect or physical or sexual abuse

- ● - Substance abuse   ─✴─ Conduct disorder

p < .0001 (Substance abuse)

p < .003 (Conduct disorder)

Number of types of abuse

% disorder

Figure 3.2 Dose effects of multiple neglect/abuse and clinical disorder in young people

The findings are consistent with the US Adverse Childhood Experiences (ACE) studies examining a wide range of childhood experiences, which summed were associated with increased rates of both clinical and physical health outcomes (Dong et al., 2004; Felitti, 2002). It also echoes the findings for sexual abuse revictimisation (Finkelhor, 1995; Finkelhor et al., 2007).

There is a body of research showing relationship between childhood abuse and PTSD (O'Connor & Elklit, 2008). A major exponent is van der Kolk, who has examined developmental trauma disorder (Van der Kolk, 2005; Van der Kolk et al., 1996). The complication with the PTSD diagnosis is that the trauma is intended to be recent, but complex PTSD recognises an early priming of childhood trauma in combination with a recent trauma experience in adulthood. PTSD diagnosis in childhood is only recently gaining credence as a new diagnosis (Ardino, 2011). In the sexual abuse domain, traumatised responses are also closely modelled (Finkelhor, 1995).

Historical abuse in the adult London women studied

When historical abuse was investigated in the same study but in the adult women (mothers), similar findings held for emotional disorder. An odds ratio of 3 was found for the presence of the index of either neglect, physical or sexual abuse and depression (Bifulco et al., 1998). In addition, an even more evident dose effect was found with rates of lifetime depression rising from 20 per cent through to 70 per cent with each additional abuse factor (Bifulco et al., 1994).

A recent publication looks at CECA child abuse in an older age sample (average age 65) and its association with lifetime emotional disorder (Bifulco et al., in press). This shows a significant association of child abuse with disorder, and this works even for those older in the sample. There does not appear to be a fall off with memory and the childhoods reflected included those in World War II and after (Bifulco, 2015). Thus, real long-term lifetime impacts seem evident. This is echoed by work on ACE childhood experiences and physical health in later life, including early mortality (Felitti et al., 1998).

Intergenerational transmission of abuse in the London studies

There is an extensive past literature on 'cycles of abuse' which emphasises the extent to which this recurs across generations (Beck-Sander, 2008). This assumes a certain fatalism of abuse continuing over time and generation, and can be stigmatising for those who had been abused in implying they in turn will be abusive (Widom, 1989). This approach has changed to a focus on pathways of abuse which looks at conditions under which abuse impacts are greatest and can extend to children. There is thus greater emphasis on resilience (impacts of abuse can be halted over time), specificity (abuse and its impacts are varied, not all lead to problem parenting) and dynamic changes in context (positive partner experiences can moderate risk). Other approaches highlight mother's postnatal depression in child's early life as key (Plant, Pariante, Sharp, & Pawlby, 2015).

Models developed using the CECA in mothers and adolescent offspring dyads (see Figure 3.3) showed that a link between mothers' own neglect/abuse in childhood and that in her offspring only occurred in the presence of either her recurrent lifetime depression, or her later vulnerability (problem relationships and low self-esteem) which mediated the experience (Bifulco et al., 2002). Also, the transmission was not only through her own maltreating parenting, but also of her partners, or in the case of sexual abuse, from other perpetrators.

The high-risk group of mid-life mothers and their adolescent offspring were examined in a paired design for intergenerational transmission of risk of child abuse. Mother's attachment style was examined as a potential mechanism for transmission along with problem partner relationship (both chronic problems in the relationship and partner's problem behaviour in terms of criminality, violence or psychiatric disorder). The resulting model (using path analysis) showed both direct and indirect effects and significant impacts of partner influence (Bifulco, Moran, Jacobs, & Bunn, 2009) (see Figure 3.4). The mother's experience of problem partner behaviour impacted her parenting competence, which significantly related to her offspring's maltreatment. Chronic problems in the partner relationship also impacted directly on offspring neglect/abuse from the mother (see Figure 3.4). Mother's insecure attachment style was a

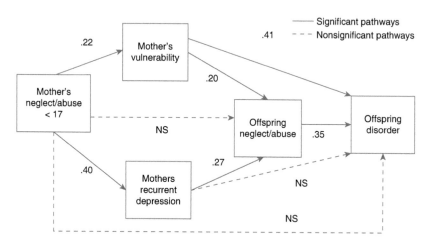

Figure 3.3 Intergenerational transmission-risk pathways in mother-adolescent dyads (Bifulco et al., 2002)

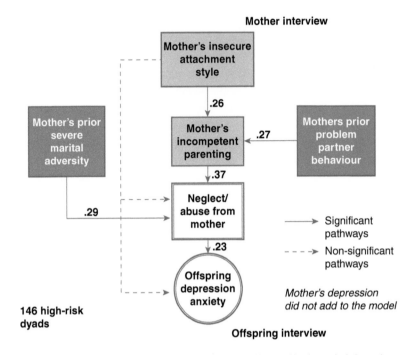

Figure 3.4 Intergenerational transmission though mother's attachment style and parenting (Bifulco et al., 2009)

significant predictor of her parenting, but not of child abuse, nor of disorder in the offspring.

The important message is that it is not a single maternal risk factor that increases the offspring risk of either maltreatment or clinical disorder, but rather a combination of factors in a more systemic family model. These implicate both mother and father behaviour and include adversity, clinical issues and attachment style. There is no intention here for 'mother blame'.[6] It is a tribute to mothers that they are more likely first to engage in intensive research studies, and second to be more likely to be present during their offsprings' early upbringing than fathers. This is why research on intergenerational transmission typically uses mother-child dyads. But it is clear that from a socio-ecological perspective that other adversities, particularly partner ones, play a part. There is also scope for resilience, with pathways only suggesting increased risk with other positive pathways emerging from different types of analysis.

Child abuse and offending or forensic disorders

Childhood abuse is also a common precursor of anti-social behaviour which leads to a criminal trajectory. The links with conduct disorder have already been briefly introduced, and this is consistently recognised as a risk factor for later anti-social personality disorder, psychopathy or violent offending Marshall & Cooke, 1999). Violent behaviour is a common outcome, more among boys, and with some genetic contribution (Caspi, 2002). Similar results are shown in UK, United States and New Zealand samples. Adverse childhood experience, including multiple victimisation, is common in all these categories (Finkelhor et al., 2007) with dose effects evident. The linkages in terms of types of abuse is sometimes surprising, with neglect a common precursor for psychopathic outcomes and sexual violence (Salter et al., 2003). The longitudinal research of Cathy Spatz Widom has been very instructive in this area. She followed up children registered with child protection agencies over a 30-year period together with a control group, and found a strong relationship with childhood abuse and delinquency and criminal behaviour (Widom, 1989a; Widom & Ames, 1994). Her specific concerns have been over accurate measurement and being wary of brief and retrospective self-reports of abuse; she has been critical of the notion of cycles of violence due to study artefacts (Widom, Czaja, & DuMont, 2015) and has found specific links to delinquency (for example from sexual abuse). More latterly she has been looking at other psychological disorder outcomes as well as negative physical health impacts in the same sample (Widom et al., 2012) described further as follows.

However, in addition to psychological disadvantage and that of opportunity, there are also direct physical health outcomes of abuse which create ramifications for the health of the nation and for health services.

Physical health outcomes of child abuse

There is now a growing body of research into adult health problems associated with childhood abuse (Dubowitz, 1991; Walker et al., 1999; Flaherty et al., 2006). This includes a meta-analysis of the various studies to establish effect sizes (Wegman & Stetler, 2009). This compared 24 studies and 78 effect sizes and 48,000 individuals. Experiencing child abuse was associated with an increased risk of negative physical health outcomes in adulthood (effect size d = 0.42, 95% Confidence Interval = 0.39–0.45). Neurological and musculoskeletal problems yielded the largest effect sizes, followed by respiratory problems, cardiovascular disease, gastrointestinal and metabolic disorders. Effect sizes were larger when the sample was exclusively female and when the abuse was assessed via self-report rather than objective, independently verifiable methods. The magnitude of the risk is comparable to the association between child abuse and poor psychological outcomes. However, studies often fail to include a diverse group of participants, resulting in a limited ability to draw conclusions about the population of child abuse survivors as a whole. Important methodological improvements are also needed to better understand potential moderators.

For example, there is raised risk of heart disease (Dong et al., 2004), adult inflammation (Danese, Pariante, Caspi, Taylor, & Poulton, 2007) and obesity (Lissau & Sorensen, 1994). Further risks are incurred from a poorer uptake of health services (Chartier, Walker, & Naimark, 2007). The ACE study of child-hood adversity also showed child abuse and related experiences to be a leading cause of death in adults (Felitti, 2002; Felitti et al., 1998). In a large survey of over 13,000 adults, they found those who experienced four or more categories of childhood adverse exposure, compared to those who had experienced none, had 4- to 12-fold increased health risks for alcoholism, drug abuse, depression and suicide attempt; a 2- to 4-fold increase in smoking, poor self-rated health, + 50 sexual intercourse partners and sexually transmitted disease; and a 1.4- to 1.6-fold increase in physical inactivity and severe obesity. The number of cat-egories of adverse childhood exposures showed a graded relationship to the presence of adult diseases including ischemic heart disease, cancer, chronic lung disease, skeletal fractures and liver disease.

Widom has spent a number of years investigating a matched case control group of children 0–11 with childhood neglect and abuse from a US Midwestern county in 1967–71 longitudinally in a 30-year follow-up when they were aged 41 (Widom et al., 2012). The tests included a medical status exam for vision and dental health and blood tests, controls were made for health behaviours (e.g. smoking) and social class and mental health. The study showed that childhood neglect/abuse predicted above normal haemoglobin A1C albumin, poor peak airflow and vision problems. Physical abuse additionally predicted malnutrition and sexual abuse hepatitis C. The authors concluded that child abuse/neglect related to long-term health outcomes increasing risk for diabetes, lung disease, malnutrition and vision problems.

However, there are some curious findings about how childhood experience is measured in relation to physical illness in adulthood. A study in Dunedin, NZ, of a cohort of children followed up into adulthood showed moderate agree-ment between measures used prospectively in childhood, based on scrutiny of child social service contacts, and structured notes from assessment staff and medical staff and then retrospective measures aged 38 using the Childhood Trauma Questionnaire (.47) (Reuben et al., 2016). Physical health was assessed by means of self-reported poor health (single item), cognitive impairment in relation to both subjective questions about memory, word finding etc. based on mild cognitive disorder report and objectively using the WAIS-IV scale, psychopathology. All measures of ACEs were significantly related to physical and psychological health scales whether retrospective or prospective. How-ever, when adjustments were made for whether the measures prospectively and retrospectively of child abuse agreed, then prospective measures alone significantly related to objectively measured health outcomes (physical health from biomarkers and cognitive health from working memory assessment). In contrast self-reported measures of physical health, cognitive health and mental health only remained for the adjusted retrospective measures of health. Differences were accounted for by neuroticism and agreeableness as measured in adulthood. One of the problems, of course, of this type of study is that the prospective childhood measure and retrospective measures are not consonant and do not give similar coverage. However, there is little doubt that however measured, there are long-term health outcomes.

Resilience to abuse

Child abuse is relatively common, but not all who experience it are equally susceptible to disorder or ill health. This is in part explained by the higher risk subset who experience multiple and cumulative abuse, but it is also evident that some children and some adults are resilient to its effects. Resilience is defined in terms of retaining good functioning in the presence of adversity or abuse. Outcomes indicating resilience have included the *absence* of psychopathology or maladaptive behaviour *or* the presence of health or social competence (Masten et al., 1999). In terms of intervention, relevant concepts include prevention (reducing the exposure to abuse), protection (moderating the effects or impacts of abuse) and counteracting (resources applied which counteract the effects of adversity by promoting the motivational state). However, in naturalistic settings in the community a range of potential protective factors have been identified which relate to better psychological outcomes when abuse is present. These include socio-environmental factors in various domains (e.g. competent parenting, closeness to a parent, good support, good educational experience and organised religion) as well as individual, psychological characteristics (e.g. high IQ, good coping skills, autonomy, empathy and sense of humour) (Fonagy, Steele, Steele, Higgitt, & Target, 1994; Luthar, 1991; Masten et al., 1988; Rutter, 1990). Resilience is thus conceptualised not merely as an attribute born into children or acquired during development, but rather as the indication of a process which characterises a complex social system at a particular point in time (Rutter, 1990). It combines the child's attributes with the family, social and cultural environments, with resilience indicated when normal child or adolescent development occurs under difficult conditions.

The London study of high risk young people found a range of experiences at age 16 were related to well-being outcomes (Bifulco, 2008). This included confiding friendships and good/safe school environments. These factors were surprisingly common in a sample of young people with high rates of abuse and disorder. Positive outcomes included secure attachment style and high self-es-teem. The two latter were the best protection against yearly disorder in the face of child abuse.

However, resilience can also be found in genetic factors. This follows from studies showing that marked variability in response occurs among people exposed to the same environmental risk (such as abuse) implying that individ-ual differences in genetic susceptibility might be at work, specifically associ-ated with stress sensitivity (Caspi, Hariri, Holmes, Uher, & Moffitt, 2010). This notion had already been current in 2008 by the work of Ellis and Boyce. They argued against the conventional view that an exaggerated biological reactiv-ity to stress is a harmful remainder of an evolutionary past in which threats to survival were more prevalent and severe (Ellis & Boyce, 2008). They point instead to evidence which indicates that effects of high reactivity on behaviour and health differ and can exert both risk-increasing and risk-protective effects, depending on the context. Thus, heightened stress reactivity may reflect increased biological sensitivity to context, with potential for negative health effects under conditions of adversity and for positive effects under conditions of support. This theoretical perspective generates a novel hypothesis: that there is a curvilinear, U-shaped relation between early exposures to adversity and the development of stress-reactive profiles, with high-reactivity pheno-types disproportionately emerging within both highly stressful and highly pro-tected early social environments.

The resilience model developed explains differential sensitivity to the environment. It is sometimes described by reference to children being either 'dandelion' (those hardier and less sensitive to stress) or 'orchid' (those more sensitive to stress). They argue that the dandelion child can remain healthy and survive in either harsh or hospitable environments but might remain aver-age or unremarkable. Orchids however require protection and shelter to thrive. Under the right circumstances remarkable blossoms may grow. A specific gene variant has been linked to 'orchid' children who have high sensitivity to their environment and are thus vulnerable to stress. The gene-marker is glucocor-ticoid receptor gene NR3C1, which influences the activity of a receptor which cortisol binds, and is directly involved in the stress response (Albert et al., 2015). In a study of first graders 75 per cent of children with the NR3C1 gene variant ('orchids') went on to develop psychological problems by age 25. The maladaptive behaviours included substance abuse, aggression and anti-social personality disorder. However, the children with this gene variant were also positively susceptible to intervention. In an intensive multi-pronged support service intervention (Fast Track Project) only 18 per cent developed psychopa-thology as adults.

> ## Case example of resilient coping (Bifulco & Moran, 1998, p 160)
>
> A woman who described extensive and multiple abuse in childhood at the hands of her stepfather described her response when she was 10 years old:
>
> *For quite a while he succeeded in making me feel worthless, and then something inside me just snapped, and I just had this feeling that I had to survive him, that I had to wait until I was old enough to walk away. I had to stop him from doing it. That's why I was the only one of the four sisters that ever stood up to him, that ever fought him physically. I'd resigned myself to the fact that there was only one person that was going to get me out of this, and that was me - my only weapon was myself. That's what I was built for.*

Discussion

Research consistently shows that childhood neglect and abuse has pernicious effects on different types of disorder from adolescence through to older age. The most recent research indicates this is through multiple channels (biological, psychological and social) and leads to both physical and psychological ill health. Odds ratios of abuse experience to disorder are highest in adolescence for psychological disorder, but in later adulthood for physical disorder. Dose effects are prevalent, so the higher severity of abuse and the greater the number of different abuses experienced, the higher the risk to health. However, some specificity of effects of experience and type of disorder are also noted.

There are various models linking abuse to disorder, and these are not mutually exclusive, but focus on different mediating variables (attachment, emotional dysregulation, dysregulated cortisol etc.). Models also extend to intergenerational transmission. Here the mother's attachment style, her parenting, but also her partner's behaviour, have key effects. Resilience is also evident, and this too can be in the social environment, psychological adaptation or genetic disposition. This ensures that not all with abuse go on to have disorder.

In terms of the contemporary issues identified, as with the increased scope of abuse, so are the increased negative outcomes. Child abuse is now a public health issue, and the implications for a range of health and social care services means that understanding of, and assessment of child abuse is required for understanding the aetiology and likely outcomes of a range of clinical and physical illnesses. Increasingly all professionals require a knowledge of childhood abuse, and assessment tools are required that can gauge an individual's status of abuse in many areas of health and social care practice. Yet this is difficult to achieve with brief self-report measures. Identifying an individual with prior or ongoing abuse also carries stigma and individuals have often become used to secrecy about their experience. These attitudes need addressing in our society if we are not protecting not only children, but their adult selves against negative consequences.

Notes

1 *www.childrenscommissioner.gov.uk/publications*
2 *www.cecainterview.com*
3 www.cecainterview.com
4 *www.cecainterview.com*
5 See DSM classifications for more details https://allpsych.com/disorders/dsm/
6 https://mothersapartproject.com/2016/05/11/picking-apart-the-mother-blaming-that-takes-place-with-abused-mothers/

4 Abuse and children's services in the UK

This chapter outlines procedures relevant to children and families involved with children's services because of child abuse or neglect. As described earlier, this occurs at 'child in need' (CiN) level where family support is provided and child protection (Section 47) levels where the child is removed from the family and services for children in care. The chapter also outlines Early Intervention (EI) initiatives which are universal or targeted services for children, usually in early years (0-5). These are preventative and geared to child well-being outcomes and to increase health and life chances. The social policy initiatives of the last ten years or so will be outlined to draw out contemporary issues for children under the twin themes of early intervention and those of safeguarding. Whilst it is beyond the scope of the book to look in detail at interventions, various approaches will be outlined.

There is no doubt about the high demand for children's services. Recent figures have been reported with newspaper headlines of 'children referred to social services in England and Wales every 49 seconds'.[1] However, these are present at a time when councils are reported as overspending and with a large funding gap predicted by 2020:

> There was a total of 646,120 referrals overall during 2016/17, up 4% on the previous year. Domestic violence was a growing cause of referrals, up from 41% of cases in 2013/14 to half now, with mental health identified as an issue 40% of the time. Council leaders have warned that children's services are dealing with pressures on a "staggering scale", with the LGA pointing to a £2bn funding gap by 2020. Three quarters of councils exceeded their budgets for children's services in the last year, with a total overspend of £605m.... With councils now having a child referred to them every 49 seconds on a daily basis, it is vital that they have the resources necessary to provide an effective response.
>
> *The Times, Page: 2 (12.1.18)*[2]

This has implications for intervention strategies from previous governments for early intervention to avert maltreatment and improve the lives of children across the country.

Two key policies have already been outlined – the first to control inter-agency working, the second to focus on working practices of social workers, their approach to assessment and their need to focus on the child. Through it all we need to remember the voice of the child and the child at the centre of proceedings.

Children, Schools and Families Act (2010) legislation followed from the review of the Baby Peter case. Harringey Local Authority came under intense criticism following Baby P's murder by his mother, her boyfriend and another individual. A joint review, undertaken by OFSTED, the regulator, the Healthcare Audit and Inspection, and the Chief Inspector of Constabulary, was completed in 2008. Lord Laming was required to produce a progress report (March 2009) which acknowledged that prior reforms had produced a firm foundation, but a renewed commitment to child protection at every level of government and across all services was required. His 58 recommendations were accepted in full and legislation was changed in relation to establishing procedures and pro-tocols for communication between agencies and opening up the LSCBs (local safeguarding boards) for greater scrutiny. The Act gave LSCBs and other agen-cies in England and Wales information-sharing powers for investigating seri-ous case reviews and child death reviews. OFSTED was authorised to conduct reviews of LSCBs. The Wood Review[3] noted problems with this and LSCBs were recently abolished under the Children and Social Work Act 2017.[4]

The Munro Review (2010–11) concluded that child protection had become too focused on bureaucratic compliance and procedures, losing its focus on the needs and experiences of individual children and recommended reforms for a more child-centred policy. The 15 recommendations to Government included a revision of the Working Together statutory guidance; a revised inspection framework; benchmarks of performance of LAs and partners on national and local levels; performance information to facilitate improvement and account-ability; early help services and a Chief Social Worker to be put in place in Gov-ernment. The recommendations were accepted and in her report on progress (May 2012) Munro stated that progress was in the right direction but needed to be swifter. In her report Munro also discussed the overuse of technology in assessment and procedures, to the exclusion of the human element in social workers relating to children and their families. She endorsed the up-skilling of social workers to help with professional judgement, flexibility on assessment forms and the appropriate use of technology whilst putting children at the cen-tre and giving professional judgement due acknowledgement.

Child safeguarding procedures

Child in need (CiN) status

Section 17 of the Children Act 1989 imposes a general duty on Children's Social Care (CSC) to safeguard and promote the welfare of children who are 'in need' and to promote the upbringing of children in need by their families by providing a range and level of services to meet those children's needs.[5]

In order to determine the needs of a child and the support that they and their family may require, CSC will carry out a 'single child and family assessment' by a qualified social worker. The assessment will involve finding out and giving due regard to the child's wishes and feelings regarding the provision of those services (as age and understanding appropriate). The assessment will also involve talking to parents, other family members where relevant and professionals involved in the child's life such as health visitor or school. Local authorities have a duty to 'safeguard and promote the welfare of children who are in need'. A child is defined as being 'in need' if:

- unlikely to achieve or maintain, or to have the opportunity of achieving or maintaining, a reasonable standard of health or development without the provision for him of services by a local authority under this Part;
- his/her health or development is likely to be significantly impaired, or further impaired, without the provision for him of such services;
- s/he is disabled (and in Scotland: s/he is affected adversely by the disability of any other person in the family).

Conversely, if the initial referral suggests that the child may be at risk of significant harm, then the professionals who work with the family will have a strategy discussion. A strategy discussion involves the social worker gathering more information from the child, parents, family members and other professionals. If the strategy discussion confirms concerns about a child, **a section 47** inquiry will start. If the strategy discussion suggests that the child may be at risk of significant harm, then the professionals who work with the family will decide if there should be section 47 inquiries. As part of the inquiry, there will be assessments of the child's welfare and safety needs. If the assessments find that the child is at risk of significant harm, then there will be a child protection conference.

Local authorities are tasked to not only safeguard but also promote the welfare of children within their area in need and to provide a range of services appropriate to such need. These cover the child but also any member of the family identified as aiding the child's welfare. In the process it is required to ascertain the child's wishes and feelings regarding the provision of those services and to give due consideration (having regard to his age and understanding) to such wishes and feelings of the child as they have been able to ascertain.

All CiN work begins with an assessment of the child and family based on section 17 of the policy described earlier. In most circumstances the single assessment should be completed, written up and signed off by a manager within 20 working days. The assessment should involve seeing the child/children and observing and talking to them (depending on their age) and listening to the family's story. The assessment also involves reviewing historical information and getting information from/talking to other professionals involved (with parental consent) to get a rounded picture of the child's needs and the support needed for parents. The completed assessment should be shared with the family and, where support is required, lead to a child in need plan.

When a single assessment is in progress or has been completed and a child and their family have identified needs that require support, either through continued social work intervention or through the provision of services, a CiN plan should be developed with the family and with any other relevant agency. This can sometimes be done by holding a child in need planning meeting with family members and agreeing with the family who else might be invited, such as school, health visitor etc. Where needed, the first CiN meeting should be chaired by a team manager and minutes taken by BSA. The first CiN meeting is often critical and extra attention needs to be paid to developing a realistic and achievable plan for the child and the family as a base for intervention. At the first meeting, the reasons and time frame for intervention should be set and agreed by the family.

The child in need plan should state what the purpose of the plan is – what it is setting out to achieve; what intervention and/or services will be provided and by whom; what the child and/or family agree to do; what the time frame for the plan is and when it will be reviewed. It should be clear about the frequency of social work visits which should be at least every six weeks (different arrangements apply for disabled children with stable packages of care). The purpose of child in need plans is to provide support and/or services in such a way that enhances the ability of parents to meet the developmental needs of their child. Social work interventions can begin, and services can be provided as soon as a need is identified, without waiting for the assessment to be completed. In Assessment and Intervention teams, short-term focused social work interventions that help parents make changes and link them up with community support are often the best way of responding to children in need, but these interventions and what they are seeking to achieve should always be set out in an agreed child in need plan.

Where a child has been subject to a child protection plan and improvements have been made so that the plan ends, and where a child in care returns home to their family, a child in need plan should be put in place to support the child's continued development. This plan should be in place for at least three months and should be reviewed before it is closed.

CiN plans should also be put in place where section 47 inquiries have not proceeded to child protection, but the child and family's need for support has been identified. CiN plans should be in place where children are at risk of entry into care, including when DBIT/MST are involved. CiN plans should also be used for children and young people with self-harming or other risky behaviour or with mental health difficulties. Children and young people with a disability, aged under 18, should have an up-to-date child in need plan if they are receiving a service such as a direct payment or overnight short-break or a social work intervention. Where children are in care or subject to a child protection plan, any child in need plan should be ended and the child in care/CP plan becomes the key plan.

The frequency of Child in Need Reviews will depend on the level of support and services that have been identified to meet need. However, the first review should be held within three months of the start of the CiN plan and further reviews should take place at least every six months thereafter. Children who have been identified as at some level of risk and/or needing a prominent level of support and services may need to be reviewed more often than those who require a minimum level of intervention.

A CiN plan is best reviewed by meeting with the family and any key professionals (teacher, health visitor e.g.) to discuss and record what has been achieved, what has gone well and not so well, and what, if anything, still needs to be done. The review should listen to and record child and family feedback about the impact the intervention or service has made. Every review should use a strengths-based approach by asking everyone to state what they think has gone well, what worries or concerns they still have and what, if anything, still needs to be achieved.

Where a child in need plan is in place and it becomes clear that the family would benefit from and are willing to work with Family Solutions, this is best achieved through a CiN review meeting to which Family Solutions are invited. Child in need cases should not be stepped down to Family Solutions until the CiN plan has been implemented for at least two months. Each review should lead to an updating of the CiN plan, unless the review concludes that the plan can end. Where child protection/section 47 inquiries arise resulting in a CP plan, or if a child comes into care, the CiN plan must be ended. CiN reviews should take place at a minimum of every 6 months. This includes reviews for children and young people with disabilities. In preparing for a review, it is best to update the single assessment and use that as the review report to be considered at the meeting.

Section 47 - child protection following significant harm

Where there is evidence of significant harm, Section 47 Inquiries should commence:

- where there is reasonable cause to suspect that a child is suffering or likely to suffer significant harm in the form of physical, sexual, emotional abuse or neglect;
- following an Emergency Protection Order and/or Police Powers of Protection.

A Section 47 Inquiry **must** always be commenced:

- immediately when there is a disclosure, allegation or evidence that a child is suffering or likely to suffer significant harm;
- where there are childcare concerns combined with domestic violence, parental mental illness, parental substance or alcohol misuse such as to cause agencies to reasonably assume the children are exposed to parenting that is not prioritising their needs;
- where there are concerns for a pre-birth child suggesting s/he is likely to suffer significant harm.

In all other situations where a Section 47 Inquiry may be initiated, the decision should consider following factors:

- severity of ill treatment;
- trauma attributed to the ill treatment;
- repetition or duration of concerns;
- vulnerability of child including any predisposing factors i.e. child looked after, age, disability etc;
- familial predisposing factors that may suggest a higher level of risk.

Threshold criteria for initiating a Section 47 Inquiry may be met at any time from the point of referral throughout the assessment process or at any time in an open case where concerns are highlighted. An Initial Child Protection Conference should always be preceded by a Section 47 Inquiry.

Those making inquiries about a child should always be alert to the potential needs and safety of any siblings or other children in the household of the child in question. In addition, inquiries may also need to cover children in other households with whom the alleged offender may have had contact. The police will have to, concurrently, (where relevant) establish the facts about any offence that may have been committed against a child and to collect evidence.

The information and conclusions of the Section 47 Inquiry will inform the full Core Assessment, which must identify family strengths, the child/ren's vulnerabilities and/or resilience as well as adverse factors to form a needs assessment as well as a risk assessment.

It is therefore critical for social workers and other professionals to understand well the threshold for early intervention; child in need; and child in danger of significant harm. This will determine the level of proceedings and the nature of the action taken. This is where the dilemma between care and investigative roles are most evident.

The profession of social work is demanding – being both carer (providing for child welfare) and controller (forensic investigator and policing role) with power over children's futures. These have been described as irreconcilable role expectations and unique to the UK (Wrennall, 2014). This dual role leads to tensions, with the result there are often shortages of social workers in child protection, and those who stay can experience burn-out. Social workers are often first blamed when child protection goes wrong and a child dies – despite the responsibility being held in multi-agency teams. This can also lead to added pressure in the profession.

Assessment, decision making and procedure in a proscribed time frame makes CP a pressured task. There are various flow charts available to social workers to indicate how the child and family need to progress through a complex process as swiftly as possible. Outcomes may be child removal to fostering

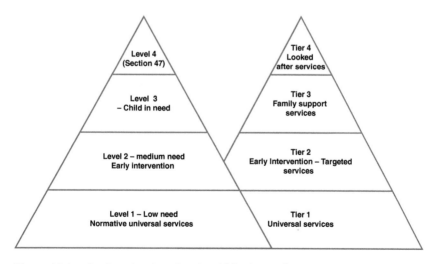

Figure 4.1 Levels of need and services for child safeguarding

and later adoption or residential care, or extra support being given to help the family cope and parent better. Responsibility for undertaking Section 47 Inquiries are held with the Local Authority in whose area the child lives, or where the alleged abuse has taken place. This can include day nurseries, schools and boarding schools, hospitals, privately fostered home, or a one-off location such as fairground, holiday home or outing. Inter-agency working includes police, health professionals, teachers and others who all contribute to assessment by providing information, and who may become part of a joint inquiry or investigation.

Where significant harm is not substantiated, social workers with their managers discuss the child together with the child, parent and any other professionals involved. This is to determine and secure support from any services which may be helpful, and to apportion responsibility for regular re-assessment of the child's health and development, where necessary. Where concerns of significant harm are substantiated, social workers and their managers convene an initial child protection conference within 15 working days of a strategy decision. They need to decide whether any specialist professionals need to be involved; ensure that the child and its parents understand the purpose of the conference, and help prepare the child for further processes, such as through advocacy services. Court action takes place for the following categories related to CP:

- emergency protection order – taking the child to a place of safety;
- exclusion order – removing abuser from the home;
- Child Assessment order – assessing child's needs if parents or carers do not give consent;
- removal by police – of a child for safety for up to 72 hours without obtaining a court order;
- female genital mutilation protection order, through family courts to protection to victims under civil law.

Children in care

Section 20 of the Children Act 1989 deals with children in care, with a requirement to provide accommodation for children who do not have a home or one which is safe. It stipulates that:

(1) Every local authority shall provide accommodation for any child in need within their area who appears to them to require accommodation as a result of –

(a) there being no person who has parental responsibility for him;

(b) his being lost or having been abandoned; or

(c) the person who has been caring for him being prevented (whether or not permanently, and for whatever reason) from providing him with suitable accommodation or care.

(2) Where a local authority provide accommodation under subsection (1) for a child who is ordinarily resident in the area of another local authority, that other local authority may take over the provision of accommodation for the child within –

(a) three months of being notified in writing that the child is being provided with accommodation; or

(b) such other longer period as may be prescribed.

Written into this legislation even then (1989) is a consideration of the child's wishes (the issues of child's 'feelings' added in the 2004 legislation (DfES, 2004):

Before providing accommodation under this section, a local authority shall, so far as is reasonably practicable and consistent with the child's welfare –

(a) ascertain the child's wishes and feelings regarding the provision of accommodation; and

(b) give due consideration (having regard to his age and understanding) to such wishes and feelings[6] of the child as they have been able to ascertain.

There are a range of arrangements possible. This can be with friends or family (kinship care) which involves less disruption. Otherwise foster arrangements are put in place, which can be more or less permanent. Foster care is usually the first arrangement for children taken away from their parents due to maltreatment and this can be of shorter or longer duration. Foster carers are reimbursed for caring for children, and this has been utilised to increase the professionalism of carers and initiatives such as therapeutic fostering developed (see therapeutic foster care section as follows in Box 4.1). The aim is to increase carer skills to handle children with complex needs and thus avert a premature breakdown of arrangements. In adoption, necessarily a later step given the legalities and the extent of the adopter assessment, the situation is somewhat different, given the legal standing of adopters as parents. But post-adoption support services are available to aid when the placement is under strain. Unfortunately, many adoptions break down.

Box 4.1

**Recent chronology of policy background
for children in care**

- **Children (Leaving Care) 2000:** Sets out duties local authorities
  must support young people leaving care from 16 to 21 years of age;
- **Adoption and Children Act 2002:** Updated the legal framework
  for domestic and inter-country adoption, duty on local authorities to
  maintain an adoption service and support services;
- **Children Act 2004:** Identified a lack of priorities and deficiencies
  in LA services. Changes included procedures for involving relevant
  professionals (children's Trusts); to extend the range of professionals
  involved in safeguarding and promoting well-being in children,
  including preventative work and the setting up of Local Safeguarding
  Children Boards (LSCBs);
- **Children and Adoption Act 2006:** Gives courts more flexible
  powers to facilitate child contact and enforce contact orders when
  separated parents are in dispute.
- **Children and Young Persons Act 2008:** Amends the Children
  Act 1989, strengthens visiting requirements and the role of the
  independent reviewing officer. Legislates for Care Matters white
  paper to provide high quality care and services for children in care.
  Residence Order or Special Guardianship Order for existing carers.
- **Children and Families Act 2014:** Encourages 'fostering for
  adoption'; a 26-week time limit for the courts to decide on child
  removal. Introduces 'staying put' arrangements with foster families
  until the age of 21 years. This is provided that both the young person
  and the foster family are happy to do so. Significantly changed the
  process for assessing foster carers through a new, two-stage process;
  shortened process for revising foster carers' terms of approval.
- **An Action Plan for Adoption - Tackling Delay (March 201):**
  Speeding up the adopter approvals process without losing any of
  its rigour. Strengthening local accountability for the timeliness of
  adoption services. Fast track process for approved foster carers and
  previous adopters. Adoption Reform Grant to local authorities, and
  grants to the Consortium of Voluntary Adoption Agencies to pass
  directly to frontline adoption agencies. Publication of an Adoption
  Passport for adopters, with adopters having a wide range of rights
  e.g. schools, council housing, adoption pay and leave.
- **The Children's Homes (England) Regulations 2015:** Sets out duties
  for those providing residential children's homes for children.
- **Residential care in England (2016):** Sir Martin Narey's independent
  review with 34 recommendations involving value for money,
  placement flexibility, cautions against criminalising children,

comments on OFSTED inspections, staff quality and work conditions, having placements close by, need for system leadership.
- **Children and Social Work Act (2017):** This introduced the concept of Corporate Parenting for Local Authorities to change the culture and consider impacts on children in care and those leaving care up to age 25. This involves promoting well-being (physical and mental health); to take into account wishes of the children; to gain them access to services; to promote high aspirations and secure best outcomes; to ensure safety and stability of children in home lives, relationships and education and work. To also prepare young people leaving care for independent living. The latter comprises a 'local offer' for help with health/well-being; relationships; education and training; employment; accommodation and participation in society. A personal adviser is offered to care leavers. With the abolishment of LSCBs, it puts duties on three safeguarding partners (LA, clinical commissioning groups and Chief Officer of Police) to make safeguarding arrangements that respond to need of children in their area.

There were 1,795 active children's homes as of 31 March 2015. This was 41 more than at the same point in 2014. Today the voluntary sector provides relatively little residential care; only about 5 per cent of children in homes; 28 per cent of children live in local authority provision, whilst the majority of children, 67 per cent, now live in private provision (Narey, 2016). In 2015, children's homes were disproportionately located in certain areas of the UK. London has only 6 per cent of children's homes whilst the North West has 24 per cent. Eleven private companies own just under a quarter of all homes although the bulk of private provision is made up of providers owning just one or two homes (71 per cent). The estimated average weekly cost of a place in a children's home (2013 costs) was approximately £3,000, with little difference in cost between local authority, voluntary sector and private sector provision (DfE, 2014). Local Authority-run homes have a higher number of staff on average (15) compared to privately run homes (11) irrespective of the size of the home. Staff in privately run homes tend to work longer hours on average (38.6 hours a week) compared to local authority-run homes (33.9 hours a week). Privately run homes currently pay significantly less per hour than local authority homes, with an average of £9.39 per hour against £13.28 in local authority-run homes. The voluntary sector figure is £10.15.

Inspection of services presents high stress for staff and managers. OFSTED has responsibility for children's homes as well as schools. The need for inspection is recognised but the number of regulations and 'single word' classification

of services which are multidimensional can prove problematic and lead to closure of provision or loss of staff. The residential care review by Sir Martin Narey
(Narey, 2016) identified issues around OFSTED. While OFSTED's new inspection
framework was generally well received, responses illustrated an imperfect system which at times places a heavy burden on already stretched providers. The
majority of those who expressed a view on regulation and inspection in residential care were positive about the voice of the child being more important
to the new process. Yet some still had concerns over the significant amount of
regulation in the sector, which they saw as 'costly', calling for a reduction in this
and an increased focus on individual needs (Narey, 2016, p. 47).

Narey recommended a greater level of dialogue between homes and OFSTED
before, during and after inspection. His report into residential care (July 2016)
resulted in 34 recommendations which Narey grouped under seven headings
(Box 4.2):

Box 4.2

Summary of Narey report recommendations

- **Obtaining value for money** (e.g. local authority consortia; new
  voluntary sector providers; numbers of staff and their attendance
  monitoring);
- **Fostering; closeness to home and size of homes** (e.g.
  positive recruitment and pay for foster carers; right placement
  more important than local placement; not to favour small
  bedded residential homes; reconsider key elements of secure
  accommodation);
- **Criminalising of children, staff confidence, setting boundaries,
  use of restraint** (e.g. restorative justice approach by police; keeping
  children safe in the homes e.g. by locking the homes; greater police
  flexibility in dealing with crime committed in residential care homes);
- **OFSTED** (e.g. good/outstanding homes only inspected yearly;
  re-examine the use of a single word judgement on homes; not rule
  out placing children in 'satisfactory' homes; revisit their inspection
  framework e.g. regarding restraint);
- **Staff qualifications, pay, recruitment** (e.g. no compromise in
  training; staff development in employment; residential placement
  included in social work training;
- **Staying close** rather than staying put (for 18-year-olds leaving
  homes to have options to 'stay put' with fostering or residential
  care to introduce 'Staying Close' with accommodation nearby to the
  previous setting provided);
- **Leadership (**residential care leadership board in DfE).

Narey's highlighting of staffing is important with staff in residential care high-lighted as often poorly paid and poorly qualified. Thus, those with least training and lowest remuneration are charged with helping the most damaged and dif-ficult children and young people. There is a need to make this a more desirable career choice. Given only 9 per cent of residential homes were found by OFSTED to be inadequate, with 75 per cent to be good or outstanding, clearly good work is being done, under difficult conditions with young people with complex needs. A key element is their ability to relate to the young people in their care. Whilst there is a call for more qualification, Narey does not advocate the requirement for graduate level as currently in place in Scotland. At present a level 3 diploma is required (and level 5 for managers) although many workers find that is not stretching. Continuing Professional Development is called for. Narey recom-mends that more social work training involves residential care placements.

Poor outcomes for children in care

Children in the UK taken into the care of the local authority (also called 'Looked After' children) tend to go first to fostering, which can be short or long term, or kinship care (by family or friends), then may proceed to adoption. For those children who don't settle in family arrangements, residential care becomes the main option, the children by then usually in teenage years. Many of these chil-dren enter their new arrangements already scarred by their early experience of neglect and abuse by parents and carers.

Figures available from 2013 indicate that 68,110 children were in care (0.6 per cent of the total population of children), that £2.5bn were spent supporting those in foster care and residential care and that 62 per cent were in care because of experiences of neglect or abuse (DfE, 2014).[7] Of those in care most (75 per cent) are fostered with costs of fostering £1.5 billion. Residential care costs total £12 billion. The average annual spend on a foster child is £29-33,00 compared to nearly three times that of £131-135,000 for a child in residential care. A third of children in care have more than one placement in a given year.

Negative impacts on their capacities including psychological, educational, relational and health make the task of caring in new families and settings dif-ficult to accomplish. Many need treatments from Child and Adolescent Mental Health Services (CAMHS), with specialised educational help and help with legal and police contact following delinquent behaviour. The challenge varies accord-ing to age group - services for infants and babies differentiated from school age and adolescent treatments and support.

However, children who have been in care have much poorer outcomes than children who stay with their birth families. Whilst much of this can be attributed to the original neglect, abuse or damaged relationships in early life, it appears that the experience of being in care may add to the emotional burden. This can be because of frequent changes of care arrangement, problematic contact with birth parents and siblings, problems with peer relationships in new settings and at school, and stigma at being in the care system. There are persistent problems with attachment issues and re-attaching to new carers. There also issues of damaged self-esteem and lack of motivation for achievement. Both the social and psychological environment becomes impoverished, often despite the best intentions and commitments of carers and care staff. Such poor outcomes are listed in Box 4.3:

Box 4.3

Figures for adult outcomes for children raised in out-of-home care[8]

- Those with three or fewer placements were more likely to finish school (65 per cent of children in foster care experienced seven or more changes in placement);
- Three times more likely than the general population to be living in poverty;
- Up to nine times more likely to become homeless;
- Five times more likely to have PTSD;
- Up to ten times *less* likely to complete a bachelor's degree;
- Sixty-six times more likely to have children needing public care.

Thus, children looked after by the State in any arrangement have poor outcomes, compared with the population of intact families, with half of these children having emotional and behavioural problems at clinical levels. However, the highest rates for poor outcome are for those in residential care which, at least in part, reflects their higher levels of dysfunction prior to being placed there (Ford, Vostanis, Meltzer, & Goodman, 2007). Longitudinal studies have found that, as adults, these individuals are more likely to become involved in criminal activity (Farrington, 1990), to be referred to forensic psychiatric services (DCSF, 2007b) and high-security hospitals (Scott, 2004). They have worse educational outcomes (NCAS, 2008), are more likely to be homeless and to become teenage parents (DfES & DoH, 2004). Those placed in residential care in the UK are usually adolescents with complex needs who have often exhausted or disrupted other types of arrangements, with residential care increasingly seen as a last resort, so residential care is not the primary cause of the problem (Colton & Hellinckx, 1994).

Interventions with children abused

Interventions for children who are abused, in need, or in care, are varied. Safe-guarding and child protection by LSCBs are perhaps the most critical, but other approaches include those preventative (for example the Early Intervention initiative or even small-scale schemes focused on neglect aspects, like school breakfast clubs or even free school meals). For the children themselves, inter-vention depends on their age group, with psychological interventions involving music or art therapy being effective although in short supply (Malchiodi, 2012). Those based around CBT for anger management[9] or self-esteem enhancement also are effective but again not widely available. As part of the healthy schools initiative (DH/DCFS, 2007) Self Esteem and Learning (SEAL) intervention was a whole schools approach to enhance self-esteem and social skills which showed promising results.[10]

> a comprehensive, whole-school approach to promoting the social and emo-tional skills that underpin effective learning, positive behaviour, regular attendance, staff effectiveness and the emotional health and well-being of all who learn and work in schools.
>
> (DCSF, 2007b, p. 4)

Other approaches are more directly linked to abuse of children. For example an initiative with parents to increase awareness of CSE with support from a Parent Liaison Officer (PLO) had positive findings as indicated by a small qual-itative research project (Shuker & Ackerley, 2017).[11] This was part of the Pace (Parents against sexual exploitation) initiative set up in Lancashire in 2014. This worked through the PLO being placed in the multi-agency 'Engage' team. The PLO offered flexible, one-to-one support to parents and families whose child was at risk or already a victim of child sexual exploitation (CSE), using the 'rela-tional safeguarding model' developed by Pace. The aims of the evaluation were to explore the impact of the PLO in relation to three key outcomes for parents: increased awareness and understanding of CSE, playing a more active part in safeguarding their child and receipt of support through the judicial process. The evaluation took the form of interviews and focus groups with parents and PLOs. There were positive impacts on parents understanding of CSE:

> All parents who took part in the evaluation reported that the PLO had helped them understand CSE. They explained that understanding how children could be manipulated, groomed and controlled helped them place respon-sibility for the abuse on the perpetrator, which in turn helped them not to blame either their child or themselves as parents. Parents also observed

that understanding the grooming process helped them to make sense of times when their child's behaviour had been avoidant, hostile or out of character, which helped them to respond more empathetically to their child.

(Shuker & Ackerley, 2017, p. 4)

Other benefits included parents being helped with the legal processes in cases of CSE, from Crown Prosecution Service referral to post-trial readjustment. Parents reported valuing the information, reassurance and practical support the PLO provided before, during and after a trial. Parents reported greater resilience, greater confidence in protecting their child and improved relationships in the home. They were able to utilise the PLOs for other related support and with other stakeholders, given the PLO was co-located with the police, children's social care, health and other agencies within the Engage team. These partners reported that the PLO role had a positive impact on their awareness of families' needs, rights and capacities. The Engage team was supported, and information sharing was improved between the team and parents. Further,

> The evaluation identified two key factors that enable Pace to achieve these outcomes. Firstly, the PLO works within a multi-agency team that has a great deal of experience of dealing with the victims and perpetrators of CSE and believes in the value of working with parents. Being co-located with other agencies is an additional benefit in terms of information sharing and building trusting relationships. Secondly, both the current and former PLO in the team have extensive experience of working with parents, and on CSE cases. Parents and professionals respect their expertise, which enhances their work and reputation in the local area.
>
> (Shuker & Ackerley, 2017, p. 5)

Other interventions have concerned specialist foster care; for example a service set up by Barnardos (Shuker, 2014) called the Safe Accommodation Project, piloted the use of specialist foster placements for young people at risk, or already victims of trafficking. The first of its kind in England, it provided training to foster carers and associated professionals and support to young people in care settings. The aim was to develop warm trusting relationships in the foster placements and effective placements supported by a team around the child, sharing a common safeguarding approach. With funding from the DfE in 2011, for a two-year project, the agency delivered 44 two-day training courses for foster carers and associated professionals to raise awareness of CSE and child trafficking. They also undertook direct work with the young people at risk, or victims of either experience. Sixteen specialist foster placements were found for young people involved with CSE or trafficking.

Findings showed that the training improved confidence in understanding CSE and trafficking and in supporting a young person with such experience. Foster carers were hesitant about taking on young people with CSE trafficking experience, but mainly wanted to understand it to better protect children in their care. The young people themselves reported greater security and sense of protection.

Another intervention funded by DfE 2016, to St Christopher's Fellowship, involved managing girls in residential care who were victims of CSE (Williams et al., 2017).[12] The Safe Steps Innovation pilot was developed as an alternative to placing young women being identified as sexually exploited, or at risk of sexual exploitation, in secure children's homes or homes far from their own area. It was based in two specially adapted London children's homes. All staff were trained in a social pedagogy model and to work in ways that emphasised relational security and a personalised approach to risk assessment. It aimed to test whether providing intensive support and supervision, while working within existing regulations on restrictions to liberty, could keep young women safe outside a secure setting. It aimed to enable young women to continue to live locally in order to limit disruption to their education and family ties, and to minimise the possibility that they will feel blamed or 'punished' for having been exploited. Outcomes for young women were partly assessed using standardised measures administered at baseline and at three-month intervals. Staff also undertook repeat risk assessments for each young woman. Evaluation suggested success in implementation and with improved outcomes. However, it was noted that setting up such accommodation involved significant time delays due to inspection regimes, which required a longer time scale to optimise success (Williams et al., 2016).

St Christopher's have also used a combined social pedagogy and attachment approach throughout their residential care for young people, a number of whom had suffered abuse (Bifulco et al., 2017). Residential care is increasingly recognised as a key service for children and young people who are unable to adapt to family settings with foster carers or adopters. Most have a high level of need, originating from the neglect and abuse experienced at the hands of parents, but often compounded by a high number of care arrangements with little chance for developing stability or strong attachments to carers. Most have mental health issues, specifically behavioural problems and difficulty with their peers and the beginning of criminal behaviour.

The project has been a sustained 'Action Research' project undertaken by the CATS team at Middlesex University over ten years. It has mainstreamed attachment assessment (both self-report and intensive interview) in relation to the social pedagogy intervention. In this it is concordant with current guidance on assessing baseline risk and change, on incorporating attachment principles and considering well-being, supplementing assessment of symptoms such as SDQ with other aspects of a child's life (Bifulco et al., 2017).

The assessment procedure has been successfully embedded within the service. In line with social pedagogy approaches, it provides the 'head' or knowledge basis to complement the 'heart' (focus on emotional adjustment) and 'hands' (practical approaches to enhancing YP well-being) (Kemp, 2011). The interventions found high baseline rates of psychological difficulty, notably behavioural problems of conduct disorder and hyperactivity. It also found high baseline rates of peer problems and low prosocial behaviour as well as both dis-organised and avoidant attachment style. Positive change at follow-up varied by care arrangement with six-month effects seen in fostering, but only 18-month effects in residential care. There was significant improvement in psychological disorder. There were modest improvements in attachment insecurity – with dis-organised style moving to single avoidant insecurity and small levels of secure style resulting. However, no change was observed in peer problems or prosocial behaviour (Bifulco et al., 2017).

Case example of angry-dismissive attachment style in young person in residential care – Leigh[13]

('Community Care Inform' 2012) Case study: Leigh – Angry Dismissive style

Leigh was 15 years old when placed, having been moved from a prior care home due to his violence towards staff. His records indicated the presence of Conduct Disorder and problems in managing anger. When interviewed with the Attachment Style Interview, ASI, he reported recent stressors around family contacts, and with the police, as well as the stress of moving home. When asked about support, he was unable to name a single person, family or friend, with whom he could share his problems, together with evidence of conflict with his birth family. He reported very high self-reliance, felt unable to get close to others and was highly mistrustful towards others in general, leading to anger and conflict. Leigh was categorised as having an Angry-Dismissive attachment style, at a marked level. This was summarised for staff, highlighting his need to cope alone and his mistrustful, angry reactions when under stress, which increased his vulnerability in day-to-day interactions and when under pressure. It was recommended that staff explore ways to relate to him to reduce his psychological barriers and increase his ability to confide and to be calmed when under pressure. Anger management techniques enabled him to identify triggers and curb his hostile responses as well as improving peer and adult interactions. One method was by encouraging Leigh to get involved in activities, which he typically avoided, and to try out experiences which 'were not under his control'. There was additional focus on monitoring contact with family members to reduce anger flashpoints and to create a safe and secure base for Leigh. At follow-up interview ten months later, Leigh was re-interviewed and found to have reduced levels of anger, reduced mistrust and his degree of confiding in staff and friends increased somewhat, although his self-reliance remained extremely high. His attachment style at follow-up was re classified as Withdrawn (highly self-reliant but without anger). This was considered a positive shift because whilst still indicating insecurity, it was at a less extreme level (moderate and not marked) due to improved relationships with staff and reduced anger and conflict in interactions. Thus, changes in his style meant that Leigh was more approachable, more careful of his interactions with others and considered easier to work with by staff.[14]

The attachment project has been an encouraging and sustained intervention project conducted by a charity in partnership with a university which has showed positive effect both in mainstreaming standardised assessment for all children in care in the organisation and showing positive effects of a social pedagogic approach to organisational culture and intervention.

Interventions for children in the care system also involve specialist aspects of educational provision and psychological services. However, these are not always widely available, for example for children with behavioural problems who are often excluded from school, and those without fixed addresses finding psychological services hard to access, with frequent non-attendance. Therefore, national approaches have tended to work with parents as a form of preventative or ameliorating action on abuse, and these have been extended to foster carers to improve the interaction and parenting of children in care. It could be argued that parenting and foster carer interventions are at more than one remove from children who suffer abuse. In this way they are similar to some of the well-being interventions which target all children. But considering parenting and foster care interventions gives us some insight into how as a society we attempt to intervene with abuse issues once formal identification of CiN or child protection is judged.

Parenting interventions

On the parenting front, the Department for Children, Schools and Families in 2011 introduced several initiatives to increase parenting programmes and their accessibility. This included for example, Parenting Early Intervention Pathfinder projects in disadvantaged areas, a parent support advisor for every school, parenting experts in each local authority and family intervention projects for those families experiencing the most difficulties. The parenting early intervention programme (PEIP), provided government funding to all 150 local authorities in England to deliver selected parenting programmes that had already proved their effectiveness. The evaluation examined five programmes (Lindsay et al., 2011)[15] which were delivered to parents in deprived settings.

- families and schools together (FAST);
- positive parenting programme (Triple P);
- strengthening families programme 10-14 (SFP 10-14);
- strengthening families, strengthening communities (SFSC);
- the incredible years.

Whilst this is data from 2011, it is relevant to examine its achievement whilst active. In general the evaluation was positive across the programmes with outcomes for parents on all four programmes significantly improved after programme completion. The PEIP findings are presented in Box 4.4:

Box 4.4

PEIP evaluation findings (Ryder, Edwards, & Clements, 2017)

- **Short-term impacts of PEIP**

- 79 per cent of parents showed improvements in their mental well-being;
- Average level of mental well-being increased from the bottom 25 per cent of population to national average;
- A considerable proportion of parents changed their parenting behaviour over the course of the programme:
- 74 per cent of parents reported reductions in their parenting laxness;
- 77 per cent of parents reported reductions in their over-reactivity;
- The percentage of parents who reported that their child had serious conduct problems reduced by a third, from 59 per cent to 40 per cent;
- Parents were highly positive about their experiences of the parenting groups they attended: 98 per cent reported that they had found the group helpful;
- 95 per cent reported that the programme had helped them deal with their problems;
- 95 per cent reported that the programme had helped them to deal with their children's behaviour;
- 86 per cent reported that they experienced fewer problems after completing the programme;

- Over 98 per cent reported that the group leader showed positive characteristics, including making them feel respected and working in partnership;
- There were differences in the effects on outcomes between the individual programmes but these were relatively small compared to the overall improvements reported by parents.

- **One year follow-up PEIP**

- Improvements in parent laxness and over-reactivity were maintained;
- Improvements in their children's behaviour were also maintained;
- There was a small reduction in parents' reported mental well-being, but this remained significantly higher than when they started their parenting programme.

Scores of randomised controlled trials (RCTs) attest to the effectiveness of good-quality parenting programmes for treating conduct problems, now recommended by the National Institute for Health and Clinical Excellence (NICE). For example, in one UK trial, local clinicians were carefully trained to deliver the basic 12-week Incredible Years programme to 3- to 8-year-olds referred to child and adolescent mental health services, and achieved a large reduction in conduct problems, and no loss of effectiveness at one-year follow-up (Scott, Spender, Doolan, Jacobs, & Aspland, 2001). Programmes were also shown to be effective for symptoms of attention-deficit hyperactivity disorder and other outcomes such as educational attainment (Scott et al., 2010). These interventions are also shown to reduce harsh parenting, so can be used more widely with parents who are at risk of abusing their children. In general, effects were largest for children with more severe problems, so it is argued that treatment of individuals referred with marked difficulties is probably more cost-effective than primary prevention for whole communities, at least in the shorter term (Dodge, 2009).

Not all interventions are effective. Evaluations of generic counselling approaches show that they may be very popular with parents, but they do not necessarily improve child outcomes. A number of widely used home-visiting schemes have no effect on child outcomes (McAuley, Knapp, Beecham, McCurry, & Sleed, 2004). Less than 10 per cent of over 150 approaches currently used in England have good evidence of effectiveness. To work, parenting programmes need to be evidence-based and delivered by skilled practitioners, since less-competent therapists often have no effect (Washington State Institute for Public Policy, 2004). Because many practitioners do not have specific skills – for example, 90 per cent of outreach workers in children's centres have no specific training at all in parenting work – there is a pressing need for training. To be effective the programmes need to have certain *content* in common: to be structured over at least an 8–12 week period, to include play, praise, incentives, setting limits and discipline. To have an emphasis on promoting sociability, self-reliant child behaviour and calm parenting, constant reference needs to be made to the parents' own experiences and circumstances. A theoretical basis for the parenting intervention is seen as a positive, and for the intervention to be evidence-based with an explicit link to research. Use of a manual to enable replicability is also seen as a positive (Scott, 2010).

In addition, the delivery needs to have systematic aspects to ensure greater success: for example, to have a collaborative approach acknowledging parents' feelings and beliefs; to normalise difficulties; and to use humour with fun encouraged. Parents need to be supported to practice innovative approaches both during the session and in homework. Parent and child need to be seen together in individual family work but with parents as a group without children in some group programmes. Facilities such as creche, refreshments and transport aid success, and therapists need regular supervision to ensure adherence to the model and to develop skills (Scott, 2010).

Currently, the many parenting programmes used in England vary greatly in theoretical orientation, quality of written materials, sophistication of training available for practitioners and evidence of effectiveness. Each local authority is required to have a Parenting Strategy and a local Parenting Commissioner who has responsibility to ensure that the right services are provided in the right places locally. Core funding for coordination and administration of local strategic multi-agency provision is from the main local providers as short-term funding on a project basis.[16]

Other parenting interventions are specifically geared to foster carers looking after children with prior abuse history who may have emotional and behavioural difficulties, and thus prove challenging to care for. Two originating in the US are highlighted: MTFC and ABC. These have some availability in the UK.

Multidimensional therapeutic foster care (MTFC)

MTFC is widely used as an intervention in foster care, originally designed in the US at the Oregon Social Learning Centre, following the work of Patterson and colleagues undertaken in the 1970s (P. A. Fisher & Chamberlain, 2000). It was introduced into the UK after extensive trial funding by the then Department of Education (Scott et al., 2001). The programme is based on social learning and behavioural change and is aimed at working with foster carers to improve interaction with the placed child to improve behavioural problems. It was later extended to consider attachment changes as an outcome (P. A. Fisher & Kim,

2007). It aimed to give parents and careers the skills needed to bring up their children and cope with problem behaviour. Weekly supervision programmes were provided for individual children held by professional therapists from the Oregon Centre. Significant reductions in anti-social behaviour were identified. This was more effective when programmes continued for longer periods. However, evaluation showed that treatment effects were not very stable and longer-term follow-ups indicated mixed results. In addition, as many as a fifth of families dropped out of the programme and another third refused to be contacted in the 12 months after completing the course. In terms of attachment, the evidence is thin, but based on foster carer's diaries, there was some indication that Secure patterns of attachment in the child were increased (P. A. Fisher & Kim, 2007). However, no further information of standardised measurement of attachment was utilised.

Attachment bio-behavioural catch-up (ABC)[17]

ABC is a US-based intervention for parent/care and young child, aimed specifically at attachment change, and with attention to enhancing children's ability to regulate their physiology and behaviour (Dozier, Peloso, Lewis, Laurenceau, & Levine, 2008). ABC has been shown to be effective in foster care settings. Its aim is to help caregivers nurture and respond sensitively to their infants, to improve child development and form healthy relationships. It is aimed at children between 6–24 months and those 24–48 months. It utilises intensive contact between parent and a trained parent coach, (10 one-hour weekly sessions) with feedback on video interactions of parent and child to increase parental sensitivity and improve positive interactions and praise to the infant. A randomised clinical trial assessed its effectiveness with regard to HPA functioning and cortisol production and enhancing cognitive skills in comparison to a non-care group of children (Bernard, Hostinar, & Dozier, 2015). Children in the ABC intervention and comparison group children showed significantly lower initial values of cortisol than children in the treatment control group. Over time and following interventions, the in-care group adjusted to being not significantly different from the non-care group. These results suggest that the ABC intervention is effective in helping children regulate biology in ways more characteristic of children who have not experienced early adversity. The study also showed that attachment insecurity increased in the child.

Such approaches are shown to be effective and have gained considerable traction in the United States. It is to be noted that the approach is designed and led by a very charismatic professional (Mary Dozier) who personally gets involved in much supervision and training and keeps the intervention en pointe. Without such leadership the results may not be so positive in other settings.

The use of volunteer practitioners for the work with parents clearly makes the costs of the intervention low, but requires greater supervision and management oversight. It is not widely available in the UK.

Another type of parental intervention is attachment-focused and based on the issue of maternal sensitivity and attunement lacking in parents who abuse, and more common in parents who were themselves abused in childhood.

Maternal sensitivity and attachment approaches

Attachment theory and practice has fitted well into children's services (described in Chapter 3) around the adoption and fostering context in finding replacement caregivers to try to ensure improved child development and well-being. Monitoring of Insecure attachment style both in children to be placed and with their adoptive or foster carers has been undertaken in research studies and has found that where the carers have Secure attachment style the children are more likely to develop greater security of attachment (Dozier, Stovall, Albus, & Bates, 2001; Hodges, Steele, Hillman, Henderson, & Kaniuk, 2003). These studies have typically used an intensive interview (the Adult Attachment Interview – AAI) to assess parental attachment style and the SST or Story Stem Test for infants and pre-school children. However, all these measures are somewhat restricted in usual social work practice given their requirement for expert use and complex administration. More mainstreamed methods are needed to replicate such assessment and monitoring in everyday adoption-fostering processes. Attachment approaches argue that carers are required to build Secure attachments in the family. This includes partners and existing children in addition to any fostered or adopted. The capacity to do so with partners and other close adults is evidenced through confiding relationships and can be assessed through exploring the existence of supportive relationships and the capacity to share difficulties and accept help. Thus, the role of support is critical to parenting capacity in determining the success and stability of future adoption or fostering placements. Assessments are therefore needed to measure the quality of support, and carers' ability to access it, in addition to their parenting competence. The problems surrounding the disruption of adoption placements and the need for additional post-placement support are well established (Rushton, 2003). The higher rate of placement breakdown in foster arrangements, particularly for children older at placement, are beginning to be equalled by those placed for adoption in recent years (Fergusson, Lynskey et al., 1995; Triseliotis, 2002). Placement instability is related both to child and carer characteristics (Quinton, Rushton et al., 1998) but few studies have looked at fostering or adoption placement specifically from the point of view of carers' coping capacity and need for support.

Attachment and parenting sensitivity Interventions which utilise adult attachment elements predominantly focus on maternal attachment style, parenting sensitivity and interaction with the baby or infant in dyadic therapeutic treatments (Bifulco & Thomas, 2012). An extensive meta-review of evaluation of 88 interventions for early childhood attachment interventions has been conducted comparing the impacts on maternal sensitivity and child attachment style (Bakermans-Kranenberg, van Ijzendoorn, & Juffer, 2003). The focus could include support, parenting sensitivity, representations of internal working models or these in combination. In terms of assessment methods, these included a range of child measures such as the HOME inventory or the SST, as well as Ainsworth sensitivity scales in addition to observational methods of the mother. The effects sizes on average were higher for maternal sensitivity change (d = 0.33) than child attachment style change (d = 0.20) but both were significant. In fact, those most effective for improving maternal sensitivity also improved child attachment security. Some results were surprising- briefer interventions were more effective, as were those by nonprofessionals, and those not involving contact (e.g. providing soft baby carriers to hold the baby close). Interventions worked whether single- or multiple-risk families were involved and those few which involved fathers were particularly successful, although had less positive effects on mothers also involved. Interventions focused on sensitivity rather than on support or on mother's representations were most effective. It was observed that attachment insecurity was harder to change and 'sleeper effects' were discussed whereby the attachment changes could occur at a later time. The focus was on positive parental behaviours including responsiveness, sensitivity or involvement, but these were restricted to observational methods of assessment. Findings showed that studies utilising SST showed less positive change.

It is relatively recently that the importance of attachment principles has been recognised in this part of children's services. National Institute on Clinical Excellence (NICE guidance 2016) has introduced quality standards incorporating attachment principles for services involved with children in care (Box 4.5). Based on the importance of parents/carers sensitivity to children and positive care, it is recognised that positive or negative experience in childhood is likely to persist into adult life and lifelong. The policy focuses on attachment difficulties which include insecure or disorganised attachment style as well as those more with what is termed attachment disorder.

The policy relates to three existing health outcomes; enduring positive experience of care; improving wider determinants of health and health improvement. It requires coordinated services; training and competencies in staff and comprehensive assessment.

Box 4.5

List of quality statements (Children's Attachment - NICE 2016)

- Statement 1 Children and young people who may have attachment difficulties, and their parents or carers, have a comprehensive assessment before any intervention programme;
- Statement 2 Children and young people with attachment difficulties have an up-to-date education plan setting out how they will be supported in school;
- Statement 3 Parents and carers of preschool-age children with or at risk of attachment difficulties are offered a video feedback programme;
- Statement 4 Health and social care provider organisations provide training, education and support programmes for carers of school-aged children and young people with attachment difficulties (2016, p.10).

- **Improved outcomes expected:**

- Children's social and emotional development;
- Children's behavioural functioning;
- Quality of parent or carer child relationship;
- Well-being and quality of life for children and parents or carers;
- Mental health problems in children and parents or carers;
- Breakdown in fostering placements or adoption;
- Youth offending rates;
- Educational progress and attainment;
- School absences and exclusions.

An attachment approach can give added insight into these young people's difficulties in forming relationships and thus help create the required stable and caring residential environments required to develop resilience. In line with attachment principles, in recent years there has been a move towards smaller residential care homes (Colton & Hellinckx, 1994). The smaller units seem to better imitate the dynamics of a 'family' and shed the negative 'institutional' connotations of larger homes (Cameron & Maginn, 2008). An emphasis is placed on attachment-related aspects such as security through stability of arrangement and bonding with the carers who in turn develop greater attunement in their care (Howe, Brandon, Hinings, & Schofield, 1999). Therapeutic interventions in residential care have been shown to be effective (Dozier, 2003; Zegers, Scheuengel, Van Ijzendoorn, & Janssens, 2006). Attachment approaches are increasingly used to supplant the unstable family models experienced and build resilience (Hawkins-Rodgers, 2007; Moore, Moretti, & Holland, 1997). Interventions in residential care have included the therapeutic community approach, where planned therapeutic help as well as education is provided on site in the home (Stevens & Furnivall, 2008). These involve a number of different theoretical approaches including CBT, but few are identified as attachment orientated.

There are a handful of studies of attachment style in young people in residential care in the UK and continental Europe. Many of these studies use the AAI to assess attachment style with nearly all young people in both German (Schleiffer & Muller, 2004) and Dutch (Zegers et al., 2008) residential care homes found to be Insecure (94 per cent). There was some gender differentiation with more girls showing Anxious/Preoccupied styles and more boys Avoidant/Dismissive. As many as 46 per cent exhibited complex (multiple) attachment styles (Disorganised). Both genders showed anti-social or aggressive behaviours with girls also having emotional disorder. Similar results have been found in the UK (Wallis & Steele, 2010) with 92 per cent Insecure with the majority (62 per cent) 'Unresolved/Cannot Classify' and 23 per cent Avoidant/Dismissive. The findings thus indicate that Insecure attachment style is rife in residential care settings with varieties of Disorganised, and Avoidant/Dismissive styles the most common categories. In view of this, the attachment-focused intervention by St Christopher's Fellowship described earlier is particularly salient.

Well-being in care

A study conducted by The National Children's Bureau (NCB) explored the measurement of well-being of children in care (Ryder et al., 2017). It explored definitions of well-being and tools used to indicate baseline and follow-up in children. It involved interviews with 114 professionals, supplemented by the views of children and young people in care. It identifies the Strengths and Difficulties Questionnaire (SDQ) as a commonly used and effective tool, but indicated its need for use alongside broader measures of well-being. Their recommendations for the Government (Box 4.6) included that it should:

Box 4.6

Recommendations for the government by NCB well-being report

- Pay particular attention to the needs of children in care in the implementation of its proposals in Transforming children and young people's mental health provision. This should include ensuring that at least one of the proposed Trailblazers focuses on the needs of these children;

- Use planned pilots of new approaches to mental health assessment to explore: Options for creating a baseline measure of children's well-being on entry to care whilst ensuring assessment of well-being is seen as an ongoing process of how access to specialist mental health services for children who need them could be made simpler;

- In consultation with children, carers and professionals, develop a definition of well-being and clear guidance on what this looks like for children in care;

- Review, tailor and supplement the SDQ to create a suite of tools that can fulfil the distinct functions of screening for mental health conditions and measuring well-being more effectively;

- Create a comprehensive outcomes framework for children in care that reflects the breadth of topics that relate to children's well-being, building on existing published data and proxy indictors. Regardless of any, professionals, local authorities and health commissioners should uphold and promote good practice within the current framework. In particular:

- Local authorities should ensure results of screening tools such as the SDQ are always taken into account in care and placement planning;

- NHS England and Clinical Commissioning Groups should work with mental health service providers to improve processes for children in care accessing mental health treatment.

The importance of measurement of well-being in children in care has been highlighted (Selwyn, Wood, & Newman, 2017). Local authorities should use a range of sources of evidence to assess the quality of care they are providing, including the views of children in care councils and professionals who do not have core responsibility for a child's care. A study using focus groups showed that children emphasised the importance of relationships with foster carers, social workers and siblings and of being able to trust the adults in their lives. Unlike children in the general population, looked after children thought that having a coherent account of their histories and knowing the reason for being in care was crucial. The study demonstrated that children as young as six years old were able to provide meaningful responses about their well-being. The challenge for practice is both to collect and to respond to those views to show their voices are heard (Selwyn et al., 2017).

Early interventions (EI) – a public policy approach

Finally, if the aim of society is to prevent or dramatically reduce the likelihood of child abuse occurring, then effective early interventions need to be put in place. This is a longer-term approach to the problem and is located within education and health as well as children's services and other related agencies. Key messages from research about the important developmental impact of life under age 5, led to a wide-ranging initiative on improving care and life chances for infants, preschoolers and those in school reception years. This has been paralleled by research into health inequalities which provide a focus for the child's earliest year to halt lifetime inequities (Marmot, 2010). In this way the child abuse and health agendas come together. However, the EI strategy is currently under threat with cuts to services and is no longer a priority under the May administration. By April 2017 nearly a quarter of children's centres were closed with 156 closing in 2015.[18] Therefore, the early promise of this intervention is unlikely to be realised, and the actions to improve life chances for children across the board, unlikely to bear fruit. The origins of the initiative are outlined here to show how this movement emerged in both health and social welfare domains, and its implication for child welfare and as an antidote to child abuse.

The Marmot review *'Fair Society, Health Lives'* identified inequalities in the nation's health. This showed that people living in the poorest neighbourhoods in England die seven years earlier than people living in the richest neighbourhoods, and spend more of their lives with disability. It also showed that, the lower one's social and economic status, the poorer one's health is likely to be. Health inequalities were noted to arise from a complex interaction of many factors - housing, income, education, social isolation, disability - all are strongly affected by economic and social status. Marmot identifies such health inequalities as largely preventable. Not only is there a strong social justice case for addressing health inequalities, there is also a pressing economic case. It is estimated that the annual cost of health inequalities is between £36 billion to £40 billion through lost taxes, welfare payments and costs to the NHS. Action on health inequalities, he argues, requires action across all the social determinants of health, including education, occupation, income, home and community. Central to the Review was the recognition that disadvantage starts before birth and accumulates throughout life. This was reflected in the six policy objectives and to the highest priority being given to the first objective:

Six policy objectives of the Marmot Review:

- giving every child the best start in life;
- enabling all children, young people and adults to maximise their capabilities and have control over their lives;
- creating fair employment and good work for all;
- ensuring a healthy standard of living for all;
- creating and developing sustainable places and communities;
- strengthening the role and impact of ill-health prevention.

This review has had impact in extending the agenda on combatting child abuse to one about child well-being and increased life chances. This turns it into a public policy which affects universal services as well as those targeted. It thus begins to affect all areas of society and professions and brings health and social justice agendas together.

A Health and Well-being report (Department of Health, 2010) stated that the key public health challenges in the early stages of life were preventing infant mortality, encouraging the good health of mothers during pregnancy and after birth, and maximising early years development. This is necessarily multi-agency and includes health visitors/perinatal staff, teachers and nursery staff and psychologists involved in parenting and mental health of both children and parents and social workers with the same remit, but also with concerns for financial and housing difficulties. Early Intervention is not restricted to age 0-5; in fact it can apply to *early* action on any emerging problem, but the early years work hopes to head off those occurring at later points. It involves both universal and targeted services, and is not restricted to families involved in CP services (such as children in need) but is concerned with those under-privileged and from socially excluded groups. It followed previous initiatives such as Every Child Matters (Department of Education, 2003), which made child opportunities a public policy issue for multiple agencies and the public. This formalised five rights of children: to be healthy, safe, to enjoy and achieve, to make a positive contribution and to achieve economic well-being. All these related to the child well-being agenda. The aim was thus not restricted to avoiding risk and adversity in children and families, but to also inculcate positive experience and aspects such as optimism and meaning and positive health. Whilst there is debate about well-being definitions, (Seligman, 2011) the PERMA model outlines five core elements of well-being and happiness which approximately correspond:

Well-being definition using the PERMA model:

- positive emotions – feeling good;
- engagement – finding flow;
- relationships – authentic connections;
- meaning – purposeful existence;
- achievement – a sense of accomplishment.

These can be seen to be higher order, and more psychological, than those identified in the now extant 'Every Child Matters' agenda but nevertheless echo similar domains, with the two highly interrelated.[19]

These initiatives strive for well-being in the young population, a universal preventative approach which is proactive and does not wait for abuse and resulting psychological disorder to occur in children and young adults. There is a lack of consensus in the literature on how well-being relates to mental health. The Office for National Statistics (2015) contends that there is a clear distinction between mental health and mental well-being with the former relating to a clinically diagnosable illness with a defined set of symptoms, and the latter about how individuals feel about their lives (Office for National Statistics, 2015). However, the World Health Organisation in 2004 proposed:

> A state of wellbeing in which the individual realises his or her own abilities, can cope with the normal stresses of life, can work productively and fruitfully, and is able to contribute to his or her community.
>
> (WHO, 2004, p.10)

Well-being can also be defined in broader terms. Guidance from the National Institute for Health and Care Excellence (NICE, 2013) describes three elements of well-being: emotional, psychological and social well-being. Katherine Weare (2015), defines social and emotional well-being as:

> A state of positive mental health and wellness. It involves a sense of optimism, confidence, happiness, clarity, vitality, self-worth, achievement, having a meaning and purpose, engagement, having supportive and satisfying relationships with others and understanding oneself, and responding effectively to one's own emotions.
>
> (Weare, 2015, p.3)

Well-being thus relates to the preventative interventions in early years and this has recently been applied to children in the care system in a review commissioned by the NCB (Ryder et al., 2017).

The remit of the EI initiative was to prevent later detrimental life outcomes in educational, clinical and criminal justice domains. It thus had a remit for child 'health and wellbeing' which extended further than merely averting risks to enhancing positive life experience. Its focus was on the first years in view of contemporary research on neurological development in early years as well as early parent-child interactions as a basis for later psychological health. Such early intervention was argued to create major societal impact, for example on educational attainment and adult social disadvantage (Field, 2010). It aimed for economic impact through improved life chances on employment and economic productivity (Doyle, Tremblay, Harmon, & Heckman, 2007). Estimates of between £4 billion to £8 billion pounds were calculated in savings (Backing the Future; (NEF/ActionforChildren, 2009). Its range of services was extensive. In education it involved increased help with Special Educational Need (SEN) and

Early Health and Care (EHC) Plans as well as Pupil Premium funding for those disadvantaged aged 3 and 4. In perinatal services it entailed additional antenatal health checks, new baby reviews, 6–8-week assessment and a one-year and then 2–2.5-year review. It also encompassed vaccination coverage and efforts to reduce infant mortality. Additional responsibilities were thus given to health visitors, perinatal nurses and family nurses. The 'Healthy Start' voucher initiative allowed for subsidy of vitamins, milk, fruit and vegetables to pregnant women and those with children under age 4. Targeted programmes, such as the Family Nurse Partnership for first-time mothers aged 19 or under, were aimed specifically at groups perceived to be at higher risk. Universal programmes by contrast, such as the now extant Sure Start programme, were aimed at all children and families and later culminated in the creation of Children's Centres as a focus for multi-agency working.

The initial EI and well-being initiative had its origins in the Sure Start services and networks instigated to aid with social development in early years. This involved varied services in disadvantaged areas to improve life chances under the labour government (House of Commons, 2013). Whilst the national evaluation had mixed results (Belsky et al., 2006; Melhuish et al., 2007), it became mainstreamed in 2010 in the form of Children's Centres to provide a universal service under local authority remit and linked closely to school and health services. It also extended to parents' services (e.g. for training and employment opportunities). The core purpose of Children's Centres was threefold: (i) child development and school readiness (ii) parenting aspirations and parenting skills and (iii) child and family health and life chances.

The Government's statutory guidance Working Together to Safeguard Children (HM Government, 2015) placed responsibility with local authorities to identify children and families who would benefit from early help. This was to include all professionals, including those in universal services and those providing services to adults with children, to understand their role in identifying emerging problems and to share information with other professionals to support early identification and assessment. Local Safeguarding Children Boards (LSCBs) were tasked to monitor and evaluate the effectiveness of training, including multi-agency training, for all professionals in the area. This included how to identify and respond early to the needs of all vulnerable children at each stage: unborn children; babies; older children; young carers; disabled children; and those in secure settings. Another key element was outlined in the Coalition Government's 'Supporting Families in the Foundation Years' and involved the provision of parenting classes for all in need (Education/Health, 2011). This was trialled in 2011–15 with favourable results (see Box 4.7).

Box 4.7

Chronology of Early Intervention policy initiatives since 2000

- **Opportunity for all: Tackling poverty and social exclusion (1999)** – to eradicate child poverty by 2020; develop Sure Start centres; 15 hours free childcare pre-school, to join up early years services. Led to **Childcare Act 2016;**
- **Early Intervention: The Next Steps** and **Early Intervention: Smart Investment, Massive Savings – (2011)** most effective models for early intervention; recommended 19 be supported by the Government. E.g., Early Intervention Foundation (EIF) to provide evidence of what works and to support local projects. Work supported through a £20m investment in a social outcomes fund;
- **The Foundation Years: Preventing poor children becoming poor adults (2010) Frank Field** to look at poverty and life chances. It recommended a new policy focus around the 'foundation years', conception to age 5, which was argued to be a crucial stage at which disadvantage can set in. Recommendations included better targeted services for the most disadvantaged families, including better outreach and the opportunity to take parenting classes; a Foundation Years Minister, sited between the Department of Health and the Department for Education;
- **The Early Years: Foundations for life, health and learning** – **(2011)** Dame Clare Tickell, proposed reforms to pre-school age education, including reform of the Early Years Foundation Stage (EYFS) assessment process and reform of safeguarding early years students;
- **The Munro Review of Child Protection (2011)** by Professor Eileen Munro, emphasised the importance of early help. Recommended a statutory duty on local authorities to secure sufficient provision of local early help services for children, young people and families. The **Government's response** accepted the importance of early help services and joint working between services, but did not commit to a statutory duty on local authorities;
- **Building Great Britons** report (2015), set out what it saw as the essentials of a good local prevention approach: including good universal services: central role of children's centres; universal early identification of need for extra support; good antenatal services; good specialised perinatal mental health services; universal assessment and support for good attunement between parent and baby; prevention of child maltreatment;
- **Life Chances Strategy** (2015); Conservative Government focused on perinatal mental health, with an announcement of £290m of funding in January 2016 and commitment to improve the life chances

of disadvantaged children and families. Early intervention would play a significant role in the strategy and increased state funding for parenting classes. In December 2016, it was confirmed that the Life Chances Strategy would no longer be published and would be replaced by a forthcoming social justice green paper. (The planned extension was however not followed through, instead incorporated into Troubled Families);

- **Troubled Families (2017):** a programme of targeted intervention for families with multiple problems, including crime, anti-social behaviour, truancy, unemployment, mental health problems and domestic abuse. Local authorities identify 'troubled families' in their area and usually assign a key worker to act as a single point of contact. Central Government pays local authorities by results for each family that meet set criteria or move into continuous employment. A total of £448 million was allocated to the first phase of the programme, which ran from 2012 to 2015;

- **Children and Social Work Act (2017):** whilst the aim was more on tertiary care, and to change structures such as LSBs, there was also an education focus on promoting the safeguarding of children by providing for relationships and sex education in schools. In addition the concept of Corporate Parenting for local authorities included aspects of child well-being in relation to health, self-expression, access to services, to be safe and have stability and to be given preparation for independent living. These latter are largely taken from EI initiatives but here applied to those children in care.

Evaluation of the national EI strategy has shown some positive results. It was implemented as the longitudinal Study of Early Education and Development (SEED) examining 5,000 children from age 2 to 7 years with a report due in 2020. The study is being carried out for the Department of Education by Nat-Cen Social Research, Frontier Economics, the University of Oxford and Action for Children. A report on the impact of early childhood education and care (ECEC) on children's school readiness and longer-term outcomes, including its impact on the most disadvantaged children, has shown that ECEC at age 2 is associated with improvement in children's cognitive and socio-emotional development at age 3 (Melhuish & Gardiner, 2017). Factors relate to quality of provision include staff training, staff retention and good pupil to staff ratio. This finding is in line with previous findings from the Effective Preschool, Primary and Secondary Education (EPPSE) study, which found that ECEC continues to relate to improved cognitive and socio-emotional development through primary and secondary school (Sylva et al., 2012). The continuing effects of disadvantage in England, to 'downward spirals' in development and to (for a minority of students) dissatisfaction and unhappiness in school persisted. But EPPSE has reported on pathways to success, on feelings of confidence and factors associated with them. Positive pre-school and school experiences can make a difference. Finally, the longitudinal nature of the rich EPPSE dataset showed the long-term effects of pre-school experiences, especially those of high quality settings.

The policies developed were all consistent with the psychological, social and health research of recent years, in providing a better start for children and therefore increasing their lifelong chances. It also accords with the Rights of the Child as a marker of a civilised society. However, the procedures put in place (Children's Centres, EY education, enhanced perinatal services, practitioner) have all been dependent on sustained funding levels and therefore proved all too vulnerable at times of austerity. Evaluation of impacts is ongoing with evidence of some improvement for example in education in teenage years, although effects of early deprivation remain evident. The initiatives extended involvement in child welfare from child protection and safeguarding to a range of services and professionals engaged in well-being. The latter is a more nebulous concept; there are multiple definitions of well-being and little consensus (Selwyn et al., 2017). Whilst there are external markers of increased life chances, subjective well-being is potentially harder to assess and may be more ephemeral with a need to root it further in social and psychological factors. Clearly it has an important relationship to mental health, both in its preventative action but also in effective management of psychological disorder and as an outcome of treatment.

Discussion

Policy initiatives for children in care have provided greater recognition of need levels in children and young people in the system and greater awareness of skills and training needed by foster carers or care providers and social workers. A focus on good assessment of children or young people is key, and standardised measures better for mainstreaming results. Models including awareness of neurological damage to children aid understanding, and attachment models provide both greater awareness and practice approaches to intervention.

The landscape of residential care has changed with greater private provision on more squeezing of voluntary and statutory provision. This can provide a more mercenary or commercial approach, with very high costs associated with having children in care, and staff salaries not always recognising of the emotional burden entailed.

Greater training both for foster carers and the need for specialist supported foster carers for staff in residential care is being recognised as well as the need for inter-agency working between educational, psychological, health and criminal justice services. A recent analysis by the NSPCC showed over 100,000 children referred to local specialist NHS mental health services were rejected for treatment over a two-year period. This is despite record numbers contacting Childline about suicidal feelings.[20] However, it is noted that YP access to CAMHS services is very limited, and those in residential care are likely to be particularly disadvantaged. Also, policy investigation of crimes within the care homes has been criticised. Often the children are not utilising educational services. So, the access of services by young people in care seems particularly disadvantaged.

Social work as a profession has come under close scrutiny in the last decade. Changes in education (providing a social work undergraduate degree and post-qualifying social work awards) have sought to raise the skill level of social work with increased CPD provided by most LAs. However, there are shortages of practitioners in some areas such as child protection, use of agency workers and international workers with less experience of home conditions. Rates of abuse cases have gone up in some areas (e.g. around neglect, emotional abuse) but also in relation to CSE. A Chief Social Worker was installed in 2013, but due to financial pressures, the College of Social Work (TCSW) was closed in 2015, disappointing for the profession in its drive to raise standards. However, funds have now gone to an initiative in Cardiff to set up a centre for 'What Works' (the CASCADE centre) to lead research and reviews for Children's Social Care funded by the Department for Education to make positive difference to practice.[21]

In 2013 the PM David Cameron praised the social work profession, but in that year there were two high profile child deaths (Keanu Williams and Hamzah Khan) and OFSTED found 20 councils to be 'inadequate'. In 2015, two chief social workers, Isabelle Trowler for children and families, and Lyn Romeo for adults, were appointed to give visibility and voice to the profession. Trowler created an initiative on leadership in 2016; trialling in 30 councils a new assessment and accreditation system for child and family social workers, and with 70 now involved in social work teaching partnerships with universities to deliver 'gold standard' training, Trowler sees the reforms becoming increasingly mainstream. However, government also reduced the social work study bursaries in 2016 which has had impact on numbers studying. Narey's focus on staff in residential care called for better salaries and work conditions but fell short of requiring graduate entry, instead calling for greater CPD opportunities.

In terms of contemporary issues in relation to child abuse, the following influence the current landscape:

Disadvantage and health: there is increasing recognition of the link between family adversity and disadvantage and child abuse and its consequences. This is also associated with lifelong problem health and mental health outcomes as well as reduced social and financial opportunities. Child abuse and its mental health correlates thus become subsumed in a wider initiative around equalising life chances and reducing long-term health impacts.

Early intervention: the research-informed understanding that the early years (0–5) are particularly critical for development, social, educational and psychological. This preventative approach aims to increase well-being universally and thus raise the positive experiences of a generation of children and seek to see their health and well-being improve longer term. However, help is still needed for children, young people and even young adults at later stages when dealing with impacts of maltreatment. A true definition of early intervention relates to help being provided early in the development of a problem. Some of these will specifically relate to teenage years (e.g. pregnancy, partner problems, some sexual exploitation) and can possibly occur even with children targeted for EI in infancy.

Well-being: there is relatively new focus on positive development, positive psychology and well-being. In some ways this is harder to categorise than the harder indicators such as educational lack of attainment, or mental health diagnostic labels, but is chosen to work towards a better adjusted population at large. It also necessitates getting the child/young person's view since it is a subjective concept. It is related to resilience, a concept also being deployed more in services, but this is more related to survival following adversity and evading specific types of dysfunction (e.g. clinical disorder) and is not necessarily a marker of 'flourishing'. Both concepts are relevant as steps to good functioning, but it is important not to raise the bar too high.

Children in need: those at risk of non-optimum parenting but not taken away from their parents require a high level of support. Some services available are now widely available (perinatal health; parenting training) but others are targeted. These need to be kept in mind whilst early intervention work and 'tier 3' specialist intervention is being undertaken. All levels of intervention/need in the pyramid need equal attention which is difficult at times of austerity. Whilst early intervention may ultimately prove highly effective, it is still necessary to help children and families at later points of need.

Multi-agency working: this becomes a necessity as the range of impacts of child abuse on the child and family become better known. Utilising the required bio-psycho-social model of impacts on the child means that all aspects involving neurological/hormonal dysfunction; psychological adjustment and mental health; social dysfunction and problem attachment style and anti-social elements; education and learning are all affected. Too many specialisms are involved for a single profession to effectively manage children damaged by maltreatment. Good communication, technological processes that work across site; working from similar theoretical models and evidence-base need refining to ensure children are not merely passed from hand to hand, continuously being assessed with long delays to treatments and interventions available. There are worries in the field about the demise of the LSCB and replacement by three partners only (children's services, health and police) tasked with safeguarding and with a 'permissive' approach for LAs to establish their own arrangements (DfE, 2017b)

'Looked After' provision: a variety of arrangements is required for children taken away from their biological parents due to maltreatment and arrangements vary from short to long term. Whilst a lot of emphasis has been put on adoption as the most desirable – foster arrangements, residential care and 16+ provision are all important aspects of the care system. These all require input of training for staff and carers to increase stability of placement. Assessment of children at baseline and during placement stay is recommended to chart change over time. Good feedback to the children and to foster carers is required.

Staff training and numbers: there has been substantial investment in social work training in the last decade or more, but this is now impacted by austerity, bursaries no longer widely available and staffing numbers cut in those Local Authorities hit by recent cuts. Such cuts are pervasive across services (e.g. Children's Centres), but social care has taken a bigger hit than health services. Given the long-term costs to society of children who grow into adults burdened by early life trauma, there needs to be balance and sustained investment not to lose the good work already being undertaken.

It is clear that successive government policies have taken child neglect and abuse seriously in its raft of policy decisions to reduce risk and increase well-being and life chances.

Notes

1 www.independent.co.uk/news/uk/home-news/children-social-services-domestic-abuse-violence-rise-uk-a8154261.html
2 www.thetimes.co.uk/article/1-770-children-a-day-referred-for-urgent-help-s55t05gdt
3 www.gov.uk/government/publications/wood-review-of-local-safeguarding-children-boards
4 www.legislation.gov.uk/ukpga/2017/16/contents/enacted
5 www.escb.co.uk/Portals/67/Documents/Local%20Practices/Children%20in%20Need%20-%20Practice%20and%20Procedures%20Jan%2014.pdf
6 'and feelings' added by the 2004 legislation www.legislation.gov.uk/ukpga/2004/31/contents
7 www.nao.org.uk/wp-content/uploads/2014/11/Children-in-care1.pdf
8 www.gov.uk/government/statistics/outcomes-for-children-looked-after-by-las-in-england
9 https://youngminds.org.uk/find-help/feelings-and-symptoms/anger/
10 www.gov.uk/government/publications/social-and-emotional-aspects-of-learning-seal-programme-in-secondary-schools-national-evaluation

11 www.beds.ac.uk/__data/assets/pdf_file/0008/551159/Empowering-Parents-UoB-Pace-Evaluation-2017.pdf

12 http://springconsortium.com/wp-content/uploads/2017/11/1.2.69-St-Christophers-Fellowship.pdf

13 Jacobs, Ilan-Clarke and Bifulco ('Community Care Inform' electronic information source. 5th March 2012)

14 1www.ccinform.co.uk/articles/2012/03/05/6604/caring+about+attachment+in+young+people+in+residential+care+the+use+of+the+attachment+style.html

15 www.gov.uk/government/publications/parenting-early-intervention-programme-evaluation

16 www.parentinguk.org/your-work/funding/

17 www.abcintervention.org/

18 *www.theguardian.com/commentisfree/2017/feb/06/sure-start-children-worked-why-theresa-may-out-to-kill-it*

19 www.researchgate.net/profile/Winton_Bates/publication/264972318_BOOK_REVIEWS_Policy_BULLET_Vol_27_No_3_BULLET_Spring_2011_Flourish_A_Visionary_New_Understanding_of_Happiness_and_Well-being/links/53f7ebc20cf2c9c3309df183.pdf

20 www.nspcc.org.uk/services-and-resources/childline/

21 https://sites.cardiff.ac.uk/cascade/what-works-centre/

5 Child victims in criminal justice systems

It is clear that child sexual and physical abuse is under-reported; these are hidden crimes that many children feel unable to discuss with adults and that often occur in the context of the family (Gekoski et al., 2016; Horvath et al., 2014). The previous chapter considered the response of social services to child abuse, while this chapter considers the response of criminal justice systems to child victimisation when abuse is reported, drawing upon research and examples of practice from the UK with examples of alternative practice from Canada, the United States and Norway.

Practice in the UK

The role of the police in the UK has recently been explicitly adapted to ensure that practice becomes more victim centred. However, research demonstrates that the families of victims and the victims of child abuse have expressed concern about police practice (McDonald & Tijierino, 2013). For example, in research conducted in Northern Ireland, a key concern expressed by parents/carers of young witnesses (including victims of CSA) was a lack of information from the police (Hayes, Bunting, Lazenbatt, Carr, & Duffy, 2011). As one parent said:

> The police... failed to return our calls.... When they did make contact her [the police officer's] attitude was disgusting – she just didn't seem interested and gave us no information at all.
>
> (Ibid., p. 36).

Research published in 2010 found that only a minority of cases of CSA are classified as detected crimes by the police. Data from case files and interviews with child protection police officers suggested that this was due to a number of factors including: poor multi-agency collaboration; high staff turnover;

inexperienced social workers and child protection officers; and problems with the Crown Prosecution Service, including slow responses, delays in making decisions, lack of communication, and low confidence in junior lawyers. The research concluded that, despite many dedicated police child protection officers, the investigative system is often failing victims (Davidson & Bifulco, 2010). To explore reasons for high Crown Prosecution Service discontinuance rates, low conviction rates and to reflect on the experience of the child, a study by Davidson and colleagues explored Metropolitan Police investigative practice with victims of intra-familial CSA (Davidson, Bifulco, Thomas, & Ramsay, 2006). Problematic issues identified included time constraints, a lack of child consultation, insufficient use of intermediaries and high police staff turnover in specialist units. Particular problems were found with police Achieving Best Evidence interviewing practice with victims; this is discussed later in this chapter.

In the UK the 2008 report from the National Registered Intermediary Conference[1] discussed the disadvantages that children and vulnerable people might encounter in the investigative interview process, especially when a case involves violence and abuse. The process of investigation can have many negative impacts on children for example re-victimisation and re-traumatisation, particularly when they have to repeat their experience to different authorities on multiple occasions. An intermediary may be either registered or non-registered. Their role is to provide support and to facilitate communication with vulnerable defendants and witnesses; as such they are able to explain questions to better enable understanding. The current statutory power to appoint an intermediary to assist a vulnerable prosecution witness to give evidence is provided by the Special Measures provisions in the Youth Justice and Criminal Evidence Act 1999, Sections 16 and 29.

In the UK the Government has recognised for some time that there is a fundamental problem in the system; in 2010 Minister Michael Gove proposed an assessment of this problem and invited Professor Eileen Munro to carry out a review of front-line child protection practice. The review began by pointing out the fact that the political agenda has focused on reforming the guidelines on protecting children from harm and abuse over the past decades, with much research and information informing reform development, such as exploring cross-examination practice and issues involving front-line workers (Platt, 2006; Westcott & Page, 2002). However, such reforms seemed to create further difficulties and did not produce the expected outcome on the front line and in practice (Munro, 2010).

The Munro review has been discussed in previous chapters with reference to the need to improve the quality of the child protection system, not only to make well-informed decisions, but also in the best interests of children and to avoid unnecessary government bureaucracy and directives. The review found that many social workers failed to address the needs of child victims because their focus had been distracted by too many rigid rules and regulations. This served to reiterate Butler-Sloss's Cleveland Report over 20 years earlier which criticised the poor treatment of sexually abused children in the justice system stating that: 'a child is a person, not an object of concern' (Butler-Sloss, 1987, p. 245). Munro identified fundamental skills for frontline staff in child protection and developing good relationships with children in need. This was hampered by changing frontline workers and having too many professionals involved in suspected child abuse cases (Munro, 2011). Similar findings relate to children in the criminal justice system.

For example, studies have shown that having a trusted and known person to support a child witness during investigative interview and court proceedings reduces stress and improves the quality of the child's statement (Hershkowitz, 2009). However, deciding who should support a child witness is often not determined by the child's individual needs but by the local practice (Plotnikoff & Woolfson, 2007; Plotnikoff & Woolfson, 2009; Plotnikoff & Woolfson, 2011; Plotnikoff & Woolfson, 2015). This is echoed by Munro's final report which highlighted the importance of learning and acting upon children's views and experiences in the child protection system:

> The new inspection framework should examine the child's journey from needing to receiving help, explore how the rights, wishes, feelings and experiences of children and young people inform and shape the provision of services, and look at the effectiveness of the help provided to children.
>
> (Munro, 2011, p. 11)

A fundamental shift from the previous 'one-size-fits-all' system to a more 'flexible and child-focused' approach was advocated. There is a need for frontline workers to be assessed on outcome for the child rather than how well they have conducted or completed certain tasks.

A number of studies have examined the approach of interviewing children, in terms of interview styles and methods. The purpose of such studies was to look at the validity and reliability of child witnesses and victims' accounts. This is already addressed in professional training as a significant part of collecting effective evidence. However, until combined with the child's experience in the criminal proceedings, such studies and practice recommendations are incomplete. These two aspects cannot realistically be separated, because if children feel comfortable in working with police or social workers, they are more likely to produce detailed and reliable information that will be viewed as reliable in court.

The registered intermediary

It is clear that many children and young people in the UK that are called upon to give evidence do not have a good experience of the criminal justice system (Plotnikoff & Woolfson, 2011; Plotnikoff & Woolfson, 2015). A report funded by the Nuffield Foundation and the NSPCC found that over half of child witnesses experienced pressure before and throughout the examinations. Over 60 per cent found this process extremely upsetting (Plotnikoff & Woolfson, 2011). Current policies state that young and vulnerable witnesses are entitled to receive appropriate support, in order to enable them to provide the best evidence with as little pressure and worry as possible.

Examples of children's experiences in CJS (Plotnikoff & Woolfson, 2004)

Many witnesses mentioned the impact of delay:

> I was sad, nervous and scared while I was waiting to go to court (Joan, age 10, a witness in a trial that took place 24 months after the offence was reported).
>
> (p. 33)

Delay sometimes resulted in other witnesses dropping out:

> Cases should come to court quicker [there was 17 months between reporting the offence and the trial]. We lost my other witnesses because it all took so long. In the end, only me and my sister told what happened.
>
> (Calum, 17) (p. 33)

In relation to lack of preparation, a parent said:

> I wasn't given any run down when we got to court about what was going to happen and the order in which the children should give evidence. The youngest was taken last on the second day. My girls were very young [eight and 10] when they first went to court but it wasn't until the fourth time [of court attendance] that a timetable for giving evidence was set that was appropriate for their ages. If I had known the first time [the first trial] what I'd learned by the fourth, I'd have insisted on a timetable for them.
>
> (Parent of Petra*, 9, and Vera*, 11) (p. 41)

In relation to support before the trial:

> I would've liked a bit more emotional help. She didn't really come enough. I'd have liked to see her every two or three weeks but she only came about once a month.
>
> (Debbie, 12)

> I felt unsupported before the trial. The young witness scheme was only in touch twice, once early on and once near the trial.
>
> (Kimberley*, 18)

> She [the young witness supporter] was really good but I had to wait for her to contact me. I would have liked a phone number for her.
>
> (Jasmin, 15)

> We would have liked earlier pro-active contact from [the young witness scheme] – not leaving it to us to call them.
>
> (Rachel*, 15) (p.66)

The Youth Justice and Criminal Evidence Act 1999[2] Part II proposed a number of 'Special Measures' to assist vulnerable and intimated witnesses during criminal proceedings. One of the Special Measures, stated in Section 29 of the Act, supports the investigative interview and examination of a vulnerable witness to be carried out by a Registered Intermediary (RI) with consent by the courts. The Ministry of Justice's Better Trials Unit initiated the pilot Witness Intermediary Scheme (WIS) in 2004, which introduced the use of Registered Intermediaries in the Criminal Justice System in England and Wales. This scheme has been implemented since the National roll-out in 2008 and has been employed by 43 police forces and Crown Prosecution Services. The role of Registered Intermediaries is to provide communication support to vulnerable and intimidated witnesses, to assist them give their best evidence in investigations and in court, and make sure that the communication process is as consistent, complete and reliable as possible. All Registered Intermediaries are monitored by the WIS's Quality Assurance Boards (QAB) to assure their professional standards.

The Ministry of Justice published the Registered Intermediaries Procedural Guidance Manual (PGM) in 2011,[3] which is proposed to be a reference paper for Registered Intermediaries in assisting them to make the justice procedures available and accessible to vulnerable people (MoJ, 2011). It may also be used as a cross-reference for other guidance such as the Achieving Best Evidence in Criminal Proceedings: Guidance on Interviewing Victims and Guidance on using

Special Measures.[4] The Registered Intermediaries Procedural Guidance Manual consists of five parts; the first part covers the role of Registered Intermediaries within the criminal justice system, its principles of practice and the procedures of handling cases. Although the first contact Registered Intermediaries make is usually with the police or other justice departments, their duty is not to work on behalf of the prosecution or the victims. Their position is neutral, and their responsibility is to assist witnesses or victims to present best evidence in court.

In terms of eligibility for using intermediary provision, section16 of the Youth Justice & Criminal Evidence Act 1999[5] provides the definition of a 'vulnerable witness' as a person who is either: (a) under the age of 17, (b) unable to provide best evidence due to mental or physical disorder, or (c) severe impairment of intelligence and communicative functioning. Moreover, under Section 19, the use of special measures needs to be approved by the judge through a 'special measures direction', either at the witness's own request or on the court's own initiative. The judge will first decide on whether any special measures are needed to assist the witness to give better evidence before identifying which special measures are suitable for them, then an appropriate direction will be made. So far, the Registered Intermediaries have helped thousands of vulnerable or intimidated witnesses to get through investigative processes and court proceedings.

The police interview: Achieving Best Evidence (ABE)

In the UK police interviews with children and other vulnerable witnesses is guided by Achieving Best Evidence (ABE), which provides a framework for practitioners. The Guidance was produced by several organisations including the Ministry of Justice, the Crown Prosecution Service, the Department of Education, the Department of Health and the Welsh Assembly.

The first edition of ABE was published in 2002 when most of Special Measures were put into practice under the Youth Justice and Criminal Evidence Act 1999. It replaced the previous professional guidance Memorandum of Good Practice for Video-interviewing Children and provided directions to police officers in conducting interviews with children. A number of major practice plans were identified including the sensitive management of victims and their families; a well-managed forensic strategy; a thorough and comprehensive search for evidence; an effective arrest strategy and case disposal. It also emphasised that the police should work closely with local authorities and other agencies by sharing information relating to child welfare with specific requirements set out for inter-agency work. The ABE guidance was later revised and re-published in 2007[6] following (a) the reform on Part II: Evidence of bad character and Hearsay evidence of the Criminal Justice Act 2003[7]), (b) the introduction of the Code of Practice for Victims of Crime under section 32 of the Domestic Violence, Crime and Victims Act 2004[8] and (c) the national roll-out of Crown Prosecution Service Care Units.

The latest publication of Achieving Best Evidence: Guidance on Interviewing Victims and Witnesses and Guidance on Using Special Measures (Ministry of Justice, 2011) replaces the two previous editions of the ABE; it explains good practice guidance for professionals who are responsible for supporting or conducting interviews with vulnerable victims or witnesses in criminal proceedings. This guidance consists of (a) the amendment to the Special Measures provisions on account of section 98-103 and 105 of the Coroners and Justice Act 2009, (b) the Advice on the Structure of Visually Recorded Interviews with Witnesses from the ACPO[9] and (c) the purpose of making improvement on the quality of video-recorded interviews.

The guidance draws attention to the necessity of a more diverse and flexible approach to the support of vulnerable witnesses, by taking account of their wishes, feelings and viewpoints. The guidance also emphasised that each witness has his or her own individual needs. It is apparent from the most recent ABE guidance that sensitivity to the child's state is explicitly indicated with extensive discussion of approved interview techniques. However, what seems less clear is the standardised content of interviews, systematic recording and categorising of information for computerisation and inter-agency sharing. Also, when specialist interviewers are required for particular types of interview methods, the guidance is rather broad and no specific interviewer approaches or techniques are discussed. The availability of training for more specialist techniques for police officers and social workers in child abuse is not indicated, but the ongoing pilot study suggests that police officers are required to take ABE training only once and that no update training courses are offered, despite regular updates on guidance by the Home Office. Research conducted by Beckett and Warrington in 2015 on ABE used with young people whose abuse was being investigated found the young people described their initial encounters with the police as lacking in sensitivity and respect, with many being made to feel in some way responsible for their abuse (Beckett & Warrington, 2015). The research included a policy and literature review; in-depth participatory research with nine young 'experts by experience'; interviews with two peer supporters along with interviews and focus groups with 38 professionals The research findings document inconsistent implementation of recognised good practice around Achieving Best Evidence interviews, specifically in relation to rapport building, reducing anxiety, questioning styles and willingness to let young people have a supporter present.[10]

Increased awareness of the impacts of stressful and emotionally traumatic events on children has led to investigations of how children process, remember and then report such events (Davidson & Bifulco, 2010; Fivush, 2002; Stein et al., 2002). This research has stemmed predominantly from forensic considerations and has focused on the accuracy and suggestibility of children's testimony as well as on techniques for evaluating the credibility of children's accounts (Ceci & Bruck, 1993; Goodman & Bottoms, 1993). Thus, research into the recall of stressful events tends to show for example that children have better recall of distinctive rather than routine events and are able to report single experiences of trauma in highly detailed reports (Fivush, 2002). It should therefore be possible to gain credible accounts of victimisation from children that meet the evidence threshold and that are able to stand up to cross-examination in court.

Research has however identified specific problems in the conduct of ABE interviews including: interviews beginning with direct questions rather than attempting to first build rapport; the interviewer jumping in with particular questions too quickly (Westcott & Kynan, 2004); too many leading and/or accusatory questions, children being barraged with questions, the use of complex language, formulaic routines that fail to account for children's differences, not allowing free narrative accounts"(Robinson, 2008); time constraints, poor interview environments, a lack of child consultation and intermediaries not being used (Davidson et al., 2006).

Within the conceptual framework of developmental victimology, recent research has approached children's emotionally traumatic experience with a special interest in the way that victims engage with services such as the police, courts and social services, and how this experience interacts with their existing trauma response (Ellison & Munro, 2016; Finkelhor, 1995; Finkelhor & Dziuba-Leatherman, 1994). These studies have sought to analyse how the environmental responses to child victimisation impact upon children at different stages of childhood. An important finding is that environmental buffers have crucial and positive bearing on individual differences in response (Finkelhor & Kendall-Tackett, 1997). As children at different stages of development operate in different social and family contexts, this can significantly alter how the victimisation affects them. For example, the way in which the child's mother responds (as non-perpetrator parent) is crucial in determining outcome, and can be more important than objective elements of the victimisation itself (Toth & Cicchetti, 1993). Thus, the reactions of institutions such as the police to school-aged children involved in intra-familial abuse have the potential to affect the impact of victimisation.

A more common view is in fact the reverse, that services inadvertently amplify the child's trauma through revisiting the painful issue and escalating the victim's feelings of helplessness and guilt. Some authors stress that the way the child is handled within the law enforcement and judicial systems in the context of victimisation can be experienced as abusive in children with primed abuse-reactive responses (VanFleet & Sniscak, 2003). This is particularly observed when the first interview is handled insensitively. The initial absence of sensitivity to the child's sense of blame for the family break-up and punishment of the primary perpetrator who may be close to the child may further impact the child's negative emotions and heighten his/her sense of guilt, shame, anger, fear and embarrassment. Failure of key adults to talk with children about these adverse experiences and emotions in ways that can facilitate both understanding and coping may serve to impact existing traumatisation and increase the child's sense of mistrust and isolation (Fivush, 2002). Early research exploring child victim's perceptions of police practice (Davidson & Bifulco, 2010; Davidson et al., 2006) found a high rate of discontinuance of intra-familial child sexual abuse cases.

There is substantially less literature on the child's experience of the investigative police process, than on the validity of the process in achieving best evidence, although these two issues are inextricably linked, the exception being the previously cited research (Beckett & Warrington, 2015). There is, however, substantial research material on methods of questioning children and children's response to potentially trauma-primed responses in the interview situation. A synthesis of the literature points to ways of achieving best evidence in the investigative interview while still attending to the child's emotional state and developmental level. Greater or more consistent attention to this during the ABE interview could result in better quality evidence with implications for lower rates of discontinuance of cases.

Analysis of police reports describing investigations of intra-familial sexual abuse from age 8 demonstrated that most victims were female and aged 13-15 (Davidson et al., 2006). Although the largest proportion of alleged perpetrators were fathers or surrogate fathers, this rate was nearly matched by the proportion of perpetrators who were male peers, including siblings and cousins - not often considered as typical perpetrators. The most common reporting source was social services, followed by reporting by the victim or the mother. Therefore, in investigating such cases particular awareness of teenage girls' vulnerabilities are required, together with awareness of situations involving alleged perpetrators who are not only fathers/surrogate fathers and family friends but also a large proportion who are peers.

The largest proportion of cases (68 per cent) were recorded as 'undetected crimes' (cases were dropped at an early stage and not presented to the Crown Prosecution Service). This was attributed by police child protection officers to a variety of factors including the unwillingness of victims to participate in the process; the lack of physical evidence given the retrospective nature of many cases; the absence of the suspect and delays by the Crown Prosecution Service in providing advice on charging. However, it was notable that detection related to reporting source – while a large proportion of cases were reported by social services, very few of these were classified as 'detected crimes', compared with over half of those reported by victim or the mother. While most victims were given ABE interviews, this constituted all of those whose cases were classified as detected crimes, but only 70 per cent of those undetected crimes. Thus, the interview was a critical if not sufficient factor in crime detection.

All Child Protection team police officers had received ABE training which is generally well regarded, but the training was reported as too short with insufficient training opportunities in child interviewing techniques and lack of 'refresher' training. Some officers felt that gaining interview experience was much more valuable than formal training but identified the need for mentoring/guidance at the outset of their post. Multi-agency working in child abuse was seen as problematic, although this varied between the two police teams participating in the research with one having a better relationship with social services than the other. Negative perceptions of social workers included high rates of social worker staff turnover, inexperienced staff and poor communication. However, it was also recognised that the police service itself in Child Protection had insufficient resourcing, lack of managerial support and recognition, high work-load and high staff turnover. The number of unresolved cases was seen as demoralising, particularly given the amount of work expended on individual cases and the high rate of undetected cases. However, satisfaction with the work included the acknowledged hard work among the officers, good level of skills and competence and satisfaction around positive results. The area of child sexual abuse was viewed as important by the officers involved, despite a perception that it was not valued by the police force in general. There was general criticism of the Crown Prosecution Service (CPS). Officers commented upon its slow response, delays in making decisions and lack of communication. Some also expressed little confidence in some junior CPS lawyers. Officers also felt deskilled by recent legal changes which have removed the power of charging from the police.

The research concludes that despite the considerable efforts and dedication demonstrated by Police Child Protection Officers, the investigative system appeared to be effectively failing many children and young people who are victims of sexual abuse perpetrated by someone known to them. A minority of cases were 'detected' with even fewer prosecuted or resulting in a conviction (Davidson et al., 2006). The experience of sexual abuse is traumatic, but this cannot be made easier by the likely failure of reported cases to lead to prosecution. The impact of this upon children and their families must be great.

This research was conducted some time ago, but is there any evidence to suggest the situation has improved? In 2014 a joint inspection of ABE in child sexual abuse cases was undertaken (HMIC, 2012). The investigation focused on both the police services use of the ABE guidance and the CPS evidential use of the ABE recorded interview. Importantly the inspection also explored to what extent the guidance enables sexually abused children to actually provide best evidence (ibid.). The findings of the inspection are shown in Box 5.1.

Box 5.1

Summary findings of the Joint Inspection of ABE in child sexual abuse cases

- There was poor compliance with the guidance. Inspectors found that there was poor compliance with the Guidance and it was prescriptive rather than as good practice by many respondents; this was despite many interviewers viewing it as prescriptive rather than best practice. Recording keeping was poor; where there was a departure from the guidance, the rationale was not recorded;
- Children are not interviewed in a child friendly setting;
- Although available, intermediaries are not generally used during the interview process, even for very young children,. The reasons for this varied, but police forces are not generally using intermediaries;
- The need to conduct better assessments of the child prior to the interview was noted; this is an issue raised by our research in 2006 (Davidson et al., 2006). The absence of an assessment is compounded by poor planning and generally poor record keeping. This links with the need to conduct better assessments of the child prior to the interview. There was a paucity of plans and record keeping was generally poor;
- The lack of good planning meant that interviewers did not deal effectively with the free narrative, and questioning often blurred the lines between the evidential and investigative packages. Little thought was given in advance to dealing with the way the child might present in interview and what approach would be adopted if this became an obstacle;
- In terms of the CPS, there was very little early investigative advice from the CPS, which could have been used to speed up the process and prevent lengthy delays between arrest and charge;
- The CPS pre-charge advice did not refer to the quality of the ABE recorded interview, nor was there any quality assurance of these interviews by CPS managers;
- There was limited feedback between the CPS and police about the quality of individual ABE interviews viewed for pre-charge advice, and subsequently about their use and effectiveness as evidence from the advocate to the case lawyer or police. Although there

was greater awareness by the CPS than the police of the benefits of intermediaries at trial, special measures meetings with the child about how their evidence would be given, which were often combined with court familiarisation visits, were conducted in the absence of the lawyer due to resource issues.

The inspection concluded that:

The evidential importance of the ABE interview cannot be overstated; this is often the key element underpinning a prosecution. In this context it is vital that there is a quality product because it invariably forms the evidence-in-chief of the witness. Currently the failure to apply the Guidance and adhere to the underpinning principles means that the best evidence is not always achieved. There is a tension between the need to obtain evidence as examination-in-chief for court and the need to obtain material for an effective investigation; the police tend to emphasise the latter, the legacy of training for statement taking and suspect interviews. The Guidance is clear that both can sit comfortably within the ABE recorded interview format, but there needs to be a clear separation. This would result in discrete recorded evidence for court, distinct from the investigative aspect of the interview, which in turn would require limited editing.

(Ministry of Justice, 2014, p. 4)

Although the ABE interview is a key element of the prosecution's case, in some cases where the interview is poor other corroborating evidence may be used by the court,. The position is summarised by a judge's comments in an alleged child sexual abuse case in which ABE guidelines had not been followed:

Where there has, as in this case, been a failure to follow the interviewing guidelines, the court is not compelled to disregard altogether the evidence obtained in interview but may rely on it together with other independent material to form a conclusion (*Re B (Allegations of Sexual Abuse: Child's Evidence)* [2006] 2 FLR 1071). However, where the court finds that no evidential weight can be attached to the interviews the court may only conclude that relies on the content of those interviews where it has comprehensively reviewed all of the other evidence.

(*TW v A City Council* [2011] 1 FLR 1597) (Cited by Burrows, 2017)[12]

In Scotland, forensic interviews with children follow the Scottish Executive (2003) guidelines using a Joint Investigative Interview Technique (JIIT). Interviews are conducted by both a police officer and a social worker; one of them carries out the interviews while the other person takes notes of the interview conversations. It was concerned that handwritten notes sometimes miss out important information and are not precise or accurate enough to serve the purpose of best evidence (Ceci & Bruck, 2000). The Scottish government piloted a two-year scheme in 2003 in which a visually recording method was used in the joint investigative interviews. The evaluation of this scheme found that recording interviews provides better quality of evidence and potentially improves the child's interview experience (Richards, Morris, Richards, & Siddall, 2007).

However, concern was raised about the quality of investigative interviews after a study conducted in Scottish police force examined how well the police interviewers followed the 2003 review by the Scottish Executive,[13] for guidelines when interviews were carried out with abused children (La Rooy, Lamb, & Memon, 2011). The findings showed that most interviewers (78 per cent) did not receive any updated training after an initial one-week course, and no interviewers obtained official feedback regarding their performance in the interviews. Moreover, similar to the ABE guidance, the Scottish Executive (2003) guidelines suggested interviewers reduce the number of interviews, concerning the risk of confused evidence and 'suggestibility' – the chance of interviewers suggesting answers without using open-ended questions. On the other hand, La Rooy and colleagues' study suggested that well-conducted multiple interviews using open-ended questions can deliver reliable evidence and help witnesses and victims recall more accurate information about their experiences (La Rooy et al., 2011).

Children in the legal system

Most work exploring child victims experience of the legal system has focused on the legal/court process, even though the vast majority of cases do not progress to this stage. However, when cases do reach court children experience difficulties, both pre- and during trial including: long waiting times for cases to come to court; inadequate support during the process; special measures not utilised and aggressive cross-examination techniques designed to undermine children's accounts; these issues are discussed as follows. Also considered is the issue of children with harmful sexual behaviours (HSB).

Inadequate support

Pre-trial issues include not all children being given court familiarisation visits and a lack of support (e.g. HMCPSI & HMIC, 2012). In a study of 50 young people

(32 of whom had been victims of sexual offences) about their experiences of being a witness in court, just under half received a pre-trial court familiarisation visit and 14 had no contact with a supporter before the trial (Plotnikoff & Woolfson, 2004). A subsequent piece of research by the same authors (Plotnikoff & Woolfson, 2009), with a larger sample size of 182 children, found that little had changed over the intervening five years, with almost exactly the same percentage of children (half) having had a pre-trial court familiarisation visit. In some instances, things had become worse, with just under half (44 per cent) of children having no contact with a supporter before the trial.

In Northern Ireland, interviews with 37 children (including victims of CSA) about their experience of pre-trial support and of giving evidence in court also found 'little in the way of pre-trial assistance' (Hayes et al., 2011, p. 64), with just over half (54 per cent) having pre-trial contact with a supporter from the NSPCC Young Witness Service and just under half (49 per cent) having a court familiarisation visit. Yet (as found by the previous two studies) when support was provided it was rated highly, with 85 per cent of children saying the supporter had made a significant difference or made it possible for them to go to court at all.

Long waiting times

Long waiting times to go to trial have been found to cause and/or exacerbate psychological and mental health problems e.g. (HMIC, 2012). In Ireland, 43 victims of CSA completed the Criminal Justice System Questionnaire, which assesses satisfaction with the system (Connon et al., 2011). Children found nine aspects of the system particularly upsetting, with the impact of waiting for court coming fourth. The children in Plotnikoff and Woolfson's (2004) study waited, on average, 11.6 months for their case to reach court. During this time 35 described themselves as very nervous or scared, nine as intimidated, and 20 spoke of symptoms of anxiety; a positive correlation was noted between pre-trial anxiety and not being kept informed about the case. The parents and carers of victims in the study by Hayes et al. (2011) also described how their children were worried, stressed, and/or intimidated by the defendant or the defendant's supporters while waiting (an average of 18.1 months) to go to court.

Special measures not utilised

The Youth Justice and Criminal Evidence Act 1999 introduced a series of 'special measures' to help children (and other vulnerable and intimidated witnesses) to give best evidence in the UK. These measures included: screens to shield the witness from the accused in court, evidence given by live link rather than in the courtroom, the courtroom being cleared so evidence can be given in private, the removal of wigs and gowns, video-recorded evidence-in-chief, video-recorded cross-examination or re-examination pre-trial, examination through an intermediary and the use of communication aids. Such measures must be approved by a judge.

Research suggests however that special measures may not always be discussed, applied for or offered to children and their families as an option. Approximately 25 per cent of the 24 parents interviewed by Hayes and colleagues said that they had not been consulted about special measures for their children (Hayes et al., 2011). Similarly, there are often assumptions made about the best methods for children to give evidence (HMIC, 2012) with children in Plotnikoff and Woolfson's (2004) study finding a lack of choice in this area. Beckett and Warrington noted in their study that even when special measures were applied, they were not properly explained to the child (Beckett & Warrington, 2015).

When special measures are implemented with victims of CSA, the outcomes tend to be very positive. This is particularly the case with measures that allow evidence to be given outside of the courtroom, such as video-recorded evidence-in-chief. For example, Plotnikoff and Woolfson's (2009) study found that of the 172 children in their study who gave evidence, 55 per cent had made a visually-recorded statement and, of these, 95 per cent used it as their evidence-in-chief, with 85 per cent saying it was helpful (Plotnikoff & Woolfson, 2009).

Similar results have been found for giving evidence via live link, either in a separate room in the courthouse or a remote location. For example, a NSPCC study found that using a remote live link reduced stress on children (McNamee, Molyneaux, & Geraghty, 2012). This makes court proceedings more likely to go ahead and children able to complete their evidence; victims of CSA may particularly benefit from the live link, as being in the witness box may be especially intimidating, embarrassing and stressful for them (ibid.).

As noted by Cooper, pre-trial video-recorded cross-examination or re-examination was not implemented along with other special measures (Cooper, 2011). However, in 2013, a pilot scheme to trial the so-called 'full Pigot' in courts in Leeds, Liverpool and Kingston-upon-Thames, was introduced. Given the distress caused by live cross-examination, as discussed next, this measure could potentially dramatically reduce secondary victimisation.

Aggressive cross-examination

The cross-examination of victims of CSA appears to be particularly problematic. Participants in (Connon et al., 2011) research reported the defence barrister to be the most upsetting aspect of the system. Analysing the cross-examination of victims of CSA, a study showed that children may be painted as 'unchildlike', 'less than innocent', 'the aggressor', and 'poor witnesses' (Westcott & Page, 2002). Elsewhere children described lawyers as aggressive, cross, rude and sarcastic. The children had problems understanding questions, finding them too complex or fast, were asked repetitive questions, were talked over and accused of lying (Plotnikoff & Woolfson, 2009). Similarly, two-thirds of the children in another study said they felt nervous, upset, tearful, scared and distressed while being cross-examined (Hayes et al., 2011). Children described questions as: long, complex, incomprehensible and repetitive; lawyers as rude and sarcastic; and the majority reported being called a liar.

Parents and carers supported these views, speaking of 'inappropriate and unnecessarily harsh questioning on the part of the defence lawyer' who 'was described as shouting and hectoring their child with little intervention from the court' (Hayes et al., 2011, p. 68). Research by Davis and colleagues also found that, while prosecutors felt the need to rely upon the judge to intervene if cross-examination was intimidating or unfair, many judges were reluctant to do so (Davis, Hoyano, Keenan, Maitland, & Morgan, 1999)

It is of considerable concern that aggressive cross-examination tactics are employed with child victims of abuse; however this style of cross-examination is a central plank of the adversarial system of justice, as the purpose is to undermine the witness's testimony, rather than to obtain the child's best evidence (Cooper, 2011). Yet this process is in direct violation of the principals involved in eliciting the most complete and accurate evidence from children (Zajac, O'Neill, & Hayne, 2012).

It is clear that despite measures to ease the courtroom experience of children, achieving best evidence guidance and the introduction of intermediaries in the UK, the system must be improved upon and must become more child friendly. We turn now to international practice and ask what lessons might be learnt.

Practice in the United States and Canada

In the United States, Children's Advocacy Centers (CACs) use a 'multi-disciplinary team interviews' method to avoid cross-examination of abused children. They are supported by the National Children's Alliance[14] which provides them with training, assistance and technical support.[15] The first CAC was established in 1985; it operates as an agency to provide support to child victims and their families, to improve the quality of child abuse examinations and reduce the chance of the victims being re-traumatised. Today, there are approximately 800 CACs throughout the United States.

CACs are served as the first stop for child witnesses and victims, before they become involved in criminal proceedings. Multi-disciplinary teams are used to engage children in interviews; these teams consist of a group of professionals from different agencies such as the police force, social services, health department, child protection teams and the legal department. This multi-disciplinary approach helps to reduce the number of interviews; hence children will be less traumatised by the investigation process.[16]

A survey sought the views of just under 100 professionals from the CACs; respondents were asked to rank 75 outcomes on a multi-disciplinary model according to their importance (Walsh, Jones, & Cross, 2003). They found that the most important outcomes expected by CACs professionals are: the effectiveness and thoroughness of investigations; increasing safety of the children; reducing the chance of children being re-traumatised; and enhancing community awareness of child victims. It is necessary to understand what outcomes are important to CACs professionals because future research could focus on these areas when evaluating the Center. An examination of the effectiveness of CACs based on the preceding 'expected outcomes' found that the use of CACs has led to greater coordination of forensic interviewing amongst professionals (Cross, Jones, Walsh, Simone, & Kolko, 2007). More recent research based on a survey of 50,000 caregivers conducted by the NCA suggests that 95 per cent of caregivers agree that CACs provide them with resources to support their children, and if caregivers knew anyone else who was dealing with a situation, 97 per cent would recommend the centre (NCA, 2016).[17] In terms of legal outcomes such as conviction rates for cases that used the CACs, a comparison was made of the trends of such rates for two areas that differed in their use of CACs for sexual abuse examinations in children (Miller & Rubin, 2009). The study found that when, between 1992 and 2002, an area tripled the number of CACs, it doubled the number of successful prosecutions. On the other hand, there was no increase in prosecution rates of child sexual abuse in an area where the use of CACs stayed constant in the same period of time. Moreover, Joa and Edelson evaluated a similar model to the CACs, namely Child Abuse Assessment Centers (CAACs), which also employed the multi-disciplinary approach in the children investigation process (Joa & Edelson, 2004). They found that 76 per cent of the CAACs cases were successfully prosecuted, which almost doubled the amount of those who employed a traditional children investigation system (39 per cent). The findings also suggested that when children's assessments involved interviews in the CAACs, the guilty perpetrators were more likely to receive longer prison sentences.

In Canada, not many programmes provide services like those of the CACs in the United States. The Zebra Child Protection Centre (ZCPC) in Edmonton was set up in 2002 and is the only programme in Canada which is associated with the National Children's Alliance (NCA). ZCPC is staffed by a multi-disciplinary panel of professionals; they include the police service, Child at Risk Response Teams, family services, Crown Prosecutors, medical professionals and volunteers.[18] ZCPC uses the 'one-stop-shop' approach which allows children who are victims of sexual abuse to have inclusive protection starting from initial examinations, interventions and legal proceedings to after-care support. In 2016, 1515 children were supported, an average of 126 per month.[19]

The advantages of using the CAC model are also found in Canada. The ZCPC has qualified forensic interviewers who conduct interviews with children. Frontline staff such as police officers and social workers observe the interviews but do not ask the child direct questions. The centre has proven outcomes that are shown to reduce the risk of re-traumatisation for child victims and improve the quality of evidence and increase conviction rates.[20]

Another Canadian establishment for supporting child abuse victims in the investigation process is 'The Gatehouse' created in 1998.[21] The difference between ZCPC and The Gatehouse is that the former is a one-stop-shop service and the latter is a child-friendly site, which is often used by police investigating team and the Child Protection Service for interviewing and investigating children who may have been sexually or physically abused. Gatehouse Investigation Support Program (GISP) provides a relaxing and non-threatening environment where children and their families can be at ease during the investigation process. The interview room in the Gatehouse is decorated as a warm living room design with 'state-of-the-art' video-recording equipment, which is separated from the room,[22] clearly a far cry from many child police interviewing facilities in the UK.

Both ZCPC and The Gatehouse use 'state-of-the-art' video-recording systems to take statements in the interviews with children, to enhance better evidence for prosecuting suspects (Cunningham & Hurley, 2007). The benefits of using the best video-recording systems are to reduce the chances of technical or human error (e.g. press the wrong button to record or cannot playback in court). Such errors mean that the child has to be re-interviewed again. Moreover, it is important that the interviewers can rely on the recording system so that they can focus on and be more confident in the interviews.

Unlike ZCPC, The Gatehouse does not have an on-site investigation team, but it provides after-care services such as call support, information on child abuse, explaining court procedures, short-term therapies and agency referral. During 2008, over 1,100 children, families and professional agencies were supported by The Gatehouse. In the same year, 75 per cent of police divisions in Toronto used The Gatehouse site to carry out child abuse investigations.

Practice in Norway

In Norway, interviewing victims of child abuse must be conducted within 15 days of the reported allegation. Interviews are carried out by specially trained police officers in video rooms. The interview process is observed by a judge and other legal professionals who may put questions to the officers during breaks in the interview. The recorded video of the interview is used as evidence in cross-examination of the victim, whose involvement in the criminal proceedings finishes within a few weeks of the initial complaint. Most stakeholders in Norway are satisfied with the current system; other countries also took on its special practices to support and protect child victims and witnesses with comparable success (Global Herald).[23] An evaluation of the 22 support centres for victims of abuse is underway by Smette and colleagues and will report in early 2018.[24]

Another support system available for victims of child abuse in Norway is the Children's Houses (Barnehuset), which was established by the Minister of Justice in 2008. There are currently houses in 11 cities throughout Norway; their goal is to create a more holistic and friendly approach in supporting children who have been victims of sexual abuse.[25] Barnehuset has adopted the 'multi-disciplinary' model from the United States. However, unlike the CACs in the United States, Barnehuset also gives support to adults with mental disability that are victims of family violence or abuse. Most Children's Houses are now initiating 'Consultation Meetings' to prepare and organise the care of children before, throughout and after the investigation in court. For the child's best interest, these meetings offer safety and care assessments on an individual basis.

An evaluation of one of the Children's Houses (in Hamar) revealed that, out of 22 users of Barnehuset, 80 per cent considered that the House provided excellent physical protection to children and families; 95 per cent felt that the waiting time for consultation was acceptable; 37 per cent said that the House's after care was good or very good and general comments from users were positive. In the responses from 97 professionals who were partners to the Barnehuset (e.g. judges, police, social workers, health care staff etc.), 58 per cent believed that the safeguards for children in terms of investigation process were appropriate, and 93 per cent found that the arrangement of tasks to all different agencies within the House was efficient. However, some professionals criticised that using a multi-agency approach in a child's investigation process might weaken each discipline's professionalism. This approach is also used in Sweden and Iceland. The Children's House Model is currently being piloted in the UK and evaluated to see if it should be rolled out nationally. There are currently two such houses in the UK. Each Child House is expected to be able to provide support to over 200 children and young people each year, aiming to provide a multi-agency, long-term support and advocacy service under one roof. Criminal justice aspects of after-care will be embedded in the service, with evidence gathering interviews led by child psychologists on behalf of the police and social workers, and court evidence provided through video links to aid swifter justice.[26]

Child offenders, criminal responsibility and harmful sexual behaviour

Much of the research conducted in developed countries ('the global north') has focused upon the treatment of children as victims of crime. There is little research addressing the needs and treatment of child offenders. In most Western European countries, the age of criminal responsibility is between the ages of 13 and 16 and is comparable to the age of consent. The UN Committee on the Rights of the Child recommended that the age of criminal responsibility should be raised in the UK (however in South Africa the age of criminal responsibility is 7). The age of criminal responsibility is still however set at 10 in England and Wales and was 8 in Scotland until a bill was recently introduced to raise the age to 12 (Scottish Government, 2017).[27]

In South Africa the Child Justice Bill was introduced in 2002. The aim of the legislation is to protect both child offenders and child victims, although the focus is predominantly upon perpetrators. After six years of debate and reworking, the Bill was enacted on 11 May 2009 and came into effect in April 2010. In an effort to both humanise the juvenile justice system and to protect the rights of children in conflict with the law, the new legislation raises the minimum age of child offenders and provides several diversion options. The key objective of the legislation is to 'entrench the notion of restorative *justice* in the criminal *justice* system in respect of *child*ren who are in conflict with the law'. Restorative justice is defined as:

> an approach to *justice* that aims to involve the *child* offender, the victim, the families concerned and community members to collectively identify and address harms, needs and obligations through accepting responsibility, making restitution, taking measures to prevent a recurrence of the incident and promoting reconciliation.[28]

(p.10)

Diversion alternatives include both family group conferencing and victim offender mediation. According to the 'minimum standards for diversion options', a diversion programme must among other things:

- impart useful skills;
- include a restorative justice element which aims at healing relationships, including the relationship with the victim;
- include an element which seeks to ensure that the child understands the impact of his or her behaviour on others, including the victims of the offence, and may include compensation or restitution.

There is increasing recognition in the UK that harmful sexual behaviour displayed by children is a child protection issue (Hackett, 2016). The NSPCC operational framework defines harmful sexual behaviours as:

> Sexual behaviours expressed by children and young people under the age of 18 years old that are developmentally inappropriate, may be harmful towards self or others, or be abusive towards another child, young person or adult.
>
> (Hackett, 2016, p. 12)

This definition is broad, including both online and offline behaviours. Also, of relevance in this context is the DfE definition of CSE:

> A form of child sexual abuse [which] occurs where an individual or group takes advantage of an imbalance of power to coerce, manipulate or deceive a child or young person under the age of 18 into sexual activity (a) in exchange for something the victim needs or wants, and/or (b) for the financial advantage or increased status of the perpetrator or facilitator. The victim may have been sexually exploited even if the sexual activity appears consensual. Child sexual exploitation does not always involve physical contact; it can also occur through the use of technology.
>
> (DfE, 2017a, p. 5)

In 2016 the NSPCC developed the Harmful Sexual Behaviour Framework which is based on the NSPCC funded work of Hackett and colleagues; the framework aims to provide an evidence informed approach to working with young people and their families and to support local work with children and young people who have displayed HSB through practice guidelines and policy (Hackett, Holmes, & Branigan, 2016). The Framework included five areas of focus:[29]

- A continuum of responses to children and young people displaying HSB.
- Prevention, identification and early assessment.
- Effective assessment and referral pathways.
- Interventions.
- Workforce development.

Recent small-scale qualitative research conducted by Hackett and Smith on behalf of the Centre of Expertise on Child Sexual Abuse[30] suggests that although HSB has often been viewed and is often approached as a specific offence category, the reality is that a *'complex set of behaviours'* (Simon Hackett & Smith, 2018, p. 21) are evident – sometimes over a long period of time in the lives of the young people who participated in the study. The investigators argue that sexual harm and exploitation had become a *'lifestyle trait'* (Simon Hackett & Smith, 2018, p. 21). Hackett and Smith suggest that one of the most striking findings from the research was the high degree of general deviance and anti-social thinking that characterised the young peoples' behaviour. However, this research is based upon anonymised police records of a sample of 14 cases of CSE where the perpetrator was under the age of 18, and as a small sample the findings are illustrative rather than representative and shed light on a complex area.

Discussion

Research from different countries indicates that a flexible, holistic and child-centred approach is necessary in supporting child witnesses, victims and child offenders. In the UK few child abuse cases are prosecuted, and the legal process can be a re-traumatising experience for children; the process is currently at best ineffective and at worst punishing. Whilst there is some good practice, research demonstrates that the key problems are as follows:

- inconsistent practice in ABE interviewing which takes no account of the child's potentially traumatised state;
- problematic inter-agency collaboration;
- lack of child friendly justice environment/interview setting;
- inadequate support for children throughout the legal process and particularly pre- and during trial;
- little use of intermediaries;
- low use of extraordinary measures that are available to child victims and the failure to routinely advise children and their families about the availability of special measures;
- long waiting times for trial which may exacerbate mental health problems;
- aggressive cross-examination practices in court designed to undermine the child's testimony rather than to achieve best evidence.

Elements of good practice with child victims include the use of the 'multi-disciplinary team interviews' approach from the child advocacy centres (CACs) in the United States which can avoid cross-examination of abused children. This approach not only reduces the chance of children being re-traumatised by having to repeat their accounts over again, it also facilitates the child victims to develop trust with a team of professionals, since they do not have to be sent to different places and meet different people during the interview process. Most importantly, the use of CACs increased the prosecution rate. Also, the 'one-stop-shop' approach employed in countries such as Canada, which allows victims of child abuse to have inclusive protection starting from initial examinations, interventions, legal proceedings to after-care support has proven to be a positive way of treating child victims. Finally, decreasing the number of times a child is required to provide evidence is preferable. In terms of the investigation time, the Norwegian statutory requires child victims to be interviewed within 15 days of the complaints. Recorded interviews are used as evidence-in-chief and cross-examination of the child, so that there's no need to be re-examined again.

Lessons should be learnt from UK and other countries' ineffective practices in order to make improvements and enhance the efficiency in current initiatives. It is important to ensure that refresher training is provided to all professionals who are involved in the child abuse investigative process; regular feedback regarding the quality of interviews is also essential for maintaining good practice; staff should be capable of handling electronic recording equipment when collecting information using recording devices; the decision of choosing the right Special Measure for a child should be determined by the child's individual needs.

Balancing the need for achieving best evidence for alleged abuse cases and at the same time acknowledging children's views and feelings requires rational and realistic measures. This requires continuous development in policies as well as learning from other countries' success, in order to achieve successful outcomes in reducing negative impact on children during the investigative interview process and during the legal process. It is hoped that the new Children's house model currently being evaluated in the UK will be rolled out nationally.

Notes

1 http://frontline.cjsonline.gov.uk/_includes/downloads/guidance/victims-and-witnesses/National_Registered_Intermediary_Conference_2008-Conference_Report.pdf
2 www.legislation.gov.uk/ukpga/1999/23/contents
3 www.justice.gov.uk/guidance/docs/achieving-best-evidence-criminal-proceedings.pdf.
4 www.cps.gov.uk/publications/docs/RI_ProceduralGuidanceManual.pdf
5 www.legislation.gov.uk/ukpga/1999/23/contents
6 *http://frontline.cjsonline.gov.uk/_includes/downloads/guidance/better-trials/Achieving_Best_Evidence_FINAL.pdf*
7 www.legislation.gov.uk/ukpga/2003/44/contents
8 www.legislation.gov.uk/ukpga/2004/28/contents
9 http://library.college.police.uk/docs/APPREF/ACPO-Witness-Interview-Structure-2013.pdf
10 www.beds.ac.uk/__data/assets/pdf_file/0005/461867/Beckett-and-Warrington-2015-Making-Justice-Work-Exec-Summary.pdf
11 *www.familylawweek.co.uk/site.aspx?i=fo30698*
12 *www.familylaw.co.uk/news_and_comment/evidence-of-sexual-abuse-in-children-proceedings-pt-2#.WjqhhlWRrlU)*
13 www.scotland.gov.uk/Resource/Doc/162579/0044250.pdf
14 www.nationalchildrensalliance.org/sites/default/files/NCAAccreditationStandards201708202015.pdf

15 *www.nationalchildrensalliance.org/our-story*
16 www.nationalcac.org/
17 *www.nationalchildrensalliance.org/measuring-cac-outcomes*
18 Zebra Child Protection Centre (2017) *Media Releases. www.zebracentre.ca/*
19 *www.zebracentre.ca/*
20 www.victimsfirst.gc.ca/
21 http://thegatehouse.org/about-us/history/
22 http://thegatehouse.org/about-us/annual-reports-and-financial-statements/
23 *http://theglobalherald.com/childrens-evidence-in-criminal-proceedings-experts-call-for-uk-reforms/17589/.*
24 www.hioa.no/eng/About-HiOA/Centre-for-Welfare-and-Labour-Research/NOVA/Prosjekter/Youth-Research-Projects/Evaluation-of-support-centres-for-victims-of-incest-and-sexual-abuse)
25 *(www.statensbarnehus.no/*
26 www.london.gov.uk/press-releases/mayoral/uks-first-child-houses-to-launch
27 www.gov.scot/Topics/Justice/policies/young-offending/MACR
28 *(www.childjustice.org.za/downloads/A75-2008.pdf).*
29 www.nspcc.org.uk/services-and-resources/research-and-resources/2016/harmful-sexual-behaviour-framework/
30 www.baspcan.org.uk/invitation-centre-expertise-child-sexual-abuse/

6 The digital world, online abuse and child safety

Online risks to children

In less than two decades, the Internet has moved from being a communications medium used by some to an everyday tool used in our homes, schools, workplaces and travels. It enables us to search for information, perform routine tasks and communicate with others. The technological aspects of the Internet are developing at the same high speed as the number of users globally. The Internet provides a social context for us to meet with others and to exchange information on a scale we would never have thought possible in the past.

The World Wide Web is a system with universally accepted standards for storing, retrieving, formatting, changing and displaying information in a networked environment. Information is stored and displayed as electronic pages that can contain numbers, text, pictures, graphics, sound and video. These web pages can be linked electronically to other Web pages, independent of where they are located, and web pages can be viewed by any type of computer.

Most research is conducted on children's exposure to risk online, some but not all of which constitutes child abuse as defined in this book. That of sexual grooming online for offline abuse is clearly included along with the creation and distribution of images of children being abused. The online sexual grooming of children is increasing and may affect up to one in ten children (Webster et al., 2015; Smith, Thompson, & Davidson, 2015). But there is need for more understanding of this among child welfare professionals and criminal justice agencies. Other harms to children online may be related to such abuse potential. For example, exposure to pornographic (adult) material is estimated to affect approximately half of all children aged 13-16, who have viewed online adult pornography with some children as young as 8 having been exposed (Martellozzo, Horvath, Davidson, & Adler, 2015). Prevalence varies however by age and gender in some instances, suggesting that the clear majority of teenagers have viewed such content. There is qualified evidence of adverse effects, including that quite young children may be learning about sex from pornography, hence the importance of sex education. What is not known is whether such risks of online harm increase likelihood of online sexual grooming for offline abuse. It may have 'normalising' effects of sexual behaviour for the young people and may be utilised as part of grooming processes.

Other risks online are more common, but these tend to include harm from peers rather than child abuse per se. For example, children are most concerned about cyberbullying, with estimated prevalence varying between 6 per cent to 25 per cent or more; this is the biggest risk faced online by children in the West (Davidson & Martellozzo, 2012; Bryce, 2009; Davidson et al., 2016; Hasebrink, Livingstone, Haddon, & Olafsson, 2009; Livingstone & Haddon, 2009). Sexting and sexual harassment are more common among teenagers developing intimate relationships. This is fuelled by lack of understanding of consent as well as gender inequalities, sexual stereotypes and coercion, which all serve to blur the boundaries between sexting and harassment. As a result, girls are more at risk, though there are grounds for concern about boys also. Finally, another source of harm is the risk of young people being targeted as consumers with age inappropriate material and potential loss of personal data.

Child Internet use in the UK

A recent literature review,[1] funded by the Department of Media, Culture and Sport (DCMS)[2] on behalf of the UK Council for Child Internet Safety Evidence Group, explored key current trends and risks associated with children's use of the Internet (Livingstone, Davidson, & Bryce, 2017). This UK review drew on key European sources. It showed that the vast majority of children in the UK have unlimited Internet access, with only a small minority of children, mostly from poorer homes, with none. But for most children, Internet use is occupying increasing amounts of time, in more locations and with more personalised devices – though tablets are preferred over smartphones by younger children. This can include younger children, for example now four in every ten children aged 3-4 has a digital device. Online opportunities for creative and civic participation are taken up only by a minority of children, though many state that they wish to be 'good digital citizens'. Risky opportunities vary – few children say they send photos to online contacts or reveal personal information, but substantial minorities use services whilst under age (Livingstone, Davidson, & Bryce, 2017). Many UK children have learnt to be cautious online, but there is little evidence that their digital skills and literacies are increasing over time, although these do improve with age. It is clear that children are using the Internet and devices from a much younger age and that usage varies greatly by age; for example annual research conducted by OFCOM suggests that in 2017 79 per cent of children aged 5-7 were online for approximately 9 hours a week, compared to 99 per cent of 12-15s who were online for approximately 21 hours per week. It is of concern that some children aged 5-7 (3 per cent) already have a social media profile however:

> almost all 8-11s and 12-15s who go online say they have been told how to use the internet safely. Nevertheless, going online can expose children to unwanted experiences: 17% of 8-11s and 29% of 12-15s who go online say they have ever seen something online that they have found worrying or nasty; 45% of 12-15s who go online say they have seen hateful content online in the last year, an increase since 2016; one in ten 12-15s have seen something online or on their phone of a sexual nature that made them feel uncomfortable; and 12% of 12-15s say they have been bullied on social media, equal to the number who say they have been bullied face to face. Many children who have these types of experiences take (positive) action in response.
>
> (OFCOM, 2018, p. 2)[3]

Children's reported experience of online risk varies: studies quote one in ten children, to one in five young teens, who report encountering something 'worrying' or 'nasty' online in the past year. Key concerns are encountering adult pornography and violence. These are more often encountered on video-sharing sites or other websites, rather than in social networks and games. Top parental concerns focus on online violence. There has been slight change in online risk in recent years, though there have been some indications of a rise in hate content and self-harm content. It is not possible to determine whether the Internet has increased the overall amount of risk children face as they grow up, or whether the Internet provides a new location for risk experiences. However, the nature of the Internet itself alters and amplifies the consequences.

Child Internet use internationally

There is a great deal of research about children's use of the Internet in the West but much less in the so-called developing world and the Middle East. However, we do know that children's use of the Internet has grown exponentially worldwide; usage in Bangladesh for example grew 143 per cent between 2000 and 2005; and in 2017 approximately 50 per cent of the population has Internet access in the region.[4] A recent survey of school children undertaken in Nepal suggests that 81 per cent of those aged 14-18 years (of a sample of 1,430) were accessing the Internet on a weekly basis, with 51 per cent of the sample having home access and many children using Internet cafes.[5] In Russia, the Foundation for Internet Development in 2009[6] reported studies in large urban centres on children and teenagers which reveals that the Internet it is a primary information source, ahead of television, books and printed mass media for those aged 14-15 and those aged 16-17. Approximately 65 per cent of the latter said that their parents allowed them free use of the Internet without imposing any time limit. In Africa, Internet use varies enormously by country with some countries equal to that of the West. In Kenya for example 89 per cent of the population has Internet access compared to only 18 per cent in Gambia as reported by Internet World Statistics, 2018.[7]

There is also growth in using alternative technological devices to go online. Mobile phone use is widespread among children and young people and an increasing number access the Internet via a mobile phone. Extensive use is made of the Internet using interactive services such as games, Social Networking Sites and instant messages, increasingly to be found as mobile phone applications. The most significant difference between Internet usage amongst children in industrialised and developing countries appears to be the mode of access, with children in developing nations increasingly accessing via mobile phones. A study undertaken by the Pew Research Center in the United States in 2015[8] of seven African countries (with a sample size of 7,052) found that approximately two-thirds of respondents owned a mobile phone, with ownership particularly high in Nigeria and South Africa. Mobile phone ownership has increased considerably in the region with 8 per cent of Ghanaians owning a mobile phone in 2002 compared to 83 per cent in 2014, a more than tenfold increase. There was however a social class divide with highly educated respondents (to degree level) being much more likely to own a mobile phone (ibid.).

Gender appears to be a key issue in terms of Internet access and usage in some countries. In certain developing nations girls are less likely to have frequent access to the Internet than boys (Gasser, MacClay, & Palfrey, 2010).

Cultural context and online behaviour

Little research has been conducted in the Middle East that has explored the use of digital technology amongst young people. One exception is an earlier study conducted in Palestine (Hijazi-Omari & Ribak, 2008). The research explores gender differences in mobile phone use amongst Palestinian girls and the way in which culturally gendered practices frame the meaning of the use of technology. The authors examine the way in which the use of mobile phones alters social dynamics, relationships and the construction of gender in Palestine. The research suggests that boys give girls mobile phones in order to communicate with them privately; the girls know that their parents would disapprove, that discovery would lead to harsh punishment, and continue to conceal the phones. Research conducted in Bahrain revealed that cultural issues do impact upon young people's use of digital media and upon parental response to the use. In some sectors of Bahraini society, for example, the act of removing the veil in a SNS photograph would be considered unacceptable (Davidson & Martellozzo, 2013):

> We have had cases of Islamic girls that took their veil off in front of the webcam and took photographs of themselves. Then they were deeply upset when their pictures were made public. You can see how their parents felt.
>
> (Teacher 3 – Bahrain study)

Stakeholders participating in the Bahrain study indicated that teenage girls are interacting with teenage boys online, via Instant Messenger (IM) or SNS. This social interaction has been hidden from parents as it is considered culturally unacceptable. In a similar fashion to the girls in the Palestinian study, the girls were aware that their behaviour was breaking cultural norms and that they would be severely punished on discovery, but they still went ahead. It could be argued that the medium allows a freedom of expression previously denied to the girls and a means to conceal the behaviour (although not always effectively). As one stakeholder suggests:

> Parents would not approve of this behaviour. It is a cultural issue.
>
> (Stakeholder 5 – Bahrain study)

When the interaction was discovered, some of the teenagers were subjected to severe physical punishment on the part of their parents. One respondent suggested that given cultural constraints placed upon some girls, interacting with and meeting strange boys is completely unacceptable and that girls are more controlled by their parents than boys:

> Girls shouldn't go out with a boy. This is not accepted in our society.
>
> (Stakeholder 6 – Bahrain study)

Unfortunately, a number of these interactions have resulted in the attempted suicide of the girls (there were seven such cases in April 2010, but cases occur on a monthly basis):

> We have had cases that the children were assaulted by parents to the degree that they were admitted to the hospital. They would arrive to us with multiple bruises and severe injuries. Sometimes they are beaten up badly with

the stick. Even if the parents know that the online relationship was innocent, even if she was just talking they would punish her. They would be punished not necessarily by the father but also by the uncles, *the brothers*.

(Stakeholder 3 – Bahrain study)

It is clear from these studies conducted with two groups of children living in very different contexts that SNS and digital media transcend geographical and social boundaries, uniting children in a shared enthusiasm for new technology. However, although children's use of digital media appears to be similar, gendered cultural issues play a significant role in shaping a response to their online behaviours; their online activities are not played out in a vacuum (Davidson & Martellozzo, 2010).

International online child risk

Children face similar online risks regardless of geographical location, but there appear to be some differences in developing nations. Although Internet usage may vary from country to country, the nature of the risks to which young people are exposed are broadly similar. This is due to the global nature of online communication, and the continuing expansion of peer-to-peer platforms and social networking sites such as Facebook (which now in terms of its population of online users is the size of a small continent). The EU Kids Online research, conducted by Livingstone and colleagues between 2006 and 2012, identified a number of risks and categorised these risks into what is now commonly referred to as the '3 Cs'. These are content, contact and conduct.

As in the UK, cyberbullying is common in developing countries – e.g. South Africa, Thailand, India and China (Gasser et al., 2010). A survey in India indicated that 65 per cent of school children claimed to have experienced cyberbullying via mobile phone (ibid.). In Bahrain, in a nationally representative survey, 38 per cent (in a sample of 2,433) reported cyberbullying, a key concern to the children, who reported feelings of depression, anxiety and helplessness and an increase in truancy and physically violent altercations with peers as a consequence (Davidson & Martellozzo, 2010).

In terms of sexual behaviour online, a national random sample of young Internet users in the United States (ages 10–17) found 13 per cent had experienced an unwanted sexual solicitation on the Internet (Mitchell, Finkelhor, & Wolak, 2005). Many of these incidents were confined to the Internet and relatively mild in nature. However, the potential for online sexual solicitation and harassment has raised obvious concerns among parents, teachers and mental health professionals. Research funded by the European Commission Safer

Internet Programme (Webster, Davidson, Bifulco, Pham, & Caretti, 2009) exploring online grooming behaviour in four European countries found that the vast majority of young people appear resilient to approach by online groomers. However offenders deliberately use SNS to target socially isolated, vulnerable young people who respond well to attention received from online contacts (Livingstone & Smith, 2014).

Only 12 per cent of young people in a pan-European study said that they had met with an acquaintance known only online, via a SNS (Livingstone, Haddon, Görzig, & Ólafsson, 2011). However, more recent research based on a victimisation survey with a group of young people aged 18-25 in three EU countries found that as many as 32 per cent of young people had experienced unwanted online sexual approaches as children (Davidson et al., 2016). This proportion is considerably higher than that found in other research and may be due to the retrospective nature of the survey. There is some evidence that children often do not recognise that an online relationship is dangerous at the time of the online contact prior to abuse (Ainsaar & Loof, 2012).[9]

Emerging research indicates that young people in countries new to Internet safety seem more likely to meet with online acquaintances. Research conducted in Brazil suggests that although children are aware that they shouldn't meet with online acquaintances, a substantial proportion still did (43 per cent) (SaferNet, 2009[10]). A study conducted in Thailand cited in Gasser and colleagues suggests that 24 per cent of those aged 7-11 had met with an online acquaintance they hadn't met before and in 58 per cent of cases the child reported this led to an unpleasant experience (Gasser et al., 2010). Research conducted in Bahrain found as many as 41 per cent of children and young people meet with online acquaintances, the rate falling to 16 per cent in 2015 (Davidson & Martellozzo, 2010) (Davidson & Martellozzo, 2013).

Thus, research undertaken in Europe and the United States as well as the UK has demonstrated that young people do engage in risk-taking behaviour online, which can also contribute to the dangers they face.

The scale of online offending

Much has been written about the way in which offenders use the Internet to meet young people and groom them for sexual abuse, how they network with other offenders and share indecent child images. However, given recent difficulty in accessing offender populations, there is little empirical evidence in this area. The Internet provides the opportunity to join a virtual community where people with similar interests can communicate and find useful information. Myspace and other similar social networking sites encompass thriving 'communities' where young people engage in countless hours of photo-sharing. In addition to Myspace, other social networking and blogging sites such as Friendster.com, Facebook.com and MyYearbook.com allow users to post pictures, videos and blogs and send emails and instant messaging. Myspace and Facebook differ in security aspects in that Myspace is open to anyone, and has loose age restrictions, while Facebook users are encouraged and often required to register using their real name (Kierkegaard, 2008). The anonymity, availability of extremely sensitive personal information and ease of contacting people make social networking sites a useful tool for online child sex offenders in general, but specifically for online groomers. While many of these sites have age restrictions, it is possible both for young people and offenders to misrepresent their age (Bergen et al., 2015). Also, to hide their IP addresses and locations, they can piggyback on Wi-Fi connections or use proxy servers. Decentralised peer-to-peer networks prevent material from being tracked to a specific server, and encryption lets them keep online chats private from those policing the Web.

There is increasing empirical evidence regarding the *modus operandi* of Internet offenders, much of which has focused on the nature, extent and use of indecent images of children (Seto & Eke, 2005). There has been a significant increase in the amount of child abuse images on the Internet over the last decade that parallels the emergence of the Internet as a facilitator of global communication (Quayle, 2017).[11] It is however very difficult to estimate the prevalence of online child sexual abuse with any accuracy or certainty (see Box 6.1). A Rapid Evidence Assessment exploring the prevalence of online child abuse has recently been published by the IICSA (Wager et al., 2018); the findings point to the difficulty associated with attempting to measure the scale of online CSA given problems associated with self-report and official statistics.[12] Estimates could and have been based upon the criteria of recorded offences, number of known victims and number of known perpetrators. However, much is not reported and there is a likely underestimation of the extent of the problem with many victims remaining unidentified. Recent research also suggests that the majority of online grooming offences are reported by the public (Davidson et al., 2016). Other issues impact upon the validity of incidence reports, these include:

- offender behaviour is increasingly sophisticated and difficult to detect;
- the use of the dark web to concealing offending;
- offenders also use Internet Protocol (IP) address anonymisation; encryption; evidence elimination software; and video and/or voice manipulation software (Global Alliance Against Child Sexual Abuse Online 2015).[13]

Box 6.1

Agency data on indecent images (Indecent Images of a Child - IIOC) incidence

- In 2013, the **Child Exploitation and Online Protection Command** (CEOP) estimated that approximately 50,000 UK-based individuals were involved in downloading and sharing indecent images of children (IIOC) during 2012;
- In 2016, the **National Police Chief's Council** reported that up to 100,000 people have viewed indecent images of children online;
- In 2015 the NCA's **Child Sexual Exploitation Referral Bureau** was receiving more than 1,800 referrals per month of indecent images of children, indecent chat and videos primarily from industry, compared with 400 per month in 2010. In 2015 the bureau received 22,606 referrals in total, 19,788 of which were from industry (*NSPCC, 2016*).[14]

Prevalence of online sexual abuse

This is estimated mainly through large-scale self-report victim studies and estimates the number of children victimised. Such victimisation surveys have tended to focus on youth-produced sexual images and experience of online child sexual exploitation or abuse, and can quantify the number affected across different time periods and in different geographical regions (Davidson et al., 2016; Hollis & Belton, 2017; L. Jonsson, Bladh, Priebe, & Svedin, 2015; L. S. Jonsson, Priebe, Bladh, & Svedin, 2014; Livingstone & Görzig, 2014; Mitchell, Finkelhor, Jones, & Wolak, 2012; Mitchell, Jones, Finkelhor, & Wolak, 2014). This approach can illuminate information otherwise hidden to services, but surveys may not be representative and can produce different estimates. These surveys generally produce higher reported rates of online child abuse than incidence reports, but the extent to which children and young people are willing to respond openly and honestly to survey is questionable, particularly where telephone interviewing in children's homes is used. The prevalence rates in these surveys vary from 9 per cent of US adolescents aged 10 to 17 who reported having experienced unwanted sexual solicitation (Jones, Mitchell, & Finkelhor, 2012); to 15 per cent of 11 to 16-year-olds in Europe who had received a sexual message online (Livingstone & Görzig, 2014); and 21 per cent of a sample of 18-25 year olds having experienced unwanted online sexual solicitation (Davidson et al., 2016). This latter retrospective victimisation survey of three EU countries (UK, Italy and Netherlands) showed that whilst the majority of young people had not experienced any negative behaviour online, of those who experienced sexual solicitation (more than half of those from the UK) the majority had been solicited by peers not adults. Under half of young people across the three countries stated that they had sent explicit material to someone online. Although the percentage of participants that engaged in the sending of explicit material varied by country with less than a quarter of young people from Italy engaging in such behaviours, young people from Italy were far more likely to seek support when they had received sexual solicitation than young people from Ireland and the UK. Less than half of young people from Ireland and the UK sought support, compared to over three-quarters of young people from Italy. This may highlight cultural differences. In terms of harassment or being threatened online, this was more common to boys, but boys also engaged in such behaviour significantly more often than girls and more often harassed/threatened someone else online.

Volume of indecent images online

Quantification of the number of images and the scale of networks has focused upon the following: number of attempts to access images; number of images viewed, downloaded or shared with others; and the geographical reach of shared images. Agencies and organisations such as the Internet Watch Foundation (IWF) and police intelligence from operations provide estimates based upon automated monitoring of specific P2P networks, industry and public reports and police operations. This information is very important in highlighting the scale of the problem faced but provides a snapshot that is reliant upon effective reporting, intelligence and investigation and that may not be representative. Box 6.2 shows the latest data available from the IWF Data for 2016 on indecent images:

Box 6.2

Volume of indecent images (IIOC) on the internet (IWF data, 2016[15]) :

- In 2016, 57,335 web pages containing child sexual abuse images or videos were removed;
- Every nine minutes the IWF's analysts encounter a webpage which shows children being sexually abused;
- 455 newsgroups were confirmed as containing indecent images;
- There has been an increase of images involving 11 to 15-year-olds, compared to children aged 10 and under. This is due to an increase in 'self-produced' content created using webcams and then shared online;

- In 2016, 28 per cent of images were category A: showing penetrative sexual activity involving children including rape or sexual torture, representing a decrease of 6 per cent compared to 2015;
- In 2016, 19 per cent of images were classified as category B: involving non-penetrative sexual activity or a decrease of 9 per cent compared to 2015;
- 92 per cent of all URLs identified as containing IIOC in 2016 were hosted in five countries; The Netherlands (20,972); the United States (12,492); Canada (8,803); France (6,099); and Russia (4,176). For other countries the combined rate is 4,793.

Such abuse is damaging and harmful for the child victims. It has been claimed that in many instances children are abused and the abuse recorded by members of their own family or people known to them (Klaine, Davis, & Hicks, 2001).[16] Many indecent images which depict the sexual abuse of children involve dual victimisation, in the abuse involved in the creation of the image and again in the distribution of the image. It could be argued that a child is re-victimised each time their image is accessed, and images on the Internet can form a permanent record of abuse. This can have an additional damaging effect on the victim.

Recently there has been considerable speculation as to whether the majority of men who download child indecent images will also have committed a contact offence against a child (e.g. Bourke & Hernandez, 2008). Other research suggests only a small number will have done so (e.g. Endrass et al., 2009), underpinned by anxieties that official data reflect only those who have been caught and convicted. Recent polygraph studies on child pornography offenders have raised concerns that such men consistently underestimate both the level of abusive content and overestimate the age of the children within the images collected, as well as underestimating the commission of offline contact offences (Bourke & Hernandez, 2008; Buschman et al., 2010). An important series of studies (Eke, Seto, & Williams, 2011; Seto & Eke, 2005) examined how traditional risk factors might apply to child pornography offenders. From their full dataset it appeared that offenders with either prior or concurrent violent offences, including sexual offences, were significantly more likely to be charged with a contact sexual recidivism compared to other offenders. There was a negative relationship between offenders who had solely child pornography offences in their criminal records and recidivism outcomes. Contact sexual recidivism was therefore predicted by criminal history (particularly violent offence history), age at the time of the first detected criminal offence (24 years and younger), and failure on conditional release.

Characteristics of online groomers

The European Online Grooming Project was funded by the European Commission Safer Internet Plus Programme and aimed to establish characteristics of convicted offenders who groomed online victims, from their interview descriptions (Webster et al., 2015). The research aimed to describe the behaviour of both offenders who groom and young people who are 'groomed' and explore differences (e.g. in demographics, behaviour or profiles) within each group and how these differences may have a bearing on offence outcome. The study also described how information and communication technology (ICT) is used to facilitate the process of online grooming and to further the current low knowledge base about the way in which young people are selected and prepared for abuse online. The aim was to make a significant contribution to the development of educational awareness and preventative initiatives aimed at parents and young people.

Findings from this research, based on depth interviews with convicted offenders is indicated in Figure 6.1 to illustrate how online groomers enter and exit particular phases of the grooming process according to their objectives and the perceived 'needs' of the young people targeted, and that not all aspects of the described process are relevant to the population of groomers. The research indicated this not to be the case. That is, although some groomers described

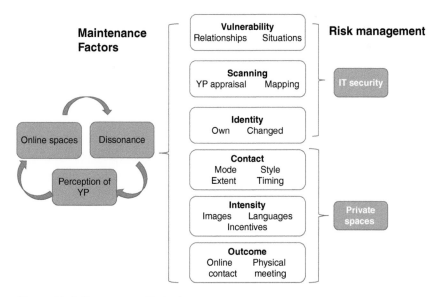

Figure 6.1 Online groomers' behaviours

Taken from (Webster et al., 2015)

taking a measured and lengthy approach through a sequence of pre-determined steps, there was also evidence of fast and almost random approaches to young people.

The model developed indicates that external factors help to *maintain* the behaviour such as the online environment, dissonance and offender's perceptions of young people and their behaviour. The research also identified *salient behaviours* in the grooming process such as: *scanning* the online environment for potential people to contact (described by one offender as a 'fishing trip'), the *identity* adopted by the groomer (be it their own or another); the *nature of contact* with the young person; the different ways in which the online groomer can *intensify* the process of grooming and the diverse range of *outcomes* toward the end of the process.

The findings from this EC-funded study have contributed to an understanding of online grooming behaviour with three grooming approaches and types of online groomer identified; the research is based upon 30 in-depth interviews with men aged 18-45 (mean age of 34), all of whom had been convicted for grooming a child online.

The first 'type' of groomer identified was the **distorted attachment** offender. Men in this group had offence supportive beliefs that involved seeing contact with the young person as a '*relationship*'. Men within this group did not have any indecent images of children, and they did not have any contact with any other sexual offenders online. This group also seemed to spend a significant amount of time online talking to the young person before they met the victim. All men in this group went on to meet the victim to develop or further the '*relationship*'.

The second type was the **adaptable online groomer**. Unlike the previous group, they did not seem to have discussed the encounter in terms of a relationship. Some men in this group had collections of indecent images of children but they were not significant collections in terms of size.

Finally, the **hyper-sexualised** group of men were characterised by extensive indecent image collections of children and significant online contact with other sexual offenders or offender groups. It is clear from the research that not all episodes of online grooming result in a physical meeting. Development of the thematic framework was followed by detailed within- and between-case analysis to identify and understand associations between broad grooming features and individual offender characteristics.

Behaviours of victims online

The EU Grooming project also identified characteristics of victims as identified by the offenders interviewed.

The most common were those **resilient** who could recognise risk and fend off any approach online they considered suspicious or 'weird'. They were more likely to acknowledge online safety messages and came from more settled family backgrounds.

The **vulnerable** group indicated a high need for affection and attentions, had difficulty in relationship with parents and problematic home lives. They were seen to be seeking 'love' on the Internet and believed the grooming relationship was a truly intimate one.

The **risk-taking** group were young people seen to be seeking adventure, disinhibited, who felt they controlled the online interaction. Less was known about their family background. These young people were more open to pressure not to disclose because they believed the groomer's view of their own cooperation and culpability with regard to the seduction.

Finally, this project speculated on a matching of the young person and offender type (see Figure 6.2. It was hypothesised that the offender seeking intimacy would gravitate to the more vulnerable victim which would satisfy both apparent sets of needs for a pseudo attachment. The hypersexualised offender is more likely to link up with the risk-taking young person, who would be less wary of such an explicitly sexual approach. Both groups of victims are likely to be targeted by the adaptable groomer who could vary his approach. However, more research is needed to identify the psychological profiles in more depth, and in particular from the victim's own account. Also, more information on attachment processes, disinhibition, context and protective factors are required to complete this tentative profiling.

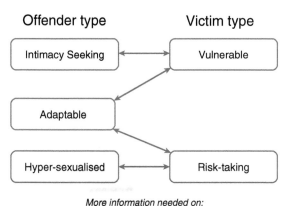

Figure 6.2 Speculative offender-young person type matching

Case example - Descriptors of vulnerable victims - EPOG project (Webster et al., 2015, p. 152)

Some victims were lonely and insecure with no friends.

(UK 1)

I chatted to one girl for half a year. She had problems in her family situation. They were all lonely in some way.

(N 2)

Many of the girls were lacking adult contact. They felt safe with me. I was there when they needed me, and I always made time. I learned about their lives and it was important to them.

(N 4)

She had low self-esteem as was overweight.

(UK 1)

These were girls who, quote unquote, were already being abused. They're aware of it, and they play along.

(B 1)[17]

Victim abused by stepfather.

(UK 4)

Deliberately targeted vulnerable young boys in Asia.

(N 3)

Some felt forgotten and lonely at home. Others would talk about how they were being urinated on (by men).

(N 4)

A project parallel to the EUOG study was called ROBERT (Risk-taking online behaviour Empowerment through Research and Training) and had this focused on child victims of online abuse (Quayle, Johnsson, & Loof, 2012). This qualitative study identified 27 children who had been victims online and were in services in six European sites. Psychological need identified included need for connectedness and security; need for identity and self-esteem; need for belonging; and prior abuse and prior sexual experience offline.

Case examples from interviews with young people abused online – ROBERT Project (Quayle et al., 2012 p. 36)

- Before I have always told my boyfriends that 'listen, if it doesn't suit piss off' and that, I have always been the one in control and almost bossed them around. Now he was the one who had taken control.
- I mean on the computer you are just sitting there and writing... you can just write anything. But when you say something then you kind of must get your arguments in order. I mean you really have to have a good reason not to go up against him. When he's sitting there talking to you. That's how I felt at least... just how you said that you didn't feel like it. And that's when he asked why. Like that.
- There had been no decision to go on a date... as in we were meant to spend time and talk. It wasn't intended to be a further contact to meet or spend time... rather it was... I don't know.... I didn't decide much about what was to be done. I guess he was the one who took the initiative or who decided.
- we started just by seeing a little television... casual and everything. Then – what's it called? He said to me that we should go to his room and I should lie down on the bed. I didn't really think about it at the time. So, when I lay down on the bed, he just casually started to take my trousers off and, well things continued from there.

- A young girl who got help
- Um... as then I was... I just wanted it to end. And then I had search online for a while and checked what there was, and I randomly found the Emergency help. That was what caught my eye. I could tell from their website that they really... that they wanted to help people. I could feel it. My gut said yes. So, I sent an email and told my story – a bit. Mostly I had emails, a couple of hours afterwards. Then I replied to that email and later that night they had their msn drop-in so then I spoke to a girl and then I said that I need to see someone, preferably tomorrow. And then I was given Lisa's telephone number and then I rang her. I don't know why I chose to tell at that precise moment... chance I guess. I couldn't take it anymore.

(Quayle et al., 2012, p. 43)

Further online victim profiling

A follow- up study to the EU online grooming project, also EU funded, com-prised a survey of young people who retrospectively reported on their online behaviour as teenagers from three EU countries (UK, Italy and Netherlands) (Davidson et al., 2016). This involved a range of risky online behaviours and a range of potential harms, not only grooming. From this large self-report survey four distinct profiles of online behaviour emerged for this wider category of young people behaviour online (Davidson et al., 2016; DeMarco et al., 2017):

- the **'adapted adolescent'** was the most well-rounded grouping with low levels of anti-social behaviour and risks;
- the **'risk-taking aggressive'** demonstrated anti-social acts and impulsivity in both the real and virtual world;
- the **'inquisitive non-sexual'** youth were most likely to have risk factors linked to online risky behaviour such as sharing information unsafely online; downloading illegal content; and accepting strangers as friends; however they had low levels of sexual requests made of them;
- **'inquisitive sexual'** youth were most likely to have risk factors linked to online sexual risky behaviour and solicitation and were most likely to be solicited by strangers online. Most young people 'never' had to deal with sexually explicit online requests. However, a significant minority did receive such requests 'often' or 'sometimes', when they were between 12 and 16 years old.

It can be seen that the adapted adolescent is similar to the previous resilient style identified from the groomers' accounts. Here there were three types of risk taking noted, the aggressive type more likely to be boys and to exhibit anti-social behaviour. The other risk-taking groups were identified as inquisitive, with the sexual group more likely to be at risk for sexual solicitation online. The non-sexual were more at risk from other sorts of harm online e.g. sharing information.

It was evident in both studies that the majority of young people showed resilience or adaptability online. These are also termed 'digitally resilient'. But those at risk offline are identified as more likely to be at risk online (Livingstone & Palmer, 2012; Webster et al., 2015). There is some research on how vulnerable children face online risk, and on how resilient children cope – but more is needed here, especially in relation to long-term outcomes. A host of risk/vulnerability factors are likely to shape children's online experiences, and this is mediated by the ways in which children develop emotionally, cognitively, in terms of their identity needs, social relationships and need for support, and their peer cultures; however, it remains difficult except in retrospect to pinpoint the moment when children succumb to specific online risks (Livingstone, Davidson & Bryce., 2017).

Protecting children online and safety initiatives

It should be imperative, as Calder rightly argues, to encourage appropriate and safe use of the Internet by assisting children and young people to feel comfortable and supported in navigating the information highway (Calder, 2004). In fact, it has been pointed out that the most critical issue surrounding child abuse and the Internet is child protection, not computer technology (Gallagher, Fraser, Christmann, & Hodgson, 2006) because technology alone is always fallible and offers no guarantees of child protection. However, if the use of technology is combined with education and awareness amongst children, parents and teachers, and effective inter-agency partnership working, it would be easier to maximise the few available resources and move closer to making cyberspace a safe place for young and vulnerable Internet users.

Awareness-raising is a central focus of the EC's Safer Internet Action Plan and this is implemented across Europe through the INSAFE[18] network of national awareness-raising nodes. Thus, a Safer Internet Day is organised by INSAFE each year to promote safer use of online technology and mobile phones. The UK INSAFE network is represented by a consortium of the awareness nodes, CEOP (Child Exploitation and Online Protection Centre), the hotline IWF (Internet Watch Foundation) and the helpline Childline. There are now Awareness Centres belonging to the INSAFE Network in 27 European countries.[19] On a broader international scale centres can also be found in Argentina, Australia, Russia and the US.

Another international initiative is that of the International Association of Internet Hotlines (INHOPE) also founded under the EC's Safer Internet Action Plan in 1999. The principal goal of INHOPE is to represent and support a global network of Internet Hotlines in their attempts to respond to reports of illegal content. Their educational efforts with policy makers and stakeholders aim to provide a way towards better cooperation internationally.

Policy seeking to strengthen child online safety has been introduced; the EU for example has decided to establish 16 as the new baseline age at which children may use social media (it was 13) but with an option for individual Member States to retain the 13 limit (they would need to legislate for this). The 'digital age of consent' refers to the age from which it is legal for data controllers to hold data gathered on children and teenagers. For children under the age of 13, parental consent will be required. This is now a hotly contested topic in the EU with states debating the pros and cons, and this has resulted in wide variance with the age of digital consent currently being 16 in Germany and 13 in Ireland. In the UK the rationale for this, it seems, is a desire to protect children's online privacy and personal data. It is also the case that some parents, particularly in poorer communities, lack basic technical knowledge and skills and their ability to regulate children's behaviour may be limited. Furthermore, the European Commission, in endeavouring to provide a 'better and safer' Internet for children, supports industry self-regulation in dealing with safety and content challenges that may arise[20] and the Council of Europe has provided recommendations to member states on children's online rights.[21]

The G8[22] countries have agreed to a strategy to protect children from sexual abuse on the Internet. Key aims include: the development of an international database of offenders and victims to aid victim identification; and offender monitoring and the targeting of those profiting from the sale of indecent images of children. Work has also been done with Internet service providers and organisations such the Association for Payment Clearing Services in the UK, and other credit card companies in different countries, in attempting to trace individuals using credit cards to access illegal sites containing indecent images of children. An attempt to put mechanisms into place to prevent online payment for illegal sites hosted outside the UK has also been made.

Many police forces both in the EU and the United States are working to trace Internet sex offenders and their victims. In the UK, National and local High Technology Crime Units currently investigate the grooming of children on the Internet and indecent online images of children. Successful prosecutions have been brought under the acts in Scotland, England and Wales, both for 'grooming' online and for the possession of indecent Internet images on the Internet following Operation Ore. This operation was launched following information provided to the UK police by the FBI in the United States, regarding peer-to-peer technology in sharing indecent images of children. The National Crime Squad (which targets serious and violent crime) has made 2,200 convictions since 2002 under Operation Ore.

Organisations like the Virtual Global Taskforce (VGT) and the Internet Watch Foundation (IWF) have made great headway in attempting to protect children online. VGT is an organisation that comprises several international law enforcement agencies from Australia, Canada, the United States, the UK and Interpol. Through the provision of advice and support to children, VGT aims to protect children online and has set up a bogus website to attract online groomers. The Internet Watch Foundation (IWF) is one of the main government watchdogs in this area.

International law enforcement in the child Internet abuse area has developed considerably in recent years but barriers to effectiveness include the preponderance of a small number of well-resourced policing units in industrialised countries leading the way and considerable differences in domestic law. Effective international law enforcement is essential in combating Internet child abuse given the global nature of the offending behaviour, and good international links should be established at local level (Martellozzo, 2013).

Interpol has a network of 187 countries and facilitates the sharing of information between police forces; as such, it provides the principal focus for much international law enforcement activity against child Internet abuse. However, the effectiveness of Interpol activity in different countries is limited despite treaty agreements and conventions by the extent to which the agreements have been ratified in national law. Interpol activity extends to many different geographical regions and regions have sub-directorates. The International Child Sexual Exploitation image database is managed by Interpol (ICSE DB) is a powerful intelligence and investigative tool which allows specialised investigators to share data internationally with police forces. Available through INTERPOL's secure global police communications system (I-247), the ICSE DB uses sophisticated image comparison software to make connections between victims and places. Backed by the G8 and funded by the European Commission, ICSE DB was launched in March 2009 as the successor to the INTERPOL Child Abuse Image Database (ICAID) which had been in use since 2001.[23]

The Europol Cybercrime Centre (EC3) based in the Hague has identified key threats in the area of online child sexual exploitation as follows:

1 **Peer-to-peer (P2P) networks and anonymised access like Darknet networks** (e.g. Tor). These computer environments remain the main platform to access child abuse material and the principal means for non-commercial distribution.

2 **Live-streaming of child sexual abuse.** Facilitated by new technology, one trend concerns the profit-driven abuse of children overseas, live in front of a camera at the request of Westerners. To a lesser degree, there is also some evidence that forms of commercial child sexual exploitation such as on-demand live streaming of abuse is also contributing to the rise of the amount of CSEM online.

3 **Live distant child abuse** has the most obvious links with commercial distribution of CSEM. As new and/or unseen CSEM is valuable currency within the offending community, live distant abuse is therefore a way to not only acquire more CSEM, but to simultaneously generate material with a high 'value'.

4 **Online solicitation and sexual extortion**. The growing number of children and teenagers who own smartphones has been accompanied by the production of self-generated indecent material. Such material, initially shared with innocent intent, often finds its way to 'collectors', who often proceed to exploit the victim, in particular by means of extortion.

5 **Networking and forensic awareness of offenders**. Offenders learn from the mistakes of those that have been apprehended by law enforcement (Source: EC3 2018).[24]

The EC3 runs produces a series of reports and runs campaigns focusing upon CSE and CSA amongst young people such as the 'Say No' Campaign[25] which includes a range of resources including videos (e.g. Anna Story[26]).

Global commitments have been made to protect children in the online and offline environments. In 1996 the First World Congress against the Commercial Sexual Exploitation of Children (CSEC) was held leading to a global declaration and timetable for action that was adopted by 122 countries. The Second World Congress was held in 2001, resulting in the Yokohama Global Commitment which commits states to national action following the First. This commitment requires states to address harms caused by new technologies. The Third World Congress led to the development of the Rio Pact which specifically refers to the prevention of online indecent child images and grooming. The Virtual Global Taskforce (VGT) has member agencies in the US, Canada, Australia and Italy. The Virtual Global Taskforce (VGT) claims that law enforcement agencies, including members of the VGT, have made 'substantial headway' in facilitating cross-jurisdictional investigations and information sharing.

Microsoft, Facebook and the National Center for Missing and Exploited Children (NCMEC) have developed a PhotoDNA programme to combat indecent child images. NCMEC's programme, using image-matching technology created by Microsoft Research in collaboration with Dartmouth College in the UK, provides online service providers an effective tool to take proactive action to stop the distribution of known images of child sexual abuse online. The PhotoDNA is provided free of charge to appropriate organisations.[27]

It is clear that much has been done, and continues to be done internationally to protect children online; however, recent literature reviews suggest that while many safety initiatives have been tried by diverse stakeholders at the national and international level, very few have been independently evaluated. This makes it difficult to determine what works and why. Such evaluations as are undertaken tend to focus on immediate outcomes (reach, appeal, etc.) rather than long term reduction in harm or improvement in well-being. Box 6.3 outlines the main points concerning increasing child safety online.

Box 6.3

Summary of child safety online messages

- Schools use a range of strategies to implement e-safety priorities – including developing children's critical abilities – but there is mixed evidence of improvement, and such programmes tend to take a standard approach and may not be suited to the specific needs of more vulnerable children;
- Awareness raising campaigns such as Safer Internet Day have been instrumental in changing attitudes and practices, but the longer-term impact of such event has not been evaluated;
- A range of industry initiatives exist in the form of agreements with the government, individual company policies and initiatives, and industry level initiatives, but there is evidence to suggest that

industry could do more to strengthen collaborative partnerships
particularly with law enforcement;
- Building children's digital resilience should have a twin focus on
developing critical ability and technical competency in terms of
education, as well as supporting children online and offline through
constructive and informed parenting practices, through safety and
privacy by design and by improving the digital expertise of relevant
welfare and other professionals who work with children. (Livingstone
et al., 2017, p. 2).

The role of industry in online safety

The role of industry in child online protection has been acknowledged for some
time now. As the providers of Internet access as well as the devices that enable
us to get online, partners from industry play a key role in many aspects of
online safety for children and young people. The ITU has produced Guidelines
for Industry on Child Online Protection[28] which addresses four key components
of industry:

- ICT industry as a whole;
- broadcasters;
- Internet Service Providers (ISPs);
- mobile operators.

The guidelines contain some key areas for consideration which are a helpful
starting point for countries embarking on the creation of an online safety strategy. The Internet will never be a completely safe space in the same way that the
world we live in cannot be. Action is therefore needed to provide users with the
technology and understanding needed to reduce the risks and develop appropriate strategies to deal with them. A balance is needed between awareness
raising and more technical solutions (tools) which allow users to make informed
choices. A positive relationship with industry is crucial in establishing the most
effective online safety provision, and there are examples where such partnerships have produced very positive outcomes. Collaboration between industry
and the European Commission has led to the development of Safer Social Networking Principles and the GSMA has produced a framework for safer mobile
use for young people to which all members have subscribed[29] (GSMA, 2014).

Perhaps one of the most significant actions taken by industry is in the fight
against online child sexual abuse images. The Mobile Alliance Against Child Sexual Abuse Content is an alliance founded by an international group of mobile

operators within the GSMA with the key aim of obstructing the use of the mobile environment by individuals or organisations wishing to consume or profit from child sexual abuse content.

Box 6.4

Measures required by industry for child safety online:

- Implementation of technical mechanisms to prevent access to websites identified by an appropriate agency as hosting child sexual abuse content;
- Implementation of notice and take down processes to enable the removal of any child sexual abuse content posted on their own services;
- Supporting and promoting hotlines or other mechanisms for customers to report child sexual abuse content discovered on the Internet or mobile content services;
- Although much has been done by industry, recent findings from our EC-funded study in four EU countries (UK, Ireland, Italy and the Netherlands) suggest that with regards to industry safety practice some young people complained that safety procedures and report mechanisms were too complicated to follow and there were also many misconceptions about reporting inappropriate material which stopped individuals from acting. This research was based upon surveys with young people and the police and industry case studies. The findings indicate that good industry practice safeguarding children online is as follows:
- A team of trusted administrators and moderators with standard procedures in place to protect site's users is a basic requirement;
- Utilising automated systems in conjunction with human moderators to ensure coverage and protection of users is recommended;
- Standardisation of procedures and thresholds constituting inappropriate and problematic content;
- Site rules which reduce the risk of under 18s being inappropriately approached by an adult;
- Site provides law enforcement with information on a user complaint or legal action;
- Proactive approach to collaborate with other industry partners.

Good industry general practice needs to include an understanding of the criminal law and communication with its representatives as well as internal policy in protecting users in a 'pre-crime' model and an appreciation and use of software and technology in assisting with prevention and in intervention. In addition, developing technologies bring dynamic risk therefore new strategies and innovative solutions are of paramount importance in safeguarding children's online world (Davidson et al., 2016).

The role of the police

While there is little recent research addressing the experience of the police in responding to online child abuse, our EC research sheds light on this critical issue in exploring the role of the police in investigating online child sexual abuse and collaboration with industry. The key findings based upon national police surveys in three EU countries (the UK, Italy and the Netherlands) (Davidson et al., 2016) are as follows:

- There are substantial challenges in investigating and prosecuting online child sexual abuse cases across jurisdictions given differing legal frameworks and legal definitions of child (age of consent to sexual relations differs across the EU);
- Law enforcement regularly encounter online child abuse cases, this was most marked in the UK; Police officers from the UK encounter online grooming cases and indecent image collection cases in equal measure; The clear majority of cases are reported to local police officers by phone in the UK (approximately half of which are reported to specialist units) and are made in person to a local police officer in Italy and the Netherlands;
- More psychological support is required for police officers, with calls for mandatory counselling and external support to be provided and it must be more accessible to investigative officers;
- There is a lack of police communication, resources, standardisation and adequate focused training;
- Police and industry professionals often differ in aims, objectives and desired outcomes in terms of strategy, operations and prioritisation when dealing with online CSA;
- There is a 'temporal incongruence' in dealing with online CSA, where the development of children, ICT devices/platforms, legislative development/ ascension of policy is 'out of sync' with one another;
- Uneven resource allocation is a reality in investigating online CSA as unequal capabilities between industry and police;
- When done well, working partnerships 'work'. They are the way forward. Models and frameworks of good practice should be sought and standardised. Prioritisation of intervention & prevention must be of a multi-disciplinary, public health approach in which all agents involved standardise their approaches, with clear and coherent primary aims and objectives;

- The invisibility and anonymity of offenders particularly on the dark or hidden web poses considerable challenges for law enforcement and little specialist training is available on this area;
- Those police officers who were often involved with online CSA cases who had received specific training, perceived themselves as 'excellently' or at least 'adequately' trained, and in most cases routinely explored online risks with child victims and investigated the online behaviours of offenders. Those who were not trained and had not been involved in investigations of this type of crime rarely routinely explored the online behaviours of victims and offenders. This might strongly limit their ability to detect and deal with online CSA. This group of officers also reported the most effective working relationships with other agencies;
- The police would welcome increased collaboration with industry in the online CSA area including: Mentoring, joint training initiatives; industry points of contact; joint work or task groups and input to educational awareness initiatives;
- There are some good examples of effective inter-agency practice, but this varies at national and international level and there is no standardisation of practice, although charities such as the Children's Society have developed some very good resources that guide the work of practitioners in this area such as the 'Seen and Heard' training package for healthcare professionals which identifies the signs of abuse.[30]

(Davidson et al., 2016)[31]

Awareness programmes and safety strategies: international examples

Measures to protect children include school-based programmes aiming to educate children, parents and teachers about the dangers posed by sex offenders in cyberspace. Such programmes are now routinely delivered to secondary school children in the UK and other countries such as the US, New Zealand and Canada; some examples are provided below.

In the United States the National Center for Missing and Exploited Children (NCMEC) has developed the. NetSmartz interactive, educational safety resource that uses age appropriate, 3-D activities to teach children and teens how to be safer when using the Internet. NetSmartz has been implemented in more than 3,000 BGCA Clubs nationally, serving more than 3.3 million young people. The programme provides parents, children and teachers with an overview of online risks. It argues that in addition to the useful educational information available on the Internet, a great deal of Internet content is not appropriate for children.

This content can include nudity or other sexually explicit material; hate or racist websites; promotional material about tobacco, alcohol or drugs; graphic violence; information about satanic or cult groups; or even recipes for making bombs and explosives at home.[32]

CEOP's ThinkUKnow Programme is now delivered to children throughout the UK. The programme seeks to impart Internet safety advice to children and young people aged 5-16. The programme includes a presentation delivered in schools (usually) and a website with different sections for different age groups, parents, teachers and trainers. Trainers are encouraged to report the number of children trained via a website link (they must go on to the website to do this). Safety advice is also provided on the website. The evaluation of CEOP's ThinkuKnow (TUK)[33] Internet safety programme summarised the findings about risk-taking on the Internet:

- a high proportion of children reported having engaged in elevated risk behaviour online (defined by degree to which they share information with and interact with strangers);
- a sizable proportion say they will continue with such behaviour (particularly 13+);
- interacting with strangers (i.e. adding them as ISM or Facebook friends and exchanging messages) is becoming an accepted behaviour not perceived as 'risk-taking'.

(Davidson, Lorenz, Grove-Hills, & Martellozo, 2009)

The UK Council for Child Internet Safety (UKCCIS) established in March 2009 unites over 100 organisations from the public and private sector working with Government to deliver recommendations from Dr Tanya Byron's report 'Safer Children in a Digital World'. Reporting directly to the Prime Minister, the Council seeks to improve the regulation and education around Internet use, tackling problems around online bullying, safer search features and violent video games. This coalition of experts and organisations will ensure that parents and young people have a voice in the development of an Internet Safety Strategy.

The strategy seeks to:

- establish a comprehensive public information and awareness and child Internet safety campaign across Government and industry including a 'one-stop-shop' on child Internet safety;
- provide specific measures to support vulnerable children and young people, such as taking down illegal Internet sites that promote harmful behaviour;
- promote responsible advertising to children online;

- establish voluntary codes of practice for user-generated content sites, making such sites commit to take down inappropriate content within a given time.

While the expansion of the Internet and the proliferation of information technology have created new opportunities for those who engage in illegal activities (Quayle & Taylor, 2003), the area of digital forensics has grown rapidly as well (Ferraro & Casey, 2005). This has helped in the discovery of new forms of criminal activity. As already known, sex offenders use the Internet to access indecent images of children, to select victims for abuse and to communicate with other sex offenders. This activity has expanded so much that law enforcement agencies have difficulties tracking down child victims and perpetrators involved unless they have the capability of professional digital forensics and intelligence.

Some good awareness-raising initiatives have been conducted recently in developing countries. The *Microsoft Internet Safety, Security & Privacy Initiative for Nigeria* (MISSPIN) began in July 2008 and was designed to move young people in Nigeria away from cybercrime to 'more positive online engagement'. Microsoft worked with a small group of young people who became ambassadors for the project – visiting schools and running workshops. All schools received *Digital Literacy Curriculum* CDs to provide training for both staff and students. (The digital literacy curriculum is also available online) and in Egypt the Suzanne Mubarak Women's International Peace Movement launched the Cyber Peace Initiative in 2007. One of the actions was to establish a youth Internet safety focus group to spread awareness about Internet safety issues to empower children and young people with the ability to identify harmful content and use computers, the Internet, IT tools and mobile phone services safely and responsibly. The group 'Net Aman' was made up of 11 members aged between 18 and 28 and had four major goals:

- research the current e-safety needs of young people in Egypt to better understand the wide range of concerns shared by youth and their families;
- assess the most appropriate guidelines for young people in safe use of the Internet;
- create and design effective education and awareness resources to communicate e-safety information to young people and their parents;
- contribute to wider strategic programmes and assess them from the youth perspective.

The Bahraini National Strategy for Child Internet Safety was developed following a study undertaken in 2010 (Davidson & Martellozzo, 2010);[34] the following recommendations for action in Bahrain can be seen in Box 6.5. Notably a follow-up study (Davidson & Martellozo, 2016) indicated that some of these recommendations have been followed.

Box 6.5

Recommendations for child online safety in Bahrain

- A committee or working group should be established to set out and ensure implementation of the Kingdom's child e-safety strategy. The Bahrain Committee for Child Internet Safety (BCCIS) should include representatives from: Government ministries; the legal profession; relevant NGOs; child welfare organisations; academia; ISPs; TRA and key community groups. The strategy should be informed by the findings from this research;
- Planned child abuse legislation should be implemented (this includes child pornography and online grooming) and implementation should be monitored by BCCIS;
- The role of the Bahraini Child Welfare Center should be enhanced to include therapeutic provision for child victims of Internet related and other forms of abuse. The centre should play an active role in training other professionals working with children;
- Training for police officer, sentencers and prosecutors should be introduced to ensure effective implementation of the new legislation;
- ISPs and the Telecommunications Regulatory Authority should play an active role in providing safety advice and technical advice on computer protection;
- A comprehensive Internet safety training programme should be developed for both the private and public school sectors as part of the national curriculum. The programme should draw upon good practice from programmes developed in other countries, but should take account of the cultural context in Bahrain. An evaluation component should be built into the programme from the outset to enable monitoring and good quality control. Young people should be consulted on the most appropriate and effective means of delivering the programme and on programme design;
- Schools should introduce a designated e-safety staff function to ensure that programmes are delivered on a rolling basis in each school and that outreach safety advice work is undertaken with parents and with communities;
- Schools and NGOs should play an active role in working with parents to raise awareness about Internet safety and about the nature of young people's online behaviour. Families in socially deprived areas might benefit from more informal advice offered by community groups and via Mosques;

- A far reaching media campaign should be organised by BCCIS using a wide range of media including: newspapers; television and radio. Safety messages should be clear and simple and designed to appeal to different audiences;
- The e-safety strategy should be developed and implemented in stages within a specified time frame. Progress against agreed objectives should be monitored and evaluated one full year following initial implementation to enable further development of the strategy.

Discussion

The world is increasingly inter-connected – the advent of the Internet and mobile technology is now all pervasive. We live in world that is more fluid where travel is easier and where geographical boundaries no longer always serve to contain and restrict populations. This inter-connectivity brings with it many positives including the ease with which it is possible to communicate with others around the world and a richness of diversity and multi-culturalism. The rise of electronic communication and this ease of movement has also resulted in and exacerbated some forms of child abuse and exploitation. The online victimisation of children continues to escalate; it also the case that diverse cultures have different views about the role of children, what age constitutes childhood and the treatment of children based upon cultural and historical norms. Rapid global development in Internet access has provided the opportunity for children to interact with friends both virtual and real, and to access information in a way that previous generations would not have thought possible, while social networking sites provide a platform for peer to peer communication previously unknown. There is increasing research evidence to suggest that young people do not distinguish between online and offline environments as the full range of digital media has become central to their lives. It seems more relevant to refer to the converged online and offline environment when referring to young people's behaviour. Although most of the research has been conducted in the West, there is increasing evidence from developing nations which indicates that digital media transcend geographical and social boundaries uniting children in a shared enthusiasm for modern technology and there is evidence to suggest that significant moves are underway to protect young people online. Although the benefits of the Internet outweigh the negative aspects, children are exposed to risk online and safety awareness education is necessary in the context of relevant and effective child safeguarding legislation. The increasingly inter-connectivity and global nature of the Internet calls for a global and coordinated response to protect children; unfortunately legislation and safety practice at national level vary enormously from country to country, inevitably leaving some children more vulnerable to abuse and exploitation.

Notes

1 www.lse.ac.uk/business-and-consultancy/consulting/consulting-reports/childrens-online-activities-risks-and-safety
2 The research informed the UK Governments Internet safety strategy (11/2017) as set out in the Green Paper.
3 OFCOM (2018) Children and Parents Media Use and Attitudes Report. www.ofcom.org.uk/__data/assets/pdf_file/0020/108182/children-parents-media-use-attitudes-2017.pdf
4 www.internetworldstats.com/stats3.htm
5 www.cwin.org.np/
6 *www.saferinternet.ru*
7 www.internetworldstats.com/stats1.htm
8 Pew Research Centre (2015) *Cell phones in Africa* www.pewglobal.org/2015/04/15/cell-phones-in-africa-communication-lifeline/
9 www.childrenatrisk.eu/robert/public/Online_behaviour_related_to_sexual_abuse.pdf
10 www.safernet.org.br/site
11 *www.barnardos.org.uk/over_the_internet__under_the_radar_literature_review.pdf*
12 file:///C:/Users/david/Downloads/RapidEvidenceAssessment-QuantifyingtheExtentofOnline-FacilitatedChildSexualAbuse.pdf
13 https://ec.europa.eu/home-affairs/what-is-new/news/news/2016/20160317_2_en
14 www.nspcc.org.uk/globalassets/documents/research-reports/online-child-sexual-abuse-images.pdf
15 https://annualreport.iwf.org.uk/
16 *www.missingkids.com/en_us/publications/NC81.pdf*
17 UK groomer ids give prison number (001–009) and then individual number for the UK group. Belgium 'B' and Norwegian 'N' cases identified by individual groomer number.
18 www.saferinternet.org/
19 https://ec.europa.eu/digital-single-market/en/news/launch-european-awareness-raising-network-insafe
20 https://ec.europa.eu/digital-single-market/en/content/safer-internet-better-internet-kids
21 www.coe.int/en/web/portal/-/council-of-europe-gives-recommendations-to-member-states-on-children-s-rights-in-the-digital-environment
22 Canada, France, Germany, Italy, Japan, Russia, UK and the United States.
23 www.interpol.int/Crime-areas/Crimes-against-children/Victim-identification
24 www.europol.europa.eu/crime-areas-and-trends/crime-areas/child-sexual-exploitation
25 www.europol.europa.eu/activities-services/public-awareness-and-prevention-guides/online-sexual-coercion-and-extortion-crime
26 *www.youtube.com/watch?v=5ttHYODhenY*), posters and web guides that seek to raise awareness about consent issues amongst young people:
27 https://news.microsoft.com/features/microsofts-photodna-protecting-children-and-businesses-in-the-cloud/
28 www.itu.int/en/cop/Pages/default.aspx
29 www.gsma.com/publicpolicy/european-framework-safer-mobile-use-younger-teenagers-children
30 www.childrenssociety.org.uk/what-we-do/commission-us/seen-and-heard
31 *www.euchildonlinesafetyproject.co.uk*
32 www.netsmartz.org/Overview/AboutUs
33 www.thinkuknow.co.uk/
34 *www.tra.org.bh/media/document/TRAAnnualReport2010_en.pdf*

7 Conclusion and key messages

In the introductory chapter, key contemporary issues were identified, and these have been explicated in the chapters that followed. This chapter seeks to revisit these issues and draw together key messages and potential ways forward in tackling them. These are summarised in Figure 7.1.

Ethics and child voice

The Rights of the Child are fundamental to understanding and intervening in abuse, with emphasis on the child's voice and participation with services and agencies. This book started with an outline of children's rights, in order to set the scene for the most important aspect of safeguarding principles. Other aspects such as harm done to children is of course critical, but even if long-term harm did not follow, abuse would still be morally wrong and have no place in a civilised society (Childs-Smith, 2017).

The Convention of the Rights of the Child, signed up to by most nations, is therefore an important step in at least ensuring that child safeguarding is accepted internationally in principle. However, the convention does not have legal force and does not require consistency of approach internationally, so national laws and policies are critical to enforcing such principles. Individual countries interpret the statutes in their own way. It would be desirable to have consistency on this, with nations using similar definitions and ways of assessing abuse and related exploitation. One of the biggest obstacles is the lack of international consensus on a definition of childhood. Wide variation exists in the age of consent to sexual relations around the world, causing considerable barriers in investigating and prosecuting cross jurisdiction child abuse cases and in reaching internationally shared definitions of child abuse.

Such rights extend to the digital world, although this is not currently reflected in the UNCRC which should be updated to include online rights. Some have argued strongly for children's digital rights. Baroness Beeban

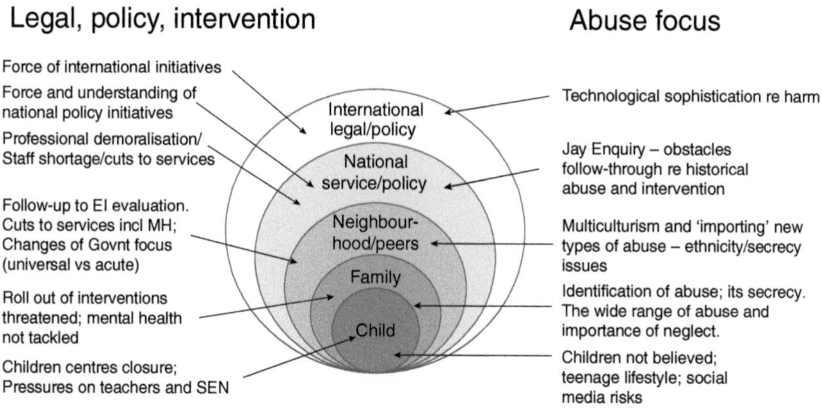

Legal, policy, intervention   Abuse focus

Force of international initiatives

Force and understanding of national policy initiatives

Professional demoralisation/ Staff shortage/cuts to services

Follow-up to EI evaluation. Cuts to services incl MH; Changes of Govnt focus (universal vs acute)

Roll out of interventions threatened; mental health not tackled

Children centres closure; Pressures on teachers and SEN

International legal/policy

National service/policy

Neighbour-hood/peers

Family

Child

Technological sophistication re harm

Jay Enquiry – obstacles follow-through re historical abuse and intervention

Multiculturism and 'importing' new types of abuse – ethnicity/secrecy issues

Identification of abuse; its secrecy. The wide range of abuse and importance of neglect.

Children not believed; teenage lifestyle; social media risks

Figure 7.1 Contemporary issues in child abuse revisited

Kidron developed in 2015 the 5Rights Framework which sets out children's digital rights. The framework was developed on the basis of research exploring children and young people's views. The five central rights are described as follows in Box 7.1:[1]

Box 7.1

The online human rights of the child

● **Right to remove** - What they have added and what has been added about them;
● **Right to know** - The right to know who and what and why and for what purposes, their data is being exchanged;
● **Right to safety and support** - From illegal and upsetting content and behaviour;
● **Right to informed and conscious choice** - Children looped in to technology that is deliberately designed to keep them attached;
● **Right to digital literacy** - Understanding the purpose of the technology.

Linked to such rights are the 'child's voice' - the principle that we need to listen to children to understand better their experience and to allow them to have at least some say in the actions taken which will affect their future life when abuse is discovered. The courts now make provision for listening to the testimony of children and young people, with varying success and have introduced special measures to ensure that children's experience in court is less intrusive. However, the research evidence suggests that children and their families still have a largely negative experience of the justice system from the investigation to the court, and there is much to be done in ensuring that child victims have full access to justice. Evaluated practice in other countries such as Canada and Norway suggest that not only does a more child-centred approach to criminal justice improve upon the child's experience, it also results in higher prosecution and conviction rates. With some exceptions in this area, the criminal justice system at present still serves to punish and humiliate the child victim and this is unacceptable. (See 'Making noise CSAFE)'[2] project for a recent investigation of the child's voice in cases of CSE (Childs-Smith, 2017).

Problems also remain in the social care system, where social workers are directed to ask children about their experience. Obstacles however abound – the tools which aid with collecting information with children, the skills needed for eliciting the information, issues around what can count as evidence and the many psychological obstacles for disclosure by children and young people following abuse experience. These obstacles to children disclosing abuse include threats of removal and separation to threaten the child's security and sense of loyalty given their attachment to their parents. This may lead to feelings of guilt. Other impediments are more affective-cognitive and concern whether the immature child's mind can encompass identifying and relating abusive experience, particularly if told to keep it secret. Psychological defences may relate to denial or 'amnesia' of abuse, or simply not being able to find words to describe horrific experience. It leads to many dilemmas.

Professionals too find it difficult to talk to children about their abuse experience, and this may account for why children are sometimes not asked 'in case it upsets them'. But numerous policies have now been identified in the UK that listening to the child is a central plank of social and criminal justice policy. There is too much evidence of children being overlooked, their views dismissed and their reputations tarnished in the collecting of evidence. One instance of such tarnishing of reputation is among adolescents, including those in care, whose behaviours, symptoms and lifestyle may antagonise professionals who fail to recognise abuse they might be experiencing, and inappropriately see them as making active choices and having control over their exploitation. This was highlighted in the UK Rotherham reports (Jay, 2014) and led to extensive abuse being left uncovered by police and social workers despite the young people affected coming forward to disclose. As a society we need to consider how we view teenagers and still accord them the protection needed as individuals who have not yet reached the age of majority and who are still very much in need of care and protection.

Key messages

- Rights of the Child need further underlining internationally, and must be even further embedded into policy and practice;

- The digital rights of the child must be recognised and enshrined in an updated version of the UNCRC;
- The child's voice needs to be heard in relation to their well-being and decisions made about their lives. More sophisticated methods of discovering children's experience and wishes needs to be established and mainstreamed;
- The child's voice must be heard more in criminal justice proceedings and the process must urgently become more child centred, really catering for the support needs of children and young people;
- We should be wary of tarnishing the reputation of young people where their behaviour is considered risky or anti-social, such that their disclosure of abuse is not believed. Young people are still developmentally vulnerable despite having greater independence than in previous years.

Internationalism and culture

We can no longer simply seek to solely minimise child abuse in our own local area or country; we need also to look worldwide as the world has become increasingly inter-connected within the context of globalisation and increased Internet penetration even in the remotest regions. Besides the obvious ethical imperative, this is because of movements of populations to and from our country, and access of children for abuse online through social media across geographic boundaries. It also has implications for practitioners who come to work in the UK, who need to hold the same values relating to Children's Rights and a developmental/health model of harm to a child. We need to avoid cultural relativism in investigating abuse, and also to overcome constraints on investigation of families from different cultures where there are biases to what their likely parenting is, or for fear of being called racist. Policies on children need to be harmonised in Europe but also ideally worldwide. The wide varieties of abuse occurring in other cultures needs to be recognised, understood and opposed.

Of course, children are raised in very different contexts and conditions from those in the UK - sometimes harsher due to poverty or third world conditions, sometimes better due to stable family and community settings in child-centred cultures. Yet the developmental issues arising from neglect or abuse of children occur cross-culturally. It behoves every society to attend to their children's well-being to ensure the future flourishing of the society.

Whilst most neglect and abuse is universal, some aspects such as FGM are specific to cultures, and others, such as child trafficking and slavery are due to economic conditions and increasingly organised international criminal networks. But all of these will increasingly affect Western countries such as the UK. So, our policy and practice on child safeguarding needs to incorporate guidance on how to recognise and overcome such types of exploitation and abuse, whilst working proactively with and across communities to foster effective communication and shared understanding.

Again, online forms of abuse are implicated here, where the perpetrators of online exploitation may reside in different countries to the children they are targeting. Geographic boundaries pose no barrier for online solicitation and other forms of child abuse such as live streaming using webcams.[3]

Culture has been identified as an issue in identifying and investigating abuse. Cultural relativism states that some forms of abuse are common and acceptable in certain cultures. For example, physical abuse is often seen as more acceptable in African-Caribbean cultures. But universal indicators of abuse are required and should be applied consistently with a view to the child's healthy development and human rights. Families, and wider groups, can be mistaken in repeating common practice from their own childhoods on the basis it is traditional, acceptable or 'never did me any harm'. This is not an adequate justification. Practitioners need to be wary of 'normalisation' grooming practice which is common in justifying sexual abuse but can actually apply to any in self- or group justification of hostile or neglectful behaviour.

This is an area of research that has also been neglected in children's use of digital media, where there is some recent evidence that cultural issues underpin online experience. For example, in some cultures the very act of interacting with members of the opposite sex on social media can lead to parental physical abuse of children. Whilst recent and current research provides an important insight into children's use of digital media in the United States and the EU, scant regard has been paid to the complex interplay between children's online and offline lives in more traditional communities and regions, and in developing countries. The research that has been conducted has tended to focus upon relatively uncontroversial issues related to digital media use and has not attempted to address more challenging obstacles to general child protection and safeguarding which are sometimes entrenched in patriarchal traditions that have long cast women and children as second-class citizens. For example, research in the Middle East has pointed to gender issues in the use of digital media with girls punished with extreme physical abuse for removing the hijab and interacting with boys on social media sites; some of the girls in this study went on to attempt suicide. In some countries intra-familial abuse is not recognised in law or punished in any way, as it is seen as the man's absolute right to control the family unit (Davidson & Martellozzo, 2010). It is very difficult to disentangle these complex issues and to focus on children's use of digital media and online abuse in isolation and without reference to their wider experience of the world. This presents a challenge, but it is one that must be addressed if we are to develop effective international safeguarding initiatives.

Key messages

- Child safeguarding policies need to be systematised internationally;
- The internationalisation of safeguarding policies must take account of the experience of other cultures and regions, not just focusing upon experience in the West and if practice can be readily transplanted into other regions;
- Policy and practice on digital media needs to set against the backdrop of general child safeguarding and child protection and not addressed in isolation;
- Children's digital rights must be acknowledged and added to the UNCRC;
- There needs to be a shared international definition of childhood and consensus on the age of informed consent to sexual relations and on the age of criminal responsibility;
- Practitioners need to be aware of a wider range of abuses, including those more common in other cultures and children trafficked across national borders;
- Practitioners need to put the child's developmental needs and rights ahead of respect for diverse cultural practice. They need to be wary of cultural relativism in condoning abuse and resist concerns about being considered racist if they investigate abuse in families from other ethnicities.

National policy response

The raft of legislative measures which has been introduced in England and Wales to protect children from sexual abuse and violence, outlined in earlier chapters, has been extensive and sustained. Some have been evaluated, yet some evaluations have floundered due to service cuts (for example cuts to Children's Centres and Early Intervention initiatives), and for others (such as the Jay report) processes are still underway. Some have proved easier to implement than others. For example, the Serious Crime Act 2015 which extended the definition of child cruelty and introduced a legal duty for professionals to report FGM in England and Wales also made important changes to the Sexual Offences Act 2003 in respect of the online grooming of a child. But this did little to address the problem of online grooming as the defendant had to communicate with a child online and to meet, arrange to meet or travel to meet the child with the intention of sexually abusing the child. This is to evidence of sexual intent. The offence of 'sexual communication with a child' was introduced through an amendment to the Serious Crime Act 2015 but not in force until 3 April 2017. The new offence required the communication to be intentionally made and either inherently sexual, objectively sexual or designed to prompt a sexual response, irrespective of whether the first communication was sexual.

The Sexual Offences Act 2003 which formed the key plank of the sexual abuse criminal legislation was important in terms of contemporary issues in including online grooming of a child for the purpose of sexual abuse for the first time (s15).[4] The last five years have seen a raft of key child protection inquiries and the introduction of new legislative measures which have seriously broadened the scope of child abuse and put more pressure on practitioners and on health, social care and criminal justice services. This adds to the anxieties in these professions where child safety is concerned. It also shows publicly the extent that child abuse has existed historically in some of our institutions, among celebrity culture and higher in the establishment. The aftermath of this is yet to be played out and the response by the criminal justice service to perpetrators, but also the help offered to victims of abuse many years earlier, is yet to be determined. In terms of contemporary forms of abuse, the policy response includes the Modern Slavery Act 2015 which consolidated and clarified existing legislation on trafficking for child trafficking and enforced child labour. Similarly, the Digital Economy Act 2017 introduced and strengthened age verification measures for children in relation to online issues. Society therefore has a substantial task in absorbing such a range of abuses, those current, those past, those more of the future and those from international sources. The area is now an extensive concern for everyday life and for professionals involved with children and with those who have suffered past abuse.

Key messages

- Professionals need continuous updating on policy and legislation in this broadened child abuse arena. Some key specialised expertise is required, for example in online harms. Ongoing training is required. This may be helped by use of multi-agency fora;
- Boundaries between types of abuse and harms are harder to establish. For example, forced labour and physical abuse; online sexting and potential grooming for offline abuse; children identified as vulnerable from prior familial abuse becoming at risk for other forms of harm;
- Images of offline familial child abuse are the basis for sharing of indecent child images and potential 'currency' in other online criminal activity and linked to further online grooming of children for abuse;
- Professionals need to be alerted to potentially new forms or modes of abuse, and new settings in which these might occur.

Identification of abuse and its impacts

Accurate identification of children who are being abused, and accurately identifying characteristics of that abuse, are central to effective safeguarding services. However, such assessments become more complex as the range of abuse experience has widened (e.g. emotional abuse, online grooming for abuse) and the known impacts have deepened to cover biological, social and psychological impacts. Because there are more aspects to identifying abuse now than would have been true two decades ago or longer, it is increasingly important to improve professionals' recognition and identification of the signs of abuse (Cossar et al., 2013; Cossar & Neil, 2015).The impacts are now known to be lifelong for some individuals and to have health consequences into old age. The impacts involve health, social care and CJS services, of both children and adults and constitute a public health concern. We have a wider range of theoretical models to explain abuse and its impacts – attachment theory encompasses much around damaged trust and relationships leading from abuse.

Social-ecological theory helps us understand systemic factors in society which make abuse more likely – poverty and deprivation, family breakdown and conflict (Belsky, 1980; Garbarino, 1997). These can emanate from wider social structures to impact directly on the child as an individual. Biological models indicate a range of pathways through which abuse can result in long-term damage. A recent one concerns how epigenetics may impart risks, through the impacts of trauma on gene-expression. This would affect children differentially, some more susceptible than others (Barnes et al., 2005). Whilst ethically the abusive behaviour is equally deplorable, the genetic profiling of children will allow us to determine ultimately the extent of the developmental damage caused. Lifespan theories of development trace problem functioning back to childhood experience and its consequences through different transitions – school leaving, pregnancy/birth, partner loss, menopause etc. This means multiple sources of evidence need to be understood in viewing the cascade impacts of abuse, but also that multi-professionals need to collect information on early life abuse to better understand the causes of illness or disorder. There is now greater understanding of resilience, which can act through biological, social and psychological mechanisms (DuMont et al., 2007). Resilience is likely to be common given the widespread nature of positive experience and relationships and well-meaning adults. We need to harness such naturally occurring aids, whilst still decrying abuse on ethical grounds when harm is reduced.

Indeed recent findings from the IICSA Research Team (C. Fisher, Goldsmith, Hurcombe, & Soares, 2017) Rapid Evidence Assessment on the impact of CSA suggest that outcomes are far reaching and can be grouped into seven key areas:[5]

1   **Physical health & Physical injuries**: High BMI, problems related to childbirth, unexplained medical problems;

2 **Emotional well-being, mental health and internalising behaviours**: emotional distress, trauma/PTSD, anxiety, depression;

3 **Externalising behaviours**: Substance misuse, 'risky' and inappropriate sexual behaviours, offending;

4 **Interpersonal relationships**: Reduced relationship satisfaction and stability and issues with intimacy and parent-child relationships;

5 **Socioeconomic**: Lower educational attainment, higher unemployment, financial instability; homelessness;

6 **Religious and spiritual belief**: Disillusionment with religion, faith as a coping mechanism;

7 **Vulnerability to revictimisation**: Sexual revictimisation in childhood and adulthood and other types of victimisation.

Source: (C. Fisher et al., 2017, p.11)

The investigators state

the way in which the outcomes or impacts in each of these areas emerge and subsequently play out in the lives of victims and survivors constitutes a complex and dynamic process. The outcomes in these areas have been shown to interact with, cause, compound or (in some cases) help to mitigate outcomes in other areas. Outcomes can occur, or recur, at any stage of the victim and survivor's life course.

(C. Fisher et al., 2017, p.11)

Abuse and its perpetration are not gendered overall. However, some types of abuse are more likely to be of females with male perpetrators (e.g. sexual abuse). Overall boys and girls are equally likely to be victims.

Key messages

- We now know abuse and exploitation is very varied and can occur in a variety of contexts by a range of perpetrators. It is important to consider both standards of care expected and signs and symptoms of significant harm in the child when making assessments;
- Practitioners need training on distinct types of abuse they may come across online and offline, and to be provided with means of assessing them;
- The impacts of abuse are numerous and long lasting. As research progresses we learn more and more about negative impacts on physical, emotional, cognitive and social development. These can last into middle age or older age and have cumulative effects of a variety of disorders and vulnerabilities;

- We need mixed causal models to explain impacts of abuse on social, psychological and biological levels. This involves inter-disciplinary and prospective research which should be ongoing due to differences in generations and cohorts;
- Evaluations of interventions need to be ongoing. Preventative actions (such as early years' intervention) need to have sustained follow-up which is not prey to party politics, budgets or political change.

Historical and organised abuse

Abuse has always been present in society, but not always recognised. In fact, much was secretive in prior decades. This was particularly true of exploitation of children by adults in institutional or organised settings where perpetrators could reach multiple children. This particularly involved sexual abuse, but by implication emotional abuse and sometimes physical abuse would be involved. Vulnerability to such approaches may also indicate prior neglect of the child. Over time different such abuses have come to light – for example, the 'Beck babies' discovery of widespread sexual abuse and paedophilia in children's residential care in the 1970s; the earlier exporting of children to the British colonies in the 1950s and the resulting abuse[6]; and abuse in the church discovered in Boston (John Jay Report, 2004). We are familiar with such stories and always hope that these no longer occur. This is false optimism on two counts – first because new institutional abuse was discovered in the last few years in Rotherham and other places in England and Wales, and second because historic abuses are still being revealed following Savile. The Inquiry into Institutional Child Sexual Abuse continues to investigate historical abuse cases committed within institutional contexts and reported by victims.[7,8]

Professionals including the police are now required to deal with historical abuse as well as ongoing and organised abuse perpetrated in institutional or group settings. Perpetrators can be well-known figures as well as those not known. Therefore, seeing abuse in terms of time is important, not least because for some victims of abuse the experience lives with them. It is likely more will emerge through the ongoing Inquiry. It raises methodological issues of how we collect information on distant abuse, and on the support provided for individuals who have been living with the burden of abuse for decades and for perpetrators as they reach old age.

The last decade has seen an avalanche of child abuse reports resulting in something of a watershed in child safeguarding and protection. The fact that the extent of abuse has come to light speaks well of our current processes and increased victim confidence, but it can give us pause to consider some dark aspects of our own society's past. It is likely that future services will always deal with a combination of ongoing, recent past and far past in prevention, investigation and in intervening with abuse. Since some risk of abuse is intergenerational, the effects need to be understood of past abuse as a current danger to children.

It is also the case that children currently inhabit a converged online/offline environment, such is the centrality of digital media in their lives. This new world brings with it new norms, practices and experience, much of which is positive but the extent of online child victimisation is an unknown given difficulties in estimating prevalence and incidence. Some forms of online abuse will quickly become historical given the rapid advancement of new technologies and the evolving nature of children's online behaviour, The Inquiry into Institutional CSA is currently exploring online abuse and the role of the Internet in facilitating online CSA (IICSA, 2018b).[9] The Internet also provides more opportunity for sex offenders to network and to share indecent images of children, and much child sex offender activity is now perpetrated on the Darknet making police investigation difficult.

Key messages

- There is extensive historical abuse which has only partly been revealed. Ongoing national inquiries will reveal more of the extent of this, embedded in institutional, establishment or organisational settings. Attention needs to be paid to the victims of such past abuse;
- We need to guard against groups of people being outside the range of safeguarding – all organisations need safeguarding oversight. No groups or age groups should be excluded from this. Independent and police investigation need to be applied where appropriate (for example in the church);
- Once historical abuse has been uncovered, we need to establish services to help adults deal with this burden. This can involve psychological/psychiatric services, health services and social services covering a wide range of domains. Intensive intervention may delay further damage and its transmission inter-generationally. This needs to be an outcome of the Jay Report. Lessons learnt may be usefully disseminated to other nations where such abuse has not been uncovered on the basis that it may yet to be recognised;
- Services need to simultaneously deal with ongoing, recent and historical abuse with a wide range of age groups. Sometimes action will need to be taken across generations;
- The Internet has played a contributory role in facilitating CSA and CSE, providing ease of access to many victims and providing offenders with an anonymous platform from which it is relatively easy to meet and network

with other offenders. Darknet activity poses serious investigative problems for the police who face the challenge of remaining a step ahead in their understanding of offender online modus operandi.

Research into abuse

Research into recognised child abuse has been highly successful in identifying the extent of the harm on the individual victim on a lifelong basis and inter-generationally. The broad domains of damage incurred to the victim (biological, psychological and social) are increasingly being investigated. However, there are subsets of abuse where more specific impacts are not yet fully understood, for example around CSE of males, or long-term effects of FMG or child trafficking. Here contexts can have their own important specific impacts. The work of researching abuse is never finalised. Contexts change, the mode of abuse can change, and even impacts may be different in varied settings. Research needs to be ongoing to understand how abuse evolves, as well as to evaluate the impact of interventions and policies which seek to reduce it. We know more now about the long-term biological impacts and the links to midlife physical illnesses which burden the health services. The research has thus been shown to underline that child abuse is a public health issue and that its impacts can be extensive, lifelong and intergenerational. Given relatively high incident rates of abuse in the community (e.g. 30 per cent), this means a very high cascade of health issues. Related to this are other social issues, for example relationship problems with partner and lack of support, and links to poverty and disadvantage. Given the wider range of abuses now covered in child safeguarding, research needs to keep up with the wider incidence and greater impact understanding. Implications include medical services knowledge of prior child abuse in diagnosing and treatment planning, and more specific mental health services geared to children and young people who have been abused, but also adults, and older adults, with a prior history of abuse. Given the outcome of the ongoing Jay Report, which includes research into organised abuse in past decades, this research needs to be disseminated. Treatment packages should also be used for individuals identified in this national inquiry. There has been substantial recent focus on CSE as the national inquiry produces output. This has led to other resources such as the recently established CSA Centre of Expertise – a significant funding venture which is currently commissioning research to inform policy and practice in this area, the Centre being funded by the Home Office and led by Barnados. The work of the Centre includes research programme findings which will inform practice and policy.[10]

Research also needs ever evolving methods. These need to be appropriate to different age groups (for example child interviews) to be amenable to different modes (for example online abuse) and to be capable of being utilised retrospectively and in different health settings (for example in relation to midlife physical illness). The ethical processes in research also need to facilitate appropriately sensitive research to continue in these areas, despite risk of 'upset' and working with vulnerable groups. The idea that some groups should be outside of research investigation violates ethical rights of children and vulnerable groups. But such methods require sensitivity and expertise, should be child centred and include advice from families (Childs-Smith, 2017). Research also needs to be intradisciplinary (e.g. different age groups, different models) and inter-disciplinary (e.g. psychology, psychiatry, neuroscience, criminology, social policy etc.). Teams need to be put in place equipped to deal with the multi-dimensions of abuse. This needs to feed into education (particularly early years), clinical practice, health practice, social work and other fields.

Funding streams for research exploring children's experience of online harm and online offending behaviour must be faster track; the fast pace of change in children's digital lives as evidenced by key annual research such as that undertaken by OFCOM[11] requires fast track funding to address issues of current and immediate concern. The current research council and charity protracted grant awarding processes can result in the investigation of issues that are potentially already out of date in the digital realm.

As discussed, it is also the case that the vast majority of research funded has been conducted in the West, with some limited research being conducted elsewhere. The lack of research in other regions of the world has resulted in something of a bias in the child Internet safety literature, with key knowledge having limited relevance beyond the West and with a preponderance of studies focusing upon the European and US perspective.

Key messages

- Although much has been learnt through research into abuse in the last 40 years or so, the effort must be ongoing to determine the exact causes and consequence of abuse in its varied types;
- Evaluative research must be ongoing with interventions and preventative initiatives in the longer term to establish their effectiveness;
- Research findings and methods of assessment and analysis can be usefully disseminated into practice. Academics have a role in helping multi-agency safeguarding teams collect and process complex case material and group data in services;
- Research needs to be undertaken on abuse in varied domains. For example, its links with physical health outcomes and mortality, and understanding of dose effects means that it should be part of assessments and treatment

plans on a routine basis. There needs to be careful use of measurement and ethical application of this;

- Funding processes for research in the digital realm must be faster track and take account of the fast-moving pace of the environment if it is to have any relevance;
- More research must be funded that explores children's and young people's experience of abuse generally and online in the developing world; it cannot be assumed that research conducted in the West has broad applicability beyond this region.

Technology and the digital world

Technology and social media has had a varied role in the child abuse domain. Whilst much is educational, entertaining and socially empowering, it can also represent harm to children. Social media can provide a point of access to victims online through different types of bullying and exploitation, but particularly for those with a sexual interest in children to locate their victims online. This widens access to children and does not require geographic closeness. It can also lead to additional contact abuse, both by perpetrators selling images of a child being abused, and by offline abuse for perpetrators who groom children online for later contact abuse. The grooming process itself can also be seen as abusive.

European safer Internet policies have put resources into seeking harmonisation in methods and research across the EU. An emerging body of work has indicated who is at risk, the harm suffered and characteristics of the perpetrators (Livingstone, Davidson, & Bryce, 2017), but there is still much to learn and whilst the area of child online behaviour has received a great deal of research funding, less funding has been directed towards online child abuse. There are several notable large-scale EU-funded studies which suggest that: online CSA is increasing; offenders use a variety of grooming approaches; police and industry collaboration must be improved upon; vulnerable young people are more likely to be abused online; the vast majority of young people online appear to be resilient; young people generate a considerable volume of self-taken indecent images and sometimes do not fully appreciate the legal implications of sharing the images with peers (Davidson et al., 2016; Quayle, 2017; Webster et al., 2015).

Technology is central to professionals processing and sharing information about children at risk and those abused. It can be an aid to practitioners in collating multiple sources of information from different agencies about the family and increase access electronically. It can also be used to aid in standardising assessments of abuse and thresholds for acting in child protection. On the other hand, electronic systems have been blamed for higher levels of bureau-cracy in services, reduction in practitioner judgement and time spent with the child or family.

Technology also evolves at a fast rate. This can hinder investigation into online harms to children, and even high-tech crime units need to move swiftly with the changing digital world in which children live. This of course is from ever younger ages as technology becomes ubiquitous. There is a danger of genera-tion gaps in technology use, with parents and professionals typically being a few steps behind both the computing experts, the new technologies and the ones the children quickly pick up. Children are being taught increasingly sophisticated IT skills at a younger age; in the UK some primary school children are now taught basic coding. Alongside the necessary focus upon their digital rights, it is impera-tive that children are taught about legal, ethical and safe use of the Internet from the moment they pick up a smartphone and by educators who really understand the issues. Recent research demonstrates that young people can easily become drawn into illegal Internet activity, including hacking, which can result in a crimi-nal record and custody in extreme cases (Aiken, Davidson, & Amann, 2016).

Criminology has had little to say about child abuse and the impact of child abuse upon adults, preferring to leave this area of study to psychologists. How-ever, the advent of the digital age and the importance of the Internet to young people makes the situation one of immense criminological significance. Inter-net activity is increasingly routine activity, providing exposure to the tools, net-works and opportunities needed both to engage in crime and to potentially be victimised. Current criminological debate has added little to an understanding of the way in which some vulnerable young people can be drawn into online criminal activity, but early criminological theory does have much to offer. Mat-za's drift idea, for example, implies a slackening of social controls and norms that can lead to and foster delinquency under certain conditions (Matza, 1964); this concept could be extended to those young people who share indecent images of partners, not realising that the behaviour is illegal. This drift idea has been also examined more recently in the context of online youth behaviour (Goldsmith & Brewer, 2014). The period of adolescence could be seen as a time of turmoil and difficulty consisting of conflict with parents/authority figures, mood disruptions, impulsivity and risky behaviour. This period may indirectly influence engagement with certain online criminality and anti-social/deviant behaviour as during this period morals are still developing, and the internali-sation of beliefs, norms, attitudes and identity are being established. All of this may occur while youths are in a state of role confusion, arguably compounded by differences between real-world norms and moral judgements, and those that prevail online. The challenge for practitioners working with children in the pro-tective services is to understand their fast-evolving use of digital media and to consider the potential impact of this upon their behaviour, while the challenge for academics is in developing relevant theoretical contexts to explain these new behaviours and the context in which they occur.

The IICSA national inquiry will for the first time investigate institutional responses to child sexual abuse and exploitation facilitated by the Internet and will also investigate the nature and extent of the use of the Internet and other digital communications technology (collectively 'the Internet') to facilitate child sexual abuse, including by way of sharing indecent images of children; viewing or directing the abuse of children via online streaming or video conferencing; grooming or otherwise coordinating contact offences against children; or by any other means. During this process, the Inquiry will consider the experiences of victims and survivors of child sexual abuse facilitated by the Internet and investigate the adequacy of government policy relevant to the protection of children from sexual abuse facilitated by the Internet. It will also investigate the adequacy of relevant statutory and regulatory framework applicable to Internet service providers, providers of online platforms, and other relevant software companies; the response of Internet service providers, providers of online platforms, and other relevant software companies to child sexual abuse facilitated by the Internet; the response of law enforcement agencies to child sexual abuse facilitated by the Internet; and the response of the criminal justice system to child sexual abuse facilitated by the Internet.

Key messages

- Harm to children through digital means is growing but also constantly changing as technology evolves. Constant vigilance and training updates are needed by services and by researchers to establish its prevalence and harmful effects;
- There needs to be international cooperation about combatting harm to children online and through social media, with children's digital rights recognised and acted upon in law;
- Practitioners need to be provided with skills to identify abuse online, and for police services the technological means of investigating it. Practitioners also need to understand children's use of digital media;
- Safeguarding children through interventions and psychoeducation about online activity needs to be undertaken and this in the context of relationships and personal and social health, rather than through technology lessons, but must also include legal and ethical use of the Internet;
- Practitioners should not substitute technological means of assessment, case processing and data sharing for contact with children and their families, but should use this to complement and enhance their work.

Service availability and effectiveness

Child abuse is sufficiently widespread that an ever-increasing pressure is placed upon child safeguarding services and criminal justice services in identifying and counteracting abuse. New policies demand additional input (e.g. early intervention services) and frequent service reorganisation or change in policies. Yet at times of austerity budgets are cut and good work in experienced teams can be lost.

There is a high level of pressure on professionals working with child abuse to keep up with the field, but also manage the emotional burden of working with dysfunctional families and damaged children. After instances of child deaths reach the media, there are always a number of practitioners who pull out of the field – particularly when their profession comes in for blame. This is particularly true in social work. There have been recent initiatives to increase training and status to social work and to roll-out safeguarding principles to a range of services, following Munro (Munro, 2011). However, child issues do not always have the highest priority, for example with the police. And the skills needed, for example in combatting online abuse, require very specialist teams.

There are continuous drives to improving the detection of abuse. It is curious that the rates of perhaps the most stigmatising (offline physical abuse and sexual abuse registered with children's services) seems to have stabilised or reduced nationally in the UK (although rates of online abuse have increased), whereas the issues around parental care (neglect, emotional abuse) are increasing and are perceived by many professionals as harder to grade in terms of severity. This can lead to some inertia within the family court system with neglect cases. These represent an absence of positive attention and nurturing to the child and invoke mothers or female carers in particular. It is also noted that early neglect can be a risk itself for later types of abuse, including CSE, so early intervention may reduce the overall load of abuse.

Modern approaches to safeguarding require multi-agency approaches to cover the necessary expertise in working with children and families. However, at times this can result in poor communication, overburdening client's assessment and delays in getting key bits of help. Munro expects all families to have a key worker to hold this together and keep the child 'in mind'. But natural circumstances with changes in staffing, ill health and other aspects means this can fall apart. There have been numerous policy reviews about childcare, pointing to different failings in the system. However, we should remember that it is parents and other carers and perpetrators who bring about abuse, and we should not underestimate their ability to lie and conceal details of their abusive parenting or other contact with children. Professionals need to be aware of such potential cynical disregard for children and for practitioners shown. With family structures more fractured, households can include a variety of adults, some there only brief periods and their contact with children needs to be established when investigating abuse.

Once in the care system, children have variable outcomes, and still have reduced life opportunities. There are many challenges to placing children in the best care arrangements and these can break down for a myriad of reasons relating to the child, the new carers, the environment etc.

A positive move is that knowledge of child safeguarding is now endemic in various professions and by the public. It is no longer acceptable to see abuse and not act. Most professionals are mandated reporters and the public increasingly sees itself in that way. However, very recent government policy changes in LSCBs may mean that the focus will become narrow again in terms of child protection rather than broader in terms of safeguarding. This is because the smaller partnerships responsible will have less resources available and will not be OFSTED inspected as before. It is important as a society we do not lose the lessons learnt about the welfare of all our children and initiatives to act in early years for preventative work.

Key messages

- Safeguarding children needs to be a concern of all professionals and the public. Training and awareness raising needs to be widespread;
- Multi-Agency working is required to combat and intervene with abuse. Different professional teams need to improve their working together, communication and processes so that no child slips through the net and that combined working does not multiply delays and bureaucracy and assessment burden on children and families;
- More intervention is needed for children in care to improve their life chances. Using models, for instance around attachment, social pedagogy and biological change markers can aid in effecting change. Ongoing assessment needed to chart change and progress;
- There is current renewed focus on neglect and related emotional abuse in children's services, since this is increasing and is reported as hard to detect by social workers in terms of its severity. Family courts often let it continue with family support even though children show signs of harm;
- Cuts to services can do damage to rolling out of policy recommendations and prevent continuation of good practice and lose experienced practitioners from the system. A move away from early intervention may ultimately be more costly, in both financial terms and of human suffering and unrealised potential.

Conclusion

Our society in the UK has made great progress in the safeguarding of children of which we should be proud. The majority of children have achieved higher well-being, are shown greater care and have better lives than in any previous era. But we cannot afford to slacken in these efforts, at time where funding is reduced. We need constant vigilance to identify and deter child abuse and to be open-minded about recognising the varied types of abuse inflicted, the mode of abuse and the range of perpetrators. It is not safe to assume that there are environments which are abuse-free, nor that any group of people is ruled out as potential perpetrators. The public are now largely aware of risky environments for children and where abuse can occur. They are more vigilant and knowledgeable about risks. More professionals are involved in safeguarding training and are mandated reporters of abuse. It is important to retain that when organisational structures for tackling abuse are reorganised.

However, the scale of child abuse internationally needs to be considered as vital in the context of contemporary concerns about child well-being. This is not only on ethical grounds, but also because globalisation can affect risk even to our own communities. Raising awareness of child well-being, healthy development and eradicating abusive practice needs to be an international concern which demands national and international collaboration and more standardised legislative frameworks coupled with child friendly criminal justice systems.

Additionally, the spotlight on abuse has extended the scope of abuse, and the range of policies enacted and thus expertise and knowledge needed by professionals in the field is extensive. We need to respond to this by providing the training and awareness needed to aid professionals in such a difficult field to ensure our children can be offered safety and protection.

This book has sought to highlight the current state of child protection knowledge, policy and practice in the UK in order to identify contemporary issues which we need to focus on to ensure that society can live up to all the demands now placed on us by our increased awareness of child abuse and its consequences. There can be no doubt that the consequences are serious, lifelong and affect not only quality of life but also over time, illness and mortality. We owe it to children to make sure they are safe, but we also owe it to ourselves as a society to reduce the pressure on services further down the line for abused children who have grown into unhappy adults and parents. This requires sustained efforts on all fronts – preventative and early intervention; universal and targeted services; and public awareness and increased sophistication in relationships. We should not slacken our resolve in this quest.

We have sought to highlight the plight of those abused. As researchers our tools are to discover and then inform those who can directly change policy and practice. We hope that in our writing we have given voice to children who suffer abuse. In the words of Ellen Bass and Laura Davies:[12]

> So often survivors have had their experiences denied, trivialized, or distorted. Writing is an important avenue for healing because it gives you the opportunity to define your own reality. You can say: This did happen to me. It was that bad. It was the fault & responsibility of the adult. I was – and am – innocent.
>
> (Bass & Davies, 2002)

Notes

1 http://5rightsframework.com/
2 www.beds.ac.uk/ic/recently-completed-projects/making-noise-csafe
3 www.europol.europa.eu/newsroom/news/live-streaming-of-child-sexual-abuse-estab lished-harsh-reality
4 England and Wales were the first EU jurisdiction to legislate against online child grooming
5 www.iicsa.org.uk/key-documents/1534/view/IICSA%20Impacts%20of%20Child%20 Sexual%20Abuse%20Rapid%20Evidence%20Assessment%20Full%20Report%20 %28English%29.pdf
6 www.bbc.co.uk/**insideout**/eastmidlands/series9/week_nine.shtml
7 www.iicsa.org.uk/
8 www.iicsa.org.uk/
9 www.iicsa.org.uk/investigations/child-sexual-abuse-facilitated-by-the-internet
10 www.csacentre.org.uk/
11 www.ofcom.org.uk/research-and-data
12 *www.goodreads.com/quotes/tag/childhood-abuse*

REFERENCES

ACPO. (2010). *Project Acumen. Setting the record. The trafficking of migrant women in the England and Wales off-street prostitution sector.* London: ACPO.

Aebi, R. (2001). *The trafficking in children for the purpose of prostitution: British Columbia, Canada.* Paper presented at the National Judicial Institute International Instruments and Domestic Law Conference, Conference proceedings, Canada.

Agnew-Blais, J., & Danese, A. (2016). Childhood maltreatment and unfavourable clinical outcomes in bipolar disorder: A systematic review and meta-analysis. *The Lancet Psychiatry, 3*(4), 342–349.

Aiken, M., Davidson, J., & Amann, P. (2016). *Youth pathways into cybercrime.* London.

Ainsaar, L., & Loof, L. (2012). *Online behaviour related to sexual abuse: Literature report.* EC Report.

Albert, D., Belsky, D. W., Crowley, D. M., Latendresse, S. J., Aliev, F., Riley, B., & Sun, C. (2015). Conduct Problems Prevention Research Group, in Dick, D. M. and Dodge, K. A. (2015), Can Genetics Predict Response to Complex Behavioral Interventions? Evidence from a Genetic Analysis of the Fast Track Randomized Control Trial. *Journal of Policy Analysis and Management, 34,* 497–518.

Allnock, D., & Miller, P. (2013). *No one listened, no one heard.* London.

American Psychiatric Association. (2013). *The diagnostic and statistical manual of mental disorders* (5th ed., DSM– 5). Washington, DC: American Psychiatric Association.

Andrews, B., & Brewin, C. R. (1990). Attributions of blame for marital violence: A study of antecedents and consequences. *Journal of Marriage and Family, 52,* 757–767.

Angelides, S. (2004). Feminism, child sexual abuse, and the erasure of child sexuality. *GLQ: A Journal of Lesbian and Gay Studies, 10*(2), 141–177.

Anning, A. (2004). The National Evaluation of Sure Start Local Programmes in England. *Child and Adolescent Mental Health, 9*(1), 2–8.

APA. (2013). *Diagnostic and statistical manual of mental disorders (DSM-5®).* Arlington, VA: American Psychiatric Association.

Ardino, V. (2011). *Post-traumatic syndromes in childhood and adolescence: A handbook of research and practice.* London, UK: Wiley.

Arnett, J. J. (2007). Emerging adulthood: What is it, and what is it good for? *Child Development Perspectives, 1*(2), 68–73.

Arnett, J. J. (2014). *Adolescence and emerging adulthood.* Boston, MA: Pearson.

Bakermans-Kranenburg, M. J., & van IJzendoorn, M. H. (2007). Research review: Genetic vulnerability or differential susceptibility in child development: The case of attachment. *Journal of Child Psychology and Psychiatry, 48*(12), 1160–1173.

Bakermans-Kranenberg, M. J., van Ijzendoorn, M. H., & Juffer, F. (2003). Less is more: Metaanalysis of sensitivity and attachment interventions in early childhood. *Psychological Bulletin, 129,* 195–215.

Barnes, J., Belsky, J., Broomfield, K. A., Dave, S., Frost, M., Melhuish, E., & The National Evaluation of Sure Start Research Team. (2005). Disadvantaged but different: Variation among deprived communities in relation to child and family well-being. *Journal of Child Psychology and Psychiatry, 46*(9), 952–962.

Bass, E., & Davies, L. (2002). *The courage to heal: A guide for women survivors of child sexual abuse.* Aberdeen: Ebury Publishing.

Beckett, H., & Pearce, J. (2017). *Understanding and responding to child sexual exploitation.* London, UK: Routledge.

Beckett, H., & Warrington, C. (2015). *Making justice work: Experiences of criminal justice for children and young people affected by sexual exploitation as victims and witnesses.* Bedfordshire University, Bedfordshire.

Beck-Sander, A. (2008). Childhood abuse in adult offenders: The role of control in perpetuating cycles of abuse. *Journal of Forensic Psychiatry,* 486–498.

Belsky, J. (1980). Child maltreatment: An ecological integration. *American Psychologist, 35*(4), 320–335.

Belsky, J. (2002). Developmental origins of attachment styles. *Attachment and Human Development, 4*(2), 166–170.

Belsky, J., Melhuish, E., Barnes, J., Leyland, A. H., Romaniuk, H., & The National Evaluation of Sure Start Research Team. (2006). Effects of Sure Start local programmes on children and families: Early findings from a quasi-experimental, cross sectional study. *British Medical Journal, 332,* 1476.

Benjet, C., Borges, G., & Medina-Mora, M. E. (2010). Chronic childhood adversity and onset of psychopathology during three life stages: Childhood, adolescence and adulthood. *Journal of Psychiatric Research, 44*(11), 732–740. doi:10.1016/j.jpsychires.2010.01.004

Bentovim, A., Cox, A., Bingley Miller, L., & Pizzey, S. (2009). *Safeguarding children living with trauma and family violence: Evidence-based assessment, analysis and planning intervention.* London, UK and Philadelphia, PA: Jessica Kingsley.

Bergen, E., Davidson, J., Schulz, A., Schuhmann, P., Johansson, A., Santtila, P., & Jern, P. (2015). The effects of using identity deception and suggesting secrecy on the outcomes of adult-adult and adult-child or -adolescent online sexual interactions. *Victims & Offenders, 9*(3), 165–188.

Bernard, K., Hostinar, C., & Dozier, M. (2015). Intervention effects on diurnal cortisol rhythms of CPS Referred infants persist into early childhood: Preschool followup results of a randomized clinical trial. *JAMA Pediatrics, 169*(2), 112–119. doi:10.1001/jamapediatrics.2014.2369

Bernstein, D. P., Fink, L., Handelsman, L., Foote, J., Lovejoy, M., Wenzel, K., ... Ruggiero, J. (1994). Initial reliability and validity of a new retrospective measure of child abuse and neglect. *American Journal of Psychiatry, 151*(8), 1132–1136.

Bifulco, A. (2008). Risk and resilience in young Londoners. In D. Brom, R. Pat-Horenczyk, & J. Ford (Eds.), *Treating traumatized children: Risk, resilience and recovery.* London, UK: Routledge.

Bifulco, A. (2015). Attachment and adversity across the lifespan. *ATTACHMENT: New Directions in Psychotherapy and Relational Psychoanalysis, 9,* 201–218.

Bifulco, A., Bernazzani, O., Moran, P., & Jacobs, C. (2005). The Childhood Experience of Care and Abuse Questionnaire (CECA.Q): Validation in a community series. *British Journal of Clinical Psychology, 44,* 1–20.

Bifulco, A., Brown, G. W., & Harris, T. O. (1987). Childhood loss of parent, lack of adequate parental care and adult depression: A replication. *Journal of Affective Disorders, 12,* 115–128.

Bifulco, A., Brown, G. W., & Harris, T. O. (1994). Childhood experience of care and abuse (CECA): A retrospective interview measure. *Journal of Child Psychology and Psychiatry, 35,* 1419–1435. doi:10.1111/j.1469-7610.1994.tb01284.x

Bifulco, A., Brown, G. W., Lillie, A., & Jarvis, J. (1997). Memories of childhood neglect and abuse: Corroboration in a series of sisters. *Journal of Child Psychology and Psychiatry, 38,* 365–374.

Bifulco, A., Brown, G. W., Moran, P., Ball, C., & Campbell, C. (1998). Predicting depression in women: The role of past and present vulnerability. *Psychological Medicine, 28*(1), 39–50.

Bifulco, A., Damiani, R., Jacobs, C., & Spence, R. (in press). Partner violence in women – associations with major depression, attachment style and childhood maltreatment. *Maltrattamento e abuse all'infanzia.*

Bifulco, A., Harris, T., & Brown, G. W. (1992). Mourning or early inadequate care? Re-examining the relationship of maternal loss in childhood with adult depression and anxiety. *Development and Psychopathology, 4,* 433–449.

Bifulco, A., & Jacobs, C. (2012). *The "childhood experience of care and abuse interview" and "parenting role interview" for child safeguarding practitioners: An evaluation in Kingston safeguarding services.* Centre for Abuse and Trauma, University of Kingston.

Bifulco, A., Jacobs, C., Ilan-Clarke, Y., Spence, R., & Oskis, A. (2017). Adolescent attachment style in residential care: The Attachment Style Interview and Vulnerable Attachment Style Questionnaire. *British Journal of Social Work, 47,* 1870–1883. doi:10.1093/bjsw/bcw117

Bifulco, A., Jacobs, C., Oskis, A., Cavana, F., & Spence, R. (in press). Lifetime trauma, adversity and emotional disorder in older age women. *Matrattamento e abuse all'infanzia, (Special Edition).*

Bifulco, A., & Moran, P. (1998). *Wednesday's child: Research into women's experience of neglect and abuse in childhood and adult depression.* London, UK and New York, NY: Routledge.

Bifulco, A., Moran, P., Baines, R., Bunn, A., & Stanford, K. (2003). Exploring psychological abuse in childhood: II Association with other abuse and adult clinical depression. *Bulletin of the Menninger Clinic, 66,* 241–258. doi:10.1521/bumc.66.3.241.23366

Bifulco, A., Moran, P., Jacobs, C., & Bunn, A. (2009). Problem partners and parenting: Exploring linkages with maternal insecure attachment style and adolescent offspring internalizing disorder. *Attachment & Human Development, 11*(1), 69–85. doi:10.1080/14616730802500826

Bifulco, A., Moran, P., Ball, C., Jacobs, C., Baines, R., Bunn, A., & Cavagin, J. (2002). Childhood adversity, parental vulnerability and disorder: Examining inter-generational transmission of risk. *Journal of Child Psychology and Psychiatry, 43,* 1075–1086.

Bifulco, A., Schimmenti, A., Jacobs, C., Bunn, A., & Rusu, A. C. (2014). Risk factors and psychological outcomes of bullying victimization: A community-based study. *Child Indicators Research, 7*(3), 633–648. doi:10.1007/s12187-014-9236-8

Bifulco, A., & Thomas, G. (2012). *Understanding adult attachment in family relationships: Research, assessment and intervention.* London, UK: Routledge.

Bourke, M., & Hernandez, A. (2008). *The Butner study Redux: A report of the incidence of hands-on child victimization by child pornography offenders.* Berlin: Springer Science.

Bowlby, J. (1988). *A secure base: Clinical application of attachment theory.* London, UK: Routledge.

Bradburn, H., & Kenyon, P. (Writers). (2010). Chocolate: The bitter truth. *BBC News Panorama.* London, UK: BBC.

Bronfenbrenner, U. (1995). Developmental ecology through space and time: A future perspective. In P. Moen & G. H. Elder, Jr. (Eds.), *Examining lives in context: Perspectives on the ecology of human development* (pp. 619–647). Washington, DC: American Psychological Association.

Bruni, F. (2002). *A Gospel of shame: Children, sexual abuse, and the Catholic Church.* London: HarperCollins.

Bryce, J. (2009). Online sexual exploitation of children and young people. In Y. Jewkes & M. Yar (Eds.), *The handbook of internet crime* (pp. 1-23). Uffculme: Willan.

Buist, A., & Janson, H. (2001). Childhood sexual abuse, parenting and postpartum depression - a 3-year follow-up study. *Child Abuse & Neglect, 25,* 909-921.

Buschman, J., Bogaerts, S., Foulger, S., Wilcox, D., Sosnowski, D., & Cushman, S. (2010). Sexual history disclosure polygraph examinations with cybercrime offences: A first Dutch explorative study. *International Journal of Offender Therapy and Comparative Criminology, 54*(3), 395-411. doi:10.1177/0306624X09334942

Butler-Sloss, L. J. E. (1987). *Report of the inquiry into child abuse in Cleveland: Presented to parliament by the secretary of state for social services.* London: HMSO.

Calder, M. C. (2004). The internet: Potential, problems and pathways to hands-on sexual offending. In M. C. Calder (Ed.), *Child sexual abuse and the internet: Tackling the new frontier* (pp. 1-23). Dorset, UK: Russell House Publishing.

Cameron, R., & Maginn, C. (2008). The authentic warmth dimension of professional childcare. *British Journal of Social Work, 38,* 1151-1172.

Carr, J. (2014). *Observations on the implementation of Article 23 of the Lanzarote convention concerning the online solicitation of children for sexual purposes, otherwise known as "grooming".* London, UK. EC Publication.

Caspi, A. (2002, August 2). Role of genotype in the cycle of violence in maltreated children. *Science, 297,* 851-854.

Caspi, A., Hariri, A., Holmes, A., Uher, R., & Moffitt, T. E. (2010). Genetic sensitivity to the environment: The case of serotonin transporter gene (5-HTTT) and its implications for studying complex diseases and traits. *American Journal of Psychiatry, 167*(5).

CEC. (2012). *Protection of children against sexual exploitation and sexual abuse.* Council of Europe, Strasbourg.

Ceci, S. J., & Bruck, M. (1993). Suggestibility of the child witness: A historical review and synthesis. *Psychological Bulletin, 113,* 403-439.

Ceci, S. J., & Bruck, M. (2000). *Why judges must insist on electronically preserved recordings of child interviews. Court Review, 37,* 10-12.

CEOP. (2010). *Strategic threat assessment child trafficking in the UK.* CEOP, London.

Chartier, M. J., Walker, J. R., & Naimark, B. (2007). Childhood abuse, adult health, and health care utilization: Results from a representative community sample *American Journal of Epidemiology, 165*(9), 1031-1038. doi:10.1093/aje/kwk113

Childs-Smith, K. (2017). *Making noise: Children's voices for positive change after sexual abuse: A study of children and young people's experiences of help-seeking and support after child sexual abuse in the family.* University of Bedfordshire, London.

Cicchetti, D., & Cohen, D. J. (2006). *Developmental psychopathology: Theory and method* (2nd ed.). New York, NY: Wiley.

Cicchetti, D., Cummings, E. M., & Greenberg, M. T. (1990). An organizational perspective on attachment beyond infancy. In M. T. Greenberg, D. Cicchetti, & E. M. Cummings (Eds.), *Attachment in the preschool years: Theory, research, and intervention.* Chicago, IL: University of Chicago.

Cicchetti, D., & Roisman, G. I. (2011). *Minnesota Symposia on child psychology, volume 36: The origins and organization of adaptation and maladaptation.* Hoboken, NJ: John Wiley & Sons.

Cloward, K. (2016). *When norms collide: Local responses to activism against female genital mutilation and early marriage.* Oxford: Oxford University Press.

Colter, M., Hobcraft, J., McLanahan, S. S., Rutherford Siegeld, S., Berg, A., Brooks-Gunne, J.,... Notterman, D. (2014). Social disadvantage, genetic sensitivity, and children's telomere length. *Proceeds of the National Academy of Science USA, 111*(16), 5944-5949. doi:10.1073/pnas.1404293111

Colton, M., & Hellinckx, W. (1994). Residential and foster care in the European community: Current trends in policy and practice. *British Journal of Social Work, 24,* 559-576.

Connon, G., Crooks, A., Carr, A., Dooley, B., Guerin, S., Deasy, D., . . . O'Flaherty, A. (2011). Child sex abuse and the Irish criminal justice system. *Child Abuse Review, 20*(2), 102-119. doi:10.1002/car.1156

Cooper, P. (2011). *ABE interviews, children's testimony and hearing the voice of the child in family cases: Are we barking up the right tree?* Paper presented at the Dartington Conference, Dartington Hall.

Cossar, J., Brandon, M., Bailey, S., Belderson, P., Biggart, L., & Sharpe, D. (2013). *"It takes a lot to build trust": Recognition and telling: Developing earlier routes to help for children and young people.* Office of the Childrens Commissioner, London.

Cossar, J., & Neil, E. (2015). Service user involvement in social work research: Learning from an Adoption Research Project. *British Journal of Social Work, 45*(1), 225-240.

Cross, T. P., Jones, L. M., Walsh, W. A., Simone, M., & Kolko, D. (2007). Child forensic interviewing in Children's Advocacy Centers: Empirical data on a practice model. *Child Abuse & Neglect, 31,* 1031-1052.

Cunningham, A., & Hurley, P. (2007). *A full and candid account', using special accommodations and testimonial aids to facilitate the testimony of children: Video-recorded evidence.* London, Ontario: Centre for Children and Families in the Justice System.

Danese, A., Pariante, C. M., Caspi, A., Taylor, A., & Poulton, R. (2007). Childhood maltreatment predicts adult inflammation in a life-course study. *Proceeds of the National Academy of Science USA, 104,* 1319-1324. doi:10.1073/pnas.0610362104

Davidson, J., & Bifulco, A. (2010). Investigating police practice in the UK: Achieving best evidence in work with young victims of abuse. *Pakistan Journal of Criminology, 1,* 19-46.

Davidson, J., Bifulco, A., Thomas, G., & Ramsay, M. (2006). Child victims of sexual abuse: Children's experience of the investigative process in the criminal justice system. *Practice, 18,* 247-263.

Davidson, J., DeMarco, J., Bifulco, A., Bogaerts, S., Caretti, V., Aiken, M., . . . Puccia, A. (2016). *Enhancing industry and police practice in the investigation of online child sexual abuse: The EU online child safety project final report.* London, UK: EU Report.

Davidson, J., Lorenz, M., Grove-Hills, J., & Martellozo, E. (2009). *Evaluation of CEOP thinkUknow internet safety programme & exploration of young people's internet safety knowledge.* Kingston University.

Davidson, J., & Martellozzo, E. (2010). *State of the nation review of internet safety in the Kingdom of Bahrain.* Bahrain: TRA.

Davidson, J., & Martellozzo, E. (2012). Exploring young people's use of social networking sites and digital media in the internet safety context: A comparison of the UK and Bahrain. *International Journal of Information, Communication and Media,* 1-21.

Davidson, J., & Martellozzo, E. (2013). Exploring young people's use of social networking sites and digital media in the internet safety context: A comparison of the UK and Bahrain. *Information, Communication & Society, 16*(9), 1456-1476. doi:10.1080/13691 18X.2012.701655

Davidson, J., & Martellozo, E. (2016). *Kingdom of Bahrain: National internet safety review.* Manama. Bahrain: TRA.

Davis, G., Hoyano, L., Keenan, C., Maitland, L., & Morgan, R. (1999). *The admissibility and sufficiency of evidence in child abuse in prosecutions.* Home Office: London, UK.

DCSF. (2007a). *The common assessment framework for children and young people: A guide for managers.* HMSO: London, UK.

DCSF. (2007b). *Impact assessment for white paper on children in care.* HMSO: London, UK.

Delap, E. (2009). *Begging for change research findings and recommendations on forced child begging in Albania/Greece, India and Senegal.* London, UK: Anti-slavery International.

DeMarco, J., Davidson, J., Bogaerts, S., Pace, U., Aiken, M., Caretti, V.,... Bifulco, A. (2017). Digital dangers and cyber victimisation: A study of European adolescent online risky behaviour for sexual exploitation. *Clinical Neuropsychiatry, 14*(1), 104-112.

Department for Education. (2015). *Characteristics of children in need in England, 2014-15.* London: Department for Education (DfE). Table D4

Department of Education. (2017). *Every child matters.* London, UK: DfE.

Department of Health. (1993). *Children Act report.* London: HMSO.

DoH. (2010). *Our health and wellbeing.* London, UK: DoH.

DfE. (2014). *Children in care.* London: House of Commons.

DfE. (2017a). *Child sexual exploitation definition and a guide for practitioners, local leaders and decision makers working to protect children from child sexual exploitation.* London, UK: DfE.

DfE. (2017b). *Children and Social Work Act.* London, UK: DfE.

DfES. (2004). *Children Act.* London, UK: DfE

DfES & DoH. (2004). *National service framework for children, young people, and maternity services: The mental health and psychological well-being of children and young people.* London, UK: DfE.

DH_DCFS. (2007). *Introduction to the National Health Schools Programme.* London, UK: DH DCFS.

DiLillo, D., Tremblay, G. C., & Peterson, L. (2000). Linking childhood sexual abuse and abusive parenting: The mediating role of maternal anger. *Child Abuse and Neglect, 24*(6), 767-779.

Dodge, K. (2009). Community intervention and public policy in the prevention of antisocial behaviour. *Journal of Child Psychology and Psychiatry, 50,* 194-200.

Dong, M., Giles, W. H., Felitti, V. J., Dube, S. R., Williams, J. E., Chapman, D. P., & Anda, R. F. (2004). Insights into causal pathways for ischemic heart disease: Adverse childhood experiences study. *Circulation, 110*(13), 1761-1766. doi:10.1161/01.CIR.0000143074.54 995.7F

Doyle, O., Tremblay, R. E., Harmon, C., & Heckman, J. J. (2007). *Early childhood intervention: Rationale, timing and efficacy.* University College Dublin, Geary Institute, Dublin.

Dozier, M. (2003). Attachment-based treatment for vulnerable children. *Attachment and Human Development, 5*(3), 253-257.

Dozier, M., Peloso, E., Lewis, E., Laurenceau, J., & Levine, S. (2008). Effects of an attachment-based intervention on the cortisol production of infants and toddlers in foster care. *Development and Psychopathology, 20*(3), 845-859. doi:10.1017/S0954579408000400

Dozier, M., Stovall, K. C., Albus, K., & Bates, B. (2001). Attachment for infants in foster care: The role of caregiver state of mind. *Child Development, 72*(5), 1467-1477.

Dubowitz, H. (1991). The impact of child maltreatment on health. In R. H. J. Starr & D. A. Wolfe (Eds.), *The effects of child abuse and neglect: Issues and research* (pp. 278-294). New York, NY: Guilford Press.

Dubowitz, H. (2017). Child sexual abuse and exploitation – a global glimpse. *Child Abuse & Neglect, 66,* 2-8.

DuMont, K. A., Widom, C. S., & Czaja, S. J. (2007). Predictors of resilience in abused and neglected children grown-up: The role of individual and neighborhood characteristics. *Child Abuse & Neglect, 31,* 255-274.

ECPAT. (2009a). *Stolen futures: Trafficking for forced child marriage in the UK.* London, UK: ECPAT UK.

ECPAT. (2009b). *Understanding child trafficking: Safeguarding children controlled through belief in ritual oaths, "child witches", or religious and traditional practices.* London, UK: ECPAT UK.

ECPAT. (2010). *Child trafficking begging and organised crime.* London, UK: ECPAT UK.

ECPAT. (2014). *The national referral mechanism: A five year review.* London, UK: ECPAT UK.

ECPAT. (2017). *Lighting the way: Steps that lawyers, legal guardians and child trafficking advocates in the UK can take to better identify and protect children who may have been trafficked.* London, UK: ECPAT UK.

DfE/DoH. (2011). *Supporting families in the foundation years.* London, UK: DfE.

Eichsteller, G. (2009). Janusz Korczak – his legacy and its relevance for children's rights today. *International Journal of Children's Rights, 17*, 377-391.

Eke, A. W., Seto, M. C., & Williams, J. (2011). Examining the criminal history and future offending of child pornography offenders: An extended prospective follow-up study. *Law and Human Behaviour, 35*(6), 466-478.

Ellis, B. J., & Boyce, W. T. (2008). Biological sensitivity to context. *Current Directions in Psychological Science, 17*(3), 183-187. doi:10.1111/j.1467-8721.2008.00571.x

Ellison, L., & Munro, V. E. (2016). Taking trauma seriously: Critical reflections on the criminal justice process. *International Journal of Evidence & Proof, 43*, 123-143.

Endrass, J., Urbaniok, F., Hammermeister, L. C., Benz, C., Elbert, T., Laubacher, A., & Rossegger, A. (2009). The consumption of Internet child pornography and violent and sex offending. *BMC Psychiatry, 9*(43). doi:10.1186/1471-244X-9-43

Farrington, D. P. (1990). Childhood aggression and early violence: Early precursers and later-life outcome. In D. J. Pepler & K. H. Rubin (Eds.), *The development and treatment of childhood aggression* (pp. 5-12). Mahwah, NJ: Lawrence Erlbaum Associates.

Farrington, D. P. (2006). Childhood risk factors and risk-focussed prevention. In M. Maguire, R. Morgan, & R. Reiner (Eds.), *The Oxford handbook of criminology* (4th ed., p. 61). Oxford: Oxford University Press.

Felitti, V. J. (2002). The relationship of adverse childhood experiences to adult health: Turning gold into lead. *Journal Psychsom Med Psychother, 48*(4), 359-369. doi:10.1176/appi.ps.53.8.1001

Felitti, V. J., Anda, R. F., Nordenberg, D., Williamson, D. F., Spitz, A. M., Edwards, V., . . . Marks, J. S. (1998). Relationship of childhood abuse and household dysfunction to many of the leading causes of death in adults: The Adverse Childhood Experiences (ACE) study. *American Journal of Preventive Medicine, 14*(4), 245. doi:10.1016/S0749-3797(98)00017-8

Fergusson, D., Boden, M., Joseph, M., & Horwood, L. J. (2006). Examining the intergenerational transmission of violence in a New Zealand birth cohort. *Child Abuse & Neglect, 30*(2), 89-108.

Fergusson, D. M., Horwood, L. J., Ridder, E. M. (2005). Show me the child at seven: The consequences of conduct problems in childhood for psychosocial functioning in adulthood. *Journal of Child Psychology and Psychiatry, 46*(8), 837-849.

Fergusson, D. M., Lynskey, M., & Horwood, L. J. (1995). The adolescent outcomes of adoption: A 16-Year Longitudinal Study. *Journal of child psychology and psychiatry.* doi:10.1111/j.1469-7610.1995.tb02316.x

Fergusson, D. M., Woodward, L. J., & Horwood, L. J. (2000). Risk factors and life processes associated with the onset of suicidal behaviour during adolescence and early adulthood. *Psychological Medicine, 30*, 23-39.

Ferraro, M. M., & Casey, E. (2005). *Investigating child exploitation and pornography: The internet, the law and forensic science.* New York, NY: Elsevier Academic Press.

Field, F. (2010). *The foundation years: Preventing poor children becoming poor adults.* Cabinet Office, London, UK.

Fink, L., Bernstein, D. P., Handelsman, J., Foote, J., & Lovejoy, M. (1995). Initial reliability and validity of the childhood trauma interview: A new multidimensional measure of childhood interpersonal trauma. *American Journal of Psychiatry, 152*, 1329-1335.

Finkelhor, D. (1984a). *Child sexual abuse: New theory and research.* New York, NY: Free Press.

Finkelhor, D. (1984b). The prevention of child sexual abuse: An overview of needs and problems. *SIECUS Reports, 12,* 1-3.

Finkelhor, D. (1995). The victimization of children in a developmental perspective. *American Journal of Orthopsychiatry, 65,* 177-193.

Finkelhor, D., & Dziuba-Leatherman, J. (1994). Victimization of children. *American Psychologist, 49*(3), 173-183.

Finkelhor, D., & Kendall-Tackett, K. (1997). A developmental perspective on childhood impact of crime, abuse and violent victimization. In D. Cichetti& S. L. Toth (Eds.), *Developmental perspectives on trauma: Theory, research and intervention* (Vol. 8). Rochester, NY: University of Rochester press.

Finkelhor, D., Ormrod, R., & Turner, H. (2007, November). Re-victimization patterns in a national longitudinal sample of children and youth. *Child Abuse and Neglect, 31,* 497-502.

Finkelhor, D., Ormrod, R. K., Turner, H. A., & Hamby, S. L. (2005). Measuring poly-victimization using the Juvenile Victimization Questionnaire. *Child Abuse & Neglect, 29*(11), 1297-1312. doi:10.1016/j.chiabu.2005.06.005

Fisher, C., Goldsmith, A., Hurcombe, R., & Soares, C. (2017). *The impacts of child sexual abuse: A rapid evidence assessment*. University of Bedfordshire, Bedfordshire.

Fisher, H., Morgan, C., Fearon, P., Morgan, K., Dazzan, P., Doody, G.,... Murray, R. (2006). Child maltreatment as a risk factor for psychosis. *Schizophrenia Research, 81*(Suppl. 1), 235.

Fisher, P. A.,& Chamberlain, P. (2000). Multidimensional treatment foster care: A program for intensive parenting, family support, and skill building. *Journal of Emotional and Behavioural Disorders, 8*(3), 155-164.

Fisher, P. A., & Kim, H. K. (2007). Intervention effects on foster preschoolers' attachment-related behaviors from a randomized trial. *Prevention Science, 8*(2), 161-170.

Fivush, R. (2002). Scripts, schemas and memory of trauma in representation, memory and development. In N. Stein, P. Bauer,& M. Rabinowitz (Eds.), *Essays in honour of Jean Mandler*. Mahwah, NJ: Lawrence Erlbaum Associates.

Flaherty, E. G., Thompson, P., Litrownik, A. J., Theodore, A., English, D. J., Black, M. M.,... Dubowitz, H. (2006). Effect of early childhood adversity on child health. *Archives of Paediatric Adolescent Medicine, 160*(12), 1232-1238. doi:10.1001/archpedi.160.12.1232

Fonagy, P., Steele, M., Steele, H., Higgitt, A.,& Target, M. (1994). The Emanuel Miller Memorial Lecture 1992: The theory and practice of resilience. *Journal of Child Psychology and Psychiatry and Allied Disciplines, 35*(2), 231-257.

Ford, T., Vostanis, P., Meltzer, H.,& Goodman, R. (2007). Psychiatric disorder among British children looked after by local authorities: Comparison with children living in private households. *British Journal of Psychiatry,* 319-325.

Gallagher, B., Fraser, C., Christmann, K., & Hodgson, B. (2006). *International and internet child sexual abuse and exploitation*. Project Report, University of Huddersfield, Huddersfield.

Garbarino, J. (1991). Not all bad developmental outcomes are the result of child abuse. *Development and Psychopathology, 3*(1), 45-50.

Garbarino, J. (1996). CAN reflections on 20 years of searching. *Child Abuse and Neglect, 20*(3), 157-160.

Garbarino, J. (1997). Growing up in a socially toxic environment. In D. Cicchetti& S. L. Toth (Eds.), *Developmental perspectives on trauma: Theory, research, and intervention. Rochester symposium on developmental psychology* (Vol. 8, pp. 141-154). Rochester, NY: University of Rochester Press.

Garrett, P. M. (2013). A "Catastrophic, Inept, Self-Serving" Church? Re-examining three reports on child abuse in the Republic of Ireland. *Journal of Progressive Human Services, 24*(1), 43-65.

Gasser, U., MacClay, C., & Palfrey, J. (2010). *Working towards a deeper understanding of digital safety for children and young people in developing nations.* Harvard University, Cambridge, MA.

Gavan, M., & van der Valk, J. (Writers). (2008). Saving Africa's witch children. In *Dispatches*. Nigeria: Red Rebel Films.

Gekoski, A., Davidson, J., & Horvath, M. A. H. (2016). The prevalence, nature, and impact of intrafamilial child sexual abuse: Findings from a rapid evidence assessment. *Journal of Criminological Research, Policy and Practice, 2*(1), 54-66. doi:10.1108/JCRPP-06-2015-0023

Gianonne, F., Schimenti, A., Caretti, V., Chiarenza, A., Ferraro, A., Guarino, S., ... Bifulco, A. (2011). Validita attendibilita e proprieta pscyhometriche dela verdsione Italiana dell'intervista CECA (Childhood Experience of Care and Abuse). *Psiciatria e Psicoterapia, 30,* 3-21.

Giardino, A. P., & Alexander, R. (2005). *Child maltreatment: A clinical guide and reference.* 3rd ed. St Louis, MO: GW Medical Publishing, Inc.

Goldsmith, A., & Brewer, R. (2014). Digital drift and the criminal interaction order. *Theoretical Criminology, 19*(1), 112-130.

Goldstein, A., Flett, G., Wekerle, C., & Wall, A-M. (2009). Personality, child maltreatment and substance use: Examining correlates of deliberate self-harm among university students. *Canadian Journal of Behavioural Science, 41*(4), 241-251.

Goodman, G. S., & Bottoms, B. (1993). *Child victims, child witnesses: Understanding and improving testimony.* New York, NY: Guilford Press.

Hackett, S., Holmes, D., & Branigan, P. (2016). *Operational framework for children and young people displaying harmful sexual behaviours.* London, UK: NSPCC.

Hackett, S., & Smith, S. (2018). *Young people who engage in child sexual exploitation behaviours an exploratory study.* Durham University, Durham.

Hasebrink, U., Livingstone, S., Haddon, L., & Olafsson, K. (2009). *Comparing children's online opportunities and risks across Europe: Cross-national comparisons for EU kids online.* London, UK: LSE.

Hawkins-Rodgers, Y. (2007). Adolescents adjusting to a group home environment: A residential care model of re-organizing attachment behaviour and building resiliency. *Children and Youth Services Review, 29,* 1131-1141.

Hayes, D., Bunting, L., Lazenbatt, A., Carr, N., & Duffy, J. (2011). *The experiences of young witnesses in criminal proceedings in Northern Ireland.* Belfast, Northern Ireland Northern Ireland & Queens University Belfast., Northern Ireland.

Hershkowitz, I. (2009). Socioemotional factors in child abuse investigations. *Child Maltreatment, 14*(2), 172-181.

Hijazi-Omari, H., & Ribak, R. (2008). Playing with fire: On the domestication of the mobile phone among Palestinian teenage girls in Israel. *Information, Communication and Society, 11*(2), 149-166.

HM Government. (2015). *Working together to safeguard children: A guide to inter-agency working to safeguard and promote the welfare of children.* London: TSO.

HMIC, H. (2012). *Joint inspection report on the experience of young victims and witnesses in the criminal justice system.* London, UK: HMIC.

Hodges, J., Steele, M., Hillman, S., Henderson, K., & Kaniuk, J. (2003). Changes in attachment representations over the first year of adoptive placement: Narratives of maltreated children. *Clinical Child Psychology and Psychiatry, 8*(3), 347-363.

Hollis, V., & Belton, E. (2017). *Children and young people who engage in technology assisted harmful sexual behaviour.* London, UK: NSPCC.

Home Office. (2009). *This report gives a renewed focus on prevention overseas, tougher action on the perpetrators and better identification and care for victims.* Home Office

Horvath, M., Davidson, J., Grove-Hills, J., Gekoski, A., & Choak, C. (2014). *It's a lonely journey: A rapid evidence assessment on intrafamilial child sexual abuse.* London, UK: Office of the Childrens Commissioner.

House of Commons. (2013). *Foundation years: Sure Start children's centres. Fifth Report of Session 2013-14*. London, UK: HMSO.

Howe, D., Brandon, M., Hinings, D., & Schofield, G. (1999). *Attachment theory, child maltreatment and family support*. Mendham, Suffolk: Palgrave Macmillan.

Humphreys, M. (2011). *Empty cradles*. London: Transworld Publishers.

IICSA. (2017). *Child sexual abuse within the Catholic and Anglican Churches: A rapid evidence assessment*. London, UK: IICSA.

IICSA. (2018a). *Inquiry publishes Child Migration Programmes report*. London, UK: IICSA, 1 March, 2018.

IICSA. (2018b). *The Internet and Child Sexual Abuse*. IICSA.

Infurna, M. R., Reichl, C., Parzer, P., Schimmenti, A., Bifulco, A., & Kaess, M. (2016). Associations between depression and specific childhood experiences of abuse and neglect: A meta-analysis. *Journal of Affective Disorders, 190*, 47-55. doi:10.1016/j.jad.2015.09.06

James, A., & Prout, A. (2015). *Constructing and reconstructing childhood: Contemporary issues in the sociological study of childhood*. London, UK: Routledge.

Jay, A. (2014). *Independent inquiry into child sexual exploitation in Rotherham 1997-2013*. Retrieved from www.rotherham.gov.uk/downloads/file/1407/independent_inquiry_cse_in_rotherham

Joa, D., & Edelson, M. G. (2004). Legal outcomes for children who have been sexually abused: The impact of Child Abuse Assessment Center evaluations. *Child Maltreat, 9*, 263-276.

John Jay Report. (2004). *The nature and scope of sexual abuse of minors by Catholic priests and deacons in the United States 1950-2002*. City University of New York, NY.

Jones, L. M., Mitchell, K. J., & Finkelhor, D. (2012). Trends in youth internet victimization: Findings from three youth internet safety surveys 2000-2010. *Journal of Adolescent Health, 50*(2), 179-186.

Jonsson, L., Bladh, S., Priebe, M., & Svedin, G. (2015). Online sexual behaviours among Swedish youth: Associations to background factors, behaviours and abuse. *European Child & Adolescent Psychiatry, 24*(10), 1245-1260.

Jonsson, L. S., Priebe, G., Bladh, M., & Svedin, C. G. (2014). Voluntary sexual exposure online among Swedish youth - social background, internet behavior and psychosocial health. *Computers in Human Behavior, 30*, 181-190.

Kaess, M., Parzer, P., Mattern, M., Resch, F., Bifulco, A., & Brunner, R. (2011, July 1). Childhood Experiences of Care and Abuse (CECA) - validation of the German version of the questionnaire and interview, and results of an investigation of correlations between adverse childhood experiences and suicidal behaviour. *Zeitschrift fur Kinder- und Jugendpsychiatrie und Psychotherapie, 39*(4), 243-252. doi:10.1024/1422-4917/a000115

Kaplan, S. J., Pelcovitz, D., & Labruna, V. (1999). Child and adolescent abuse and neglect research: A review of the past 10 Years. Part I: Physical and emotional abuse and neglect. *Journal of the American Academy of Child & Adolescent Psychiatry, 38*(10), 1214-1222. doi:10.1097/00004583-199910000-00009

Kemp, R. (2011). Social pedagogy: Differences and links to existing child care practices. *Children Australia, 36*(4). doi:10.1375/jcas.36.4.199

Kierkegaard, S. (2008). Cybering, online grooming and ageplay. *Computer Law & Security Report, 24*, 41-55.

Kim, D-H., Kim, K-I., Park, Y-C., Zhang, L. D., Lu, M. K., & Li, D. (2000). Children's experience of violence in China and Korea: A transcultural study. *Child Abuse & Neglect, 24*(9), 1163-1173. doi:10.1016/S0145-2134(00)00175-7

Kirby, S., & Peal, K. (2015). The changing pattern of domestic cannabis cultivation in the UK and its impact on the cannabis market. *Journal of Drug Issues, 45*(3), 279-292.

Kirschner, R. H., & Stein, R. J. (1985). The mistaken diagnosis of child abuse: A form of medical abuse? *American Journal of Diseases of Children, 139*(9), 873-875.

Klaine, E., Davis, H., & Hicks, M. (2001). *Child pornography: The criminal justice system response*. National Centre for Missing and Exploited Children, Washington, DC.

La Rooy, D., Lamb, M. E., & Memon, A. (2011). Forensic interviews with children in Scotland: A survey of interview practices among police. *Journal of Police and Criminal Psychology, 26*(1).

Laming, L. (2003). *The Victoria Climbie inquiry: Report of an inquiry by Lord Laming*. London, UK: HMSO.

Larkin, H., Felitti, V., & Anda, R. F. (2014). Social work and adverse childhood experiences research: Implications for practice and health policy. *Social Work and Public Health, 29*(1), 1-16.

Lightfoot, S., & Evans, I. M. (2000). Risk factors for a New Zealand sample of sexually abusive children and adolescents. *Child Abuse and Neglect, 24*(9), 1185-1198.

Limanowska, B. (2005). *Trafficking in human beings in Southern Europe*. UNICEF, Sarajevo, Bosnia and Herzegovina.

Lindsay, G., Strand, S., Cullen, M. A., Cullen, S., Band, S., Davis, H., ... Evan, R. (2011). *Parenting early intervention programme*. Research Report, DFE-RR047, CEDAR University Warwick.

Lissau, I., & Sorensen, T. I. A. (1994). Parental neglect during childhood and increased risk of obesity in young adulthood. *The Lancet, 343*(8893), 324-327. doi:10.1016/S0140-6736(94)91163-0

Livingstone, S., Davidson, J., & Bryce, J. (2017). *Children's online activities, risks and safety*. London, UK: LSE.

Livingstone, S., & Görzig, A. (2014). When adolescents receive sexual messages on the internet: Explaining experiences of risk and harm. *Computers in Human Behavior, 33*, 8-15.

Livingstone, S., & Haddon, L. (2009). EU Kids online. *Zeitschrift Für Psychologie/Journal of Psychology, 217*(4), 236.

Livingstone, S., Haddon, L., Görzig, A., & Ólafsson, K. (2011). *Risks and safety on the internet. The perspective of European children. Final findings from the EU Kids Online survey*. London, UK: LSE.

Livingstone, S., & Palmer, C. (2012). *Identifying vulnerable children online and what strategies can help them, report of a seminar arranged by the UKCCIS evidence group*. London, UK: LSE.

Livingstone, S., & Smith, P. K. (2014). Annual research review: Harms experienced by child users of online and mobile technologies: The nature, prevalence and management of sexual and aggressive risks in the digital age. *Journal of Child Psychology and Psychiatry, 55*(6), 635-654.

Luthar, S. S. (1991). Vulnerability and resilience: A study of high-risk adolescents. *Child Development, 62*(3), 600-616.

Malchiodi, C. A. (2012). Art therapy and the brain. In C. Malchiodi (Ed.), *Handbook of art therapy*. New York, NY: Guilford Press.

Marmot, M. (2010). *Marmot review, fair society, healthy lives*. London, UK: Guilford Press.

Marshall, L. A., & Cooke, D. J. (1999). The childhood experiences of psychopaths: A retrospective study of familial and societal factors. *Journal of Personality Disorders, 13*(3), 211-225.

Martellozzo, E. (2013). *Online child sexual abuse: Grooming, policing and child protection in a multi-media world*. London, UK: Routledge.

Martellozzo, E., Horvath, M., Davidson, J., & Adler, J. (2015). *'I wasn't sure it was normal to watch it': Young people and adult pornography*. NSPCC & Office of the Childrens Commissioner, London, UK.

Masten, A. S., Garmezy, N., Tellegen, A., Pellegrini, D. S., Larkin, K., & Larsen, A. (1988). Competence and stress in school children: The moderating effects of individual and family qualities. *Journal of Child Psychology and Psychiatry and Allied Disciplines, 29*(6), 745-764.

Masten, A. S., Hubbard, J. J., Gest, S. D., Tellegen, A., Garmezy, N., & Ramirez, M. (1999). Competence in the context of adversity: Pathways to resilience and maladaptation from childhood to late adolescence. *Development and Psychopathology, 11*(1), 143-169.

Matza, D. (1964). *Delinquency and drift.* New York, NY: Wiley.

McAuley, C., Knapp, M., Beecham, J., McCurry, N., & Sleed, M. (2004). *The outcomes and costs of home-start support for young families Under Stress.* Joseph Rowntree Foundation, London, UK.

McCrory, E., de Brito, S., & Viding, E. (2010). Research review: The neurobiology and genetics of maltreatment and adversity. *Journal of Child Psychology and Psychiatry, 5*(10), 1079-1095.

McCrory, E. J., De Brito, S., & Viding, E. (2012). The link between child abuse and psychopathology: A review of neurobiological and genetic research. *Journal of the Royal Society of Medicine, 105*(4), 151-156. doi:10.1258/jrsm.2011.110222

McDonald, S., & Tijierino, A. (2013). *Male survivors of sexual abuse and assault: Their experiences.* Justice Canada, Canada.

McKenzie, K., Scott, D. A., Waller, G. S., & Campbell, M. (2011). Reliability of routinely collected hospital data for child maltreatment surveillance. *BMC Public Health.* doi:10.1186/1471-2458-11-8

McNamee, H., Molyneaux, F., & Geraghty, T. (2012). *Key stakeholder evaluation of NSPCC young witness service remote live link (Foyle).* London, UK: NSPCC.

Melhuish, E., Belsky, J., Anning, A., Ball, M., Barnes, J., Romaniuk, H.,... Team, N. R. (2007). Variation in community intervention programmes and consequences for children and families: The example of Sure Start Local Programmes. *Journal of Child Psychology and Psychiatry, 48*(6), 543-551.

Melhuish, E., & Gardiner, J. (2017). *Study of Early Education and Development (SEED): Study of quality of early years provision in England.* Department for Education, London, UK.

Mickelson, K. D., Kessler, R. C., & Shaver, P. R. (1997). Adult attachment in a nationally representative sample. *Journal of Personality and Social Psychology, 73*(5), 1092-1106. doi:10.1037/0022-3514.73.5.1092

Miller, A., & Rubin, D. (2009). The contribution of children's advocacy centers to felony prosecutions of child sexual abuse. *Child Abuse & Neglect, 33*(1), 12-18.

Ministry of Justice. (2011). *Achieving best evidence in criminal proceedings: Guidance on interviewing victims and witness, and guidance on using special measures.* Home Office London, UK.

Ministry of Justice. (2014). *Achieving best evidence in child sexual abuse investigations: A joint inspection.* Home Office: London, UK.

Mitchell, K. J., Finkelhor, D., Jones, L. M., & Wolak, J. (2012). Prevalence and characteristics of youth sexting: A national study. *Pediatrics, 129*(1), 13-20.

Mitchell, K. J., Finkelhor, D., & Wolak, J. (2005). *Internet and family and acquaintance sexual abuse.* Thousand Oaks, CA: Sage.

Mitchell, K. J., Jones, L., Finkelhor, D., & Wolak, J. (2014). *Trends in unwanted online experiences and sexting: Final report.* University of New Hampshire, Durham and New Hampshire.

MoJ. (2011). *Achieving best evidence in criminal proceedings: Guidance on interviewing victims and witness, and guidance on using special measures.* Great Britain: MoJ.

Moore, K., Moretti, M. M., & Holland, R. (1997). A new perspective on youth care programs: Using attachment theory to guide interventions for troubled youth. *Residential Treatment for Children and Youth, 15*(3), 1-24.

Moran, P. M., Bifulco, A., Baines., R., Bunn, A., & Stanford, K. (2003). Exploring psychological abuse in childhood: I. Developing a new interview scale. *Bulletin of the Menninger Clinic, 66*, 213-240. doi:10.1521/bumc.66.3.213.23367

Munro, E. (2010, June). *The Munro review of child protection.* Department of Education, London.

Munro, E. (2011). *The Munro review of child protection – interim report: The child's journey.* GR Government Report. London: Dfe

Munro, E. (2011). *The Munro review of child protection: Final report: A child-centered system.* [Press release]

Mutiga, M., & Flood, Z. (2016, August 8). Africa calling: mobile phone revolution to transform democracies. *The Guardian.*

Narey, M. (2016). *Residential care in England: Report of Sir Marin Narey's independent review of children's residential care.* National Care Advisory Service (NCAS), London, UK.

NCAS. (2008). *Introduction to leaving care.* NCAS, London, UK.

NEF/Action for Children. (2009). *Backing the future.* Action for Children, London, UK.

Ney, P. G., Fung, T., & Wickett, A. R. (1993). Child neglect: The precursor to child abuse. *Pre and Peri Natal Psychology Journal, 8(2),* 95–112.

Ney, P. G., Fung, T., & Wickett, A. R. (1994). The worst combinations of child abuse and neglect. *Child Abuse and Neglect, 18(9),* 705–714.

NICE. (2013). *Social and emotional wellbeing for children and young people.* NICE, London, UK.

O'Connell Davidson, J. (2005). *Children in the Global Sex trade Polity.*

O'Connor, M., & Elklit, A. (2008). Attachment styles, traumatic events, and PTSD: A cross-sectional investigation of adult attachment and trauma. *Attachment & Human Development, 10(1),* 59–71.

Office for National Statistics. (2015). *Measuring national wellbeing: Insights into children's mental health and well-being.* London, UK: ONS.

Parker, G. (1990). The parental bonding instrument – a decade of research. *Social Psychiatry and Psychiatric Epidemiology, 25,* 281–282.

Pearce, J. (2017). Preventing CSE: Would an international age of consent to sexual activity help secure the welfare of children. In P. Dolan & N. Forst (Eds.), *The Routledge handbook of global child welfare* (pp. 153–165). London, UK: Routledge.

Pearce, J. J., Hynes, P., & Bovarnick, S. (2013). *Trafficked young people: Breaking the wall of silence.* London, UK: Routledge Falmer.

Piercea, L., & Bozalekb, V. (2004). Child abuse in South Africa: An examination of how child abuse and neglect are defined. *Child Abuse & Neglect, 28,* 817–832.

Plant, D. T., Pariante, C. M., Sharp, D., & Pawlby, S. (2015). Maternal depression during pregnancy and offspring depression in adulthood: Role of child maltreatment. *British Journal of Psychiatry, 207(3),* 213–220. doi:10.1192/bjp.bp.114.156620

Platt, D. (2006). Investigation or initial assessment of child concerns? The impact of the refocusing initiative on social work practice. *British Journal of Social Work, 36,* 267–281.

Plotnikoff, J., & Woolfson, R. (2004). *In their own words the experiences of 50 young witnesses in criminal proceedings.* London, UK: NSPCC.

Plotnikoff, J., & Woolfson, R. (2007). *Evaluation of young witness support: Examining the impact on witnesses and the criminal justice system.* Hitchin, Herts: Lexicon Limited.

Plotnikoff, J., & Woolfson, R. (2009). *Measuring up? Evaluating implementation of government commitments to young witnesses in criminal proceedings.* London, UK: NSPCC.

Plotnikoff, J., & Woolfson, R. (2011). *Registered intermediaries in action: Messages for the CJS from the witness intermediary scheme smartSite.* London, UK: NSPCC & MoJ.

Plotnikoff, J., & Woolfson, R. (2015). *Intermediaries in the criminal justice system.* Bristol: Policy Press.

Quayle, E. (2017). *Over the internet, under the radar: Online child sexual abuse and exploitation: A brief literature review.* Edinburgh University, Edinburgh.

Quayle, E., Johnsson, L., & Loof, L. (2012). *Online behaviour related to child sexual abuse: Interviews with affected young persons.*

Quayle, E., & Taylor, M. (2003). Model of problematic internet use in people with a sexual interest in children. *Cyberpsychology and Behaviour, 6(1),* 93–106.

Radford, L., Corral, S., Bradley, C., Fisher, H. L., Bassett, C., Howat, N., & Collishaw, S. (2011). *Child cruelty in the UK 2011*. London, UK: NSPCC.

Reuben, A., Moffitt, T. E., Caspi, A., Belsky, D. W., Harrington, H., Schroeder, F., . . . Danese, A. (2016). Lest we forget: Comparing retrospective and prospective assessments of adverse childhood experiences in the prediction of adult health. *Journal of Child Psychology and Psychiatry, 57*, 1103-1112. doi:10.1111/jcpp.1262

Reza, A., Breiding, M. J., Gulaid, J., Mercy, J. A., Blanton, C., Mthethwa, Z., & Anderson, M. (2009). Sexual violence and its health consequences for female children in Swaziland: A cluster survey study. *The Lancet, 373*(9679), 1966-1972. doi:10.1016/S0140-6736(09)60247-6

Richards, P., Morris, S., Richards, E., & Siddall, K. (2007). *On the record: Evaluation the visual recording of joint investigative interviews with children*. Edinburgh, Scotland: Scottish Executive.

Robinson, B. (2008, July 8). ABE interviews: Is the child's "best evidence" being achieved in alleged sexual abuse cases? (Part 1). *Family Law Week*.

Rushton, A. (2003). Support for adoptive families, a review of current evidence on problems, needs and effectiveness. *Adoption & Fostering, 27*(3), 41-49.

Rushton, A., Quinton, D., Dance, C., & Mayes, D. (1998). Preparation for permanent placement: Evaluating direct work with older children. Adoption and Fostering, *21*(4), 41-48

Rutter, M. (1990). Psychosocial resilience and protective mechanisms. In J. E. Rolf & A. S. Masten (Eds.), *Risk and protective factors in the development of psychopathology* (pp. 181-214). New York, NY: Cambridge University Press.

Ryder, R., Edwards, A., & Clements, K. (2017). *Measuring the wellbeing of children in care*. National Childrens Bureau, London

Salter, D., McMillan, D., Richards, M., Talbot, T., Hodges, J., Bentovim, A., . . . Skuse, D. (2003). Development of sexually abusive behaviour in sexually victimised males: A longitudinal study. *The Lancet, 361*, 471-476.

Schimmenti, A., & Bifulco, A. (2015). Linking lack of care in childhood to anxiety disorders in emerging adulthood: The role of attachment styles. *Child and Adolescent Mental Health, 20*, 41-48. doi:10.1111/camh.12051

Schleiffer, R., & Muller, S. (2004). Attachment representations of adolescents in institutional care. *International Journal of Child & Family Welfare, 7*(1), 60-77.

Scott, S. (2004). Reviewing the research on the mental health of looked after children: Some issues for the development of more evidence informed practice. *International Journal of Child & Family Welfare, 7*(2-3), 86-97.

Scott, S. (2010). National dissemination of effective parenting programmes to improve child outcomes. *The British Journal of Psychiatry, 196*, 1-3. doi:10.1192/bjp.bp.109.067728

Scott, S., Spender, Q., Doolan, M., Jacobs, B., & Aspland, H. (2001). Multicentre controlled trial of parenting groups for childhood antisocial behaviour in clinical practice. *BMJ, 323*, 194-197.

Scott, S., Sylva, K., Doolan, M., Price, J., Jacobs, J., Crook, C., & Landau, S. (2010). Randomised controlled trial of parent groups for child antisocial behaviour targeting multiple risk factors: The SPOKES project. *Journal of Child Psychology and Psychiatry, 51*(1), 48-57. doi:10.1111/j.1469-7610.2009.02127.x

Seligman, M. E. P. (2011). *Flourish: A visionary new understanding of happiness and well-being*. Sydney: William Heinamann.

Selwyn, J., Wood, M., & Newman, T. (2017). Looked after children and young people in England: Developing measures of subjective well-being. *Child Indicators Research, 10*(2), 363-380.

Seto, M. C., & Eke, A. W. (2005). Criminal histories and later offending of child pornography offenders. *Sexual Abuse: A Journal of Research & Treatment, 17*, 201-210.

Shen, H. (2005). The hard science of oxytocin. *Nature, 522*.

Shore, A. N. (2003). *Affect dysregulation and disorders of the self*. New York, NY: Norton and Sons.

Shuker, L. (2014). *Evaluation of Barnardo's safe accommodation project for sexually exploited and trafficked young people*. London, UK: Barnados.

Shuker, L., & Ackerley, E. (2017). *Empowering parents evaluation of parents as partners in safeguarding children and young people in Lancashire project 2014-2017*. University of Bedfordshire, Bedfordshire.

Smith, P. K., Thompson, F., & Davidson, J. (2015). Cyber safety for adolescent girls: Bullying, harassment, sexting, pornography, and solicitation. *Current Opinion in Obstetrics and Gynecology, 26*(5).

Spence, R., Nunn, S., & Bifulco, A. (in press). The long-term effects of childhood financial hardship mediated by physical abuse, shame, and stigma on depression in women. *Matrattamento e abuse all'infanzia*.

Stein, H., Allen, J. G., Bifulco, A., Allen, D., Lantz, K., Wheat, K., . . . Wisman, M. (2002). A common framework for evaluating risk and protective factors in childhood. *Psychology and Psychotherapy. Theory, Research and Practice, 75*(1), 77-91.

Stevens, I., & Furnivall, J. (2008). Therapeutic approaches in residential child care. In A. Kendrick (Ed.), *Residential child care: Prospects and challenges* (Vol. 47 of Research highlights in social work). London, UK and Philadelphia, PA: Jessica Kingsley.

Straus, M. (1979). Measuring intrafamily conflict and violence: The Conflict Tactics (CT) scales. *Journal of Marriage and Family, 41*(1), 75-88. doi:10.2307/351733

Surtees, R. (2005). *Second annual report on victims of trafficking in South-Eastern Europe 2005*. International Organization for Migration and the Regional Clearing Point, Geneva.

Sylva, K., Melhuish, E. C., Sammons, P., Siraj-Blatchford, I., Taggart, B., Toth, K., . . . Welcomme, W. (2012). *Effective pre-school, primary and secondary education 3-14 project (EPPSE 3-14)-Final report from the Key Stage 3 phase: Influences on students' development from age 11-14*. University of Oxford, Oxford.

Toth, S. L. (1997). Representations of self and other in the narratives of neglected, physically abused, and sexually abused preschoolers. *Development and Psychopathology, 9*, 781-796.

Toth, S. L., & Cicchetti, D. (1993). Child maltreatment: Where do we go from here in our treatment of victims? In D. Cicchetti & S. L. Toth (Eds.), *Child abuse, child development and social policy* (pp. 399-438). Norwood, NJ: Ablex.

Toth, S. T., Cicchetti, D., Macfie, J., Maughan, A., & Vanmeenen, K. (2000). Narrative representations of caregivers and self in maltreated pre-schoolers. *Attachment and Human Development, 2*(3), 271-305.

Triseliotis, J. (2002). Long-term foster care or adoption? The evidence examined. *Child and Family Social Work, 7*, 23-33.

UN General Assembly. (2000). *United Nations convention against transnational organized crime and the protocols thereto*. UN General Assembly.

UNCF_UNICEF. (2011). *Violence against children in Tanzania findings from a national survey 2009*. Tanzania: UNICEF.

UNCRC. (1989). *United Nations Convention on the Rights of the Child (UNCRC): how legislation underpins implementation in England*. UNCRC.

UNICEF. (2017). *No time to lose: On child marriage and female genital mutilation/cutting*. UNICEF.

UNICEF. (2018a). *Close to 300 million children aged 2 to 4 worldwide (3 out of 4) experience violent discipline by their caregivers on a regular basis*. UNICEF.

UNICEF. (2018b). *No time to lose: On child marriage and female genital mutilation/cutting*. UNICEF.

UNODC. (2011). *The role of organized crime in the smuggling of migrants from West Africa to the European Union*. Vienna: UNODC.

Van der Kolk, B. A. (2005). Developmental trauma disorder. *Psychiatric Annals, 35*(5), 401-408.

Van der Kolk, B. A., & Fisler, R. E. (1994). Childhood abuse and neglect and loss of self-regulation. *Bulletin of the Menninger Clinic, 58*(2), 145-168.

Van der Kolk, B. A., Pelcovitz, D., Roth, S., Mandel, F. S., McFarlane, A., & Herman, J. L. (1996). Dissociation, somatization, and affect dysregulation: The complexity of adaption to trauma. *American Journal of Psychiatry, 153*(Suppl.), 83-93.

VanFleet, R., & Sniscak, C. (2003). Crimes against children. In *State, municipal and police training manual*. Boiling Springs, PA: Play Therapy Press.

Wager, N., Armitage, R., Christmann, K., Gallagher, B., Ioannou, M., Parkinson, S., . . . Synnott, J. (2018). *Rapid evidence assessment: Quantifying the extent of online-facilitated child sexual abuse. Report for the independent inquiry into child sexual abuse*. London, UK: Home Office.

Walker, E. A. U. J., Rutter, C., Gelfand, A., Saunders, K., VonKorff, M., Koss, M. P., & Katon, W. (1999). Costs of health care use by women HMO members with a history of childhood abuse and neglect. *Archives of General Psychiatry, 56*(7), 609-613. doi:10.1001/archpsyc.56.7.609

Wallis, P., & Steele, H. (2010). Attachment representations in adolescence: Further evidence from psychiatric residential settings. *Attachment & Human Development, 3*, 259-268. doi:10.1080/14616730110096870

Walsh, W., Jones, L., & Cross, T. (2003). Children's Advocacy Centers: One philosophy, many models. *American Professional Society on the Abuse of Children, 15*(3), 1-6.

Warner, S. (2009). *Understanding the effects of child sexual abuse: Feminist revolutions in theory, research and practice*. Oxon, UK: Routledge.

Washington State Institute for Public Policy. (2004). *Outcome evaluation of Washington State's research-based programs for juvenile offenders*. Washington, DC: Public Policy.

Weare, K. (2015). *What works in promoting social and emotional well-being and responding to mental health problems in schools?* London, UK: Public Health England.

Webster, S., Davidson, J., & Bifulco, A. (2015). *Online offending behaviour and child victimisation. New findings and policy*. Basingstoke and New York, NY: Palgrave Macmillan.

Webster, S., Davidson, J., Bifulco, A., Pham, T., & Caretti, V. (2009). *European online grooming project: Progress report covering period: 1 June 2009-31 December 2009*. London: NATCEN.

Wegman, H. L., & Stetler, C. (2009). A meta-analytic review of the effects of childhood abuse on medical outcomes in adulthood. *Psychosomatic Medicine, 71*(8), 805-812. doi:10.1097/PSY.0b013e3181bb2b46

Westcott, H. L., & Kynan, S. (2004). The application of a "storytelling" framework to investigate interviews for suspected child sexual abuse. *Legal and Criminological Psychology, 9*, 37-56.

Westcott, H. L., & Page, M. (2002). Cross-examination, sexual abuse and child witness identity. *Child Abuse Review, 11*, 137-152.

WHO. (2017). *Promoting mental health: Concepts; emerging evidence; practice*. WHO, Geneva.

Widom, C. S. (1989a). Child abuse, neglect, and adult behavior: Research design and findings on criminality, violence, and child abuse. *American Journal of Orthopsychiatry, 59*(3), 355-367.

Widom, C. S. (1989b). Does violence beget violence? A critical examination of the literature. *Psychological Bulletin, 106*, 3-28.

Widom, C. S., & Ames, M. A. (1994). Criminal consequences of childhood sexual victimization. *Child Abuse and Neglect, 18*, 303-318.

Widom, C. S., Czaja, S. J., Bentley, T., & Johnson, M. S. (2012). A prospective investigation of physical health outcomes in abused and neglected children: New findings from a 30-year follow-up. *American Journal of Public Health, 102*(6), 1135-1144. doi:10.2105/ALPH.2011.300636

Widom, C. S., Czaja, S. J., & DuMont, K. A. (2015). Intergenerational transmission of child abuse and neglect: Real or detection bias? *Science, 347*(6229), 1480-1485. doi:10.1126/science.1259917

Williams, J., Scott, S., & Ludvigsen, A. (2017). *Safe Steps CSE Innovation Project*. Evaluation report. Department of Education, London.

Wrennall, L. (2014, December 2). *Miscarriages of justice in child protection: A brief history and proposals for change*. Paper presented at the parliamentary conference held by the All Party Group on Abuse Investigations, Attlee Suite, Portcullis House, London.

Zajac, R., O'Neill, S., & Hayne, H. (2012). Disorder in the courtroom? Child witnesses under cross-examination. *Developmental Review, 32*(3), 181-204.

Zegers, M. A. M., Scheuengel, C., van Ijzendoorn, M. H., & Janssens, J. M. A. M. (2006). Attachment representations of institutionalized adolescents and their professional caregivers: Predicting the development of therapeutic relationships. *American Journal of Orthopsychiatry, 76*(3), 325-334.

Zegers, M. A. M., Schuengel, C., van Ijzendoorn, M. H., & Janssens, J. M. A. M. (2008). Attachment and problem behaviour of adolescents during residential treatment. *Attachment & Human Development, 10*(1), 91-103. doi:10.1080/14616730701868621

INDEX

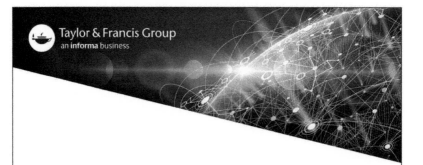